THE BUSINESSMAN'S GUIDE TO SPEECH-MAKING
AND TO THE LAWS AND CONDUCT OF MEETINGS

EWAN MITCHELL

The businessman's guide to
Speech-making
and to the laws and conduct of
Meetings

SECOND EDITION

Illustrations by Mel Calman

BUSINESS BOOKS
COMMUNICA - EUROPA

First published 1968
Second impression 1969
Third impression 1973
Fourth impression 1974
Second edition 1977

ISBN 0 220 66343 2

Printed and bound in Great Britain by
Morrison & Gibb Ltd., London and Edinburgh
for the publishers, Business Books Limited,
24 Highbury Crescent, London N5

For
MY FATHER
with admiration
and affection

OTHER BOOKS BY EWAN MITCHELL

Contents

**Book I   THE BUSINESSMAN'S GUIDE TO SPEECH-
MAKING**

**Part I   THE SPEECH – ITS STRUCTURE AND
CONTENTS**

Part II   THE ARTS OF DELIVERY

Part III   OCCASIONS

Part IV   IN COURTS AND TRIBUNALS

Book II THE BUSINESSMAN'S GUIDE TO THE LAWS AND CONDUCT OF MEETINGS

Part I MEETINGS

Part II THE CHAIRMAN — AND CHAIRMANSHIP

APPENDICES

Introduction

This is two books in one. The first is a guide to speech-making, the second a guide to the conduct of meetings and to the laws which govern them.

No modern businessman can make all his speeches in private. Whether he likes it or not, he will have to address his staff, his customers, and his sales force. There will be Board meetings, company meetings, shareholders' meetings and (possibly, alas!) creditors' meetings to contend with. He may have to take the chair at a company gathering, a public meeting, a political session, or a private dinner. There are presentations and awards to give and to receive. He may even have to venture into court.

Then there are overseas customers, clients or suppliers to be addressed . . . personnel to harangue and enthuse . . . the Press to be dealt with. The higher you get, the more often you must speak in public. And the better you speak, the higher you are likely to climb.

Here, then, culled from a quarter-century of public speaking, debating, lecturing, chairing meetings, making after-dinner speeches . . . controlling, wheedling, persuading, trying to convince company and organizational meetings of many kinds . . . are the main rules.

Naturally, the best way to learn to speak in public is to steel yourself and to do it. If you have sufficient flair, you can learn through experience and mistakes. But it is a good deal easier to base your experience upon the mistakes (and the triumphs) of others. This book provides some of the basic principles of successful public speaking, in most of the circumstances you are likely to meet.

The public speaker has many weapons. There is tact, humour, persuasion, passion . . . even silence. Each has its place and, in most cases, its chapter. No one would think of constructing a building without preparing the plans. No one who wishes to make a good speech should try to avoid preparing it in advance. The more careful the preparation, the less it is likely to show. Book One explains how best to create the skeleton of a speech and later to clothe it in words.

You must know how to tackle Press and public . . . to judge your audience . . . to control your voice, stance, and gestures. Each speaker's style will differ, but many of the rules are common to all. Here is your guide to those you should follow if you want your speech to be a success . . . if you would like to retain your seat on the Board . . . to be invited back to speak another day.

Book Two is intended to be of special help to those who must organize and control meetings—including company chairmen and secretaries. So we deal with order and disorder, with rules of debate and laws of defamation, with meetings of members, directors and creditors of companies, with resolutions and notices, with votes, proxies, agenda.

I hope that you will not only enjoy reading this Guide, but will also find it useful enough to keep in your desk or on your bookshelf. I am very grateful to those who have (in many cases unwittingly) provided the material for these books. One of the penalties of being a speaker is that you have to listen to the speeches of others. If you are a golf enthusiast, you will try to learn from the other man's swing. I have (not invariably with enjoyment) watched, listened (and sometimes slept through) many thousands of speeches. One way or another, their makers have all contributed to this book.

I am very grateful to Dr Desmond Morris and to his U.K. and U.S.A. publishers (Jonathan Cape and McGraw Hill Book Company) for permission to use the quotation from *The Naked Ape* on page 53.

My special thanks, though, to Mr Brian Clapham, to Lord Morris of Kenwood and to my wife for their suggestions and help in the preparation of this book, and particularly for reading it in manuscript or in proof. I hope that they will take pleasure in the result.

EWAN MITCHELL

The Temple,
London EC4
June 1968

Introduction to the Second Edition

The art of speech-making—like the art of lovemaking—is basically eternal and unchanging. But after ten years of service as a business man's *vade mecum*, this book was ripe for revision—largely because of the increase in the amount of speech-making which the law is now forcing upon the unsuspecting executive.

So here is a new Part, setting out the structure of Courts and Tribunals and how to win cases in them. Checklists on how to cope in the witness box or as an advocate (in industrial tribunals, you may have to represent your own company or firm) . . . hence on how to avoid court or tribunal hearings are (I hope) all as useful as their need is inevitable. And with a statute requiring the setting up of safety committees by 1 October 1978 I have added a chapter to the chairmanship Section, on coping with these crucial committees.

My thanks to those who have wittingly helped to produce this edition and especially to my wife and to June Hill for their proof reading—and to my unwitting helpers, too, whose own speeches (and whose reactions to the speeches of others, including my own) have provided so much of the raw material for this work.

GREVILLE JANNER
(Ewan Mitchell)

The Temple,
London EC4
July 1977

Book I

*The businessman's guide
to speech-making*

First I'll say I'm glad to be here, then I'll tell them the one about the Bishop, then I'll say I'm going to be brief, then I'll talk for half an hour and then sit down to thunderous applause...

. . . .

Part I

The speech—its structure and contents

Introduction
Thinking on your feet

The art of good public-speaking is to be able to think while on your feet. Whether you are debating or orating, you are not engaged in an exercise in reading, elocution or recitation. You are trying to put across ideas or thoughts to an audience, in your own words. And if your speech has been written for you, there is even more reason to attempt to make it appear your own.

There are many reasons for avoiding too careful preparation of the precise wording of a speech. Interruption (intentional or otherwise) can so easily throw you off your stride. Your ability to draw from your surroundings . . . to refer to speeches that have gone before or speakers that are to come after . . . these are inevitably affected. The speech loses spontaneity—and hence much of its charm and effect.

Here, then, are the techniques of thinking whilst speaking—an art which every public speaker must acquire, if he seeks success.

1 The skeleton of a speech

The human spirit can live, flourish and be much admired even when the human body is frail, ugly or misshapen. There are some brilliant minds which can capture and hold an audience with a rambling, poorly-formed oration. Meaning and sincerity shine through and all is forgiven. But to the businessman who wishes to make a speech in a businesslike way . . . to the average speaker who wishes to put on an above-average performance . . . to the poor or timorous orator, forced into public speech-making . . . the structure of the speech is of supreme importance. Create the skeleton, clothe it with sensible thought and all that remains is to put it across. But without a healthy skeleton, the entire speech collapses. So here are the rules on forming a well-built talk.

*   *   *

Any speech may conveniently be divided into three parts—the opening, the body and the closing. Let us take them in turn.

The first and last sentences of a speech are crucial. The importance of a clear, resounding and striking first sentence and a well-rounded peroration cannot be over-emphasized. You must catch the interest of your audience from the start and send them away satisfied at the end. So, when building your skeleton, spend time on the 'topping and tailing' process. Many speakers actually write out their opening and closing sentences, even if the rest is left entirely in skeleton form.

Assume, now, that you have established a relationship with your audience. You have led in with your thanks for the invitation to speak . . . your topical references . . . your personal remarks, introductory witticisms and greetings to old friends. Now comes the substance of the speech—any speech. It must flow.

Like a first-class book or chapter or article, most fine speeches start their substance with a general introductory paragraph which sums up what is to come, catches the attention of the audience and indicates the run of the speaker's thought. Each idea should then be taken in sequence, and should lead on logically to the next. Just as each bone of the human body is attached to its fellow, so the ideas in a speech should be jointed. The flow of ideas needs rhythm. Disjointed ideas . . . dislocated thoughts . . . fractured theories . . . these are the hall-mark of a poor speech.

So jot down the points you wish to make. Then set them out in logical order, so that one flows from the next. Connect them up, if you like, with a general theme. Start with that theme— and then elaborate, point by point.

Suppose, for instance, that you are explaining the virtues of a new product to your own sales staff. You begin in the usual way by asking for silence, smiling, looking round your audience and saying: 'Ladies and Gentlemen, sales staff of the X Company . . . it is a pleasure to see you here today, in spite of our reluctance to deprive the company's customers of your services . . .' Refer to Mr Y and Mr Z by name, congratulating them on their successes. Put your audience at ease. Tell them a joke, if you like. And then launch into your theme.

'I have called you together today to introduce our new pro- duct.' (There it is, in a sentence.) 'Our research department has produced it. It will now be up to you to sell it. If you understand and exploit its full potentialities, you will not only benefit the company but you should also add considerably to your own earnings. I only hope that the Chancellor of the Exchequer will not consider this in any way unpatriotic in the light of the country's present financial situation. For surely there was never a time when a substantial volume of home sales was more essen- tial to help us build up the productive capacity we need to produce our goods sufficiently cheaply to capture the vast export markets which we all desire.' (So you have offered your audience a real incentive to listen . . . have introduced a touch of humour . . . have whetted your listeners' appetites for what is to come.)

Now for the speech proper. First, you name and describe the product in broad terms. Next, preferably with the assistance of diagrams or slides, you describe the product in detail. Then you take its selling features, one by one. 'The following features are entirely new . . .' Spell them out and explain them. 'But the following features are retained—they were too valuable to be lost . . .' (Once again, the logical sequence is maintained.)

'So there, ladies and gentlemen, we have our new product— and you are the first to know about it. You will be supplied with full sales literature within the next week. It will be available for your customers by the first of next month. The rest is up to you. I wish you the very best of good fortune.' A good, sound ending to a well-constructed speech.

Precisely the same rules of construction can be applied to any other sort of discourse. Whether you are pronouncing a funeral oration over a deceased colleague or congratulating an employee on completing 25 years' service . . . whether you are making an after-dinner speech or haranguing your workers at the factory gates . . . whatever the circumstances, wherever the speech is made, if its skeleton is sound and solid, then even if the body is not as strong as it might be, there's an excellent chance that the audience will not notice. But ignore the skeleton and the odds are that the speech will prove a rambling disaster.

2 The end of a speech

There is nothing that so becomes a good speech as a fine ending. And nothing can be more ruinous than a weak termination trailing off into silence. Just as much care needs to be given to the tail of a talk as to the top.

Consider some common flops:

Mr Brown rushes his last few sentences, gathers his notes and slides almost surreptitiously back into his seat.

Mr Black ends his talk in what appears to be the middle of a sentence or the centre of an anti-climax.

Mr Grey, who had been allotted thirty minutes to speak, ran out of material after twenty but was determined 'not to let the audience down', and said: 'In conclusion', 'finally', 'before I conclude', 'lastly', and 'to end up with', at least twice each—each time rekindling hope in the minds of his audience that he really meant it.

Mr Green thought that he was narrating a serial story and left his audience in suspense by overrunning his time, panicking and then forgetting to propose the resolution which was the sole object of his speech.

Mr Blue realizes that he is not going to conclude his prepared talk if he keeps going at the same speed. So he runs out of script and breath at the same moment, leaving his audience miles behind.

Mr Dark forgets that a peroration should be brief—and drags it out interminably, embellishing thoughts which were in the body of the speech, introducing new ideas in the guise of a summary of what he had said and is not only woolly-minded but shows it.

What, then, makes a really good ending or peroration? It should round off the speech and, in most cases, include the following:

1 A summary, in a sentence or two, of the main purport of the speech.
2 Any proposal or resolution arising out of the body of the speech, and
3 A call for support or warm words of thanks, as the case may be.

Some say that if you were to attach the peroration to the opening, they should between them contain the core of the entire speech. The opening says what is coming; the closing says what has gone and what is to come.

Here are some examples of good closing gambits:

'So this project does have great possibilities for our company. But to achieve success, it is essential that we at once take the steps I have suggested. I therefore ask you all not merely to support the resolution which stands in my name but to help put it into useful and urgent effect.'

'And so, Mr Chairman, my argument is closed. I have tried to suggest the appropriate action which this company could now take. I believe that if the resolution which stands in my name is passed and put into urgent effect, it will transform the company's finances. I trust that no one will vote against it without the most careful thought. I submit, Mr Chairman, that it presents the best possible way out of our current difficulties.'

'And so this company stands in grave peril. To my mind, the way out is clear. The action I recommend could transform the situation. I am pleased to have had the opportunity to put forward the resolution which stands in my name and I am grateful to all of you for having listened so attentively to my arguments. I trust that they will not lightly be rejected.'

'There is, then, no need for despair. The future presents great opportunities. But we must not only resolve to carry out the procedure proposed in my resolution but also ensure that the action which must follow will have the urgent and active support of us all. I therefore move that . . .'

'So those are the possibilities open to us. And only one of them really carries any hope of real success. It is the duty of this Board to protect and advance the interests of our shareholders. That duty can only be performed if steps are taken in accordance with the resolution which stands in my name. I urge, with all the earnestness I can command, that it be accepted—fully, whole-heartedly and without amendment.'

*   *   *

There are many roads to Rome and countless ways to construct the end of the same speech. There is no need for the old clichés: 'My time is running short . . . I see that my time is nearly up and I must close . . .' Still worse: 'I see that you are beginning to get restless . . . I have no wish to bore you any further . . .' Make your summary and your appeal—for support, for money, for understanding.

Try not to mix your metaphors. 'We have so many irons in the fire that some of them are bound to come home to roost . . .' brings laughter. But by all means adapt a well-known metaphor to your own use. 'This company is the finest in the chicken business . . . and our shareholders will continue to see the profits come home to roost . . .' Or 'Thanks to the happy relations between management and labour in this business, our many irons are kept white hot in the fire . . .' The new twist on the old words brings life to many a dead topic.

*   *   *

Other recommended endings:

'And so, Mr Chairman, I would like to end as I began—with my warm thanks for your kind hospitality.'

'Ladies and Gentlemen, it has been a delight to be with you. I hope that my words will have been of some help in promoting the cause for which you work and in which I—like you—believe so firmly. I wish you, Mr Chairman, your honorary officers, executives, members and workers, every possible success in your great venture.'

'And so our Conference is over. It has been a tremendous experience to meet you all. I trust that we shall see each other on many more such happy and useful occasions. Meanwhile, I know that I am expressing the warm feelings of all of us when I wish you God-speed on your journeys home, every success in all your ventures, and a speedy return to our midst.'

'I know that the views I have put forward are unusual and, in some quarters, unpopular. But I know, too, that you would not have wished me to do otherwise than to speak my mind. That I have done, most earnestly. I do hope that the suggestions I have made will be adopted, or at least adapted. But whatever decision you take, I would like you to know how much I have appreciated the kind attention which you have given to me—and how much I have the future of this organization at heart.'

*   *   *

Some people end by saying: 'Thank you' or 'Good Night'. But a climax is better. A last, powerful phrase, left hovering in the air—and beckoning on the applause. Then do not rush back to your seat, flop quickly down into your chair, whip out your cigarette-case and light up. Like any good trouper, wait for the applause. If it comes, smile or bow slightly in acknowledgement. If it does not, then look your audience straight in the eye. Pause. And then sit down. The end of your speech should make quite as solid an impact as its start.

3 Notes

Some speeches are so important that they have to be read. Every word counts and the occasion is so fraught with peril that you cannot risk setting a foot wrong. But read speeches tend to be a bore. Even Parliament, some of whose debates are an agony to endure, forbids the reading of speeches. The Mother of Parliaments has to suffer enough without allowing its members to exchange debates for a series of written essays, probably the product of the minds of others. Remove the element of the impromptu and the likelihood of the speech proving interesting is minimal. As the audience knows this truth, instead of looking forward to hearing the speaker it prepares for slumber and boredom. As soon as the speaker starts reading from a script, his audience begins to curl up—mentally if not physically.

But to the average, non-professional speaker, the difficulty of constructing a speech as he goes along is almost insurmountable. Even for the expert, preparation is a necessity—and the more complex the speech, the more essential it is to be reminded of its main points, so that none is left out. The compromise, then? Notes. The skeleton of the speech (see Chapter 1) committed to paper, leaving the speaker to clothe it with words, embellish it with new ideas and thoughts, and enliven it with wit as he goes along.

What, then, should good notes contain? The first sentence plus the last sentence plus the skeleton. The flow of ideas. The thread of the speech. Brief phrases to indicate the contents of even lengthy paragraphs. And notes to remind you of themes. Pegs on which to hang your thoughts.

What you need are brief headings for the eye, to direct the flow of speech but not to interrupt it. Except where you must indulge in quotations, the shorter and clearer the note, the better. By all means divide up the note itself by using block capitals for the main headings and a small type of script for subsidiary items.

Underline in red, blue, green. Set the notes themselves into columns and lay them out so as to catch your eye, just as you seek to lay out your speech to catch the minds and imaginations of your listeners.

Notes are best made on cards, preferably not larger than normal postcard size. Each theme, each paragraph, each range of ideas can then be put on to a separate card. Use one side only. When the ground on a card has been covered, you turn it over. If you have a desk, table or stand to operate from, well and good. But if not—as when you are speaking from the floor, at a meeting—then you are not burdened by clumsy sheets, paper that tends to slip through your fingers, scraps of notes which you lose at the crucial moment, so sending yourself into that very fluster which the notes were intended to avoid. You simply return each card to the bottom of the pack as soon as you are through with it. Just in case you drop your notes, number each card clearly, at the top, right-hand corner.

Another advantage of the card system is that if you run out of time, the chances are that you can simply skip two or three of the less essential cards—or at least summarize them in sentences and turn them over at speed. They provide your guide without restricting you to an itinerary. They leave you room for manœuvre, and the ability to think on your feet.

4 Brevity is the soul of success

Mr Mort Mendels, long-time Secretary of the World Bank and sufferer from the speeches of others, boasted a cartoon on his office wall. It showed a man being carried out of the Senate on a stretcher. 'Talked to Death' was the caption. The corpse might just as easily have been emerging from any one of hundreds of meetings anywhere in Britain.

The man who stands in front of the mirror admiring himself for long periods, is rightly regarded as a freak. But at least he disturbs no one else. The man who so rejoices in the sound of his own words that he imposes them at great length upon his fellows should be relegated to the same privacy.

Have you ever heard an audience complain that the speaker did not go on long enough? On the contrary, far more listeners complain at the sluggishness of their watch hands. And on the rare occasions when they do want more from the speaker—well, he can always be invited again.

'If you cannot strike oil within 15 minutes, stop boring,' the oil man is alleged to have told his apprentices. He could have been talking to a course on public-speaking.

Incidentally, the importance of this chapter should not be judged by its brevity.

5 *Wit and humour*

Every comedian works extremely hard for his living. If he is renowned for his wit, then he may be able to make his audience laugh (if they are in the right mood) where no laughter is really deserved. Part of the art of any speaker is to let his hearers know what is coming . . . to lead them up to the climax . . . to prepare them to react as he intends. The well-known wit has his groundwork laid ready for him. He no sooner comes to the stage or the platform or up to the microphone, shakes his head or performs some other famous gesture—and the audience begins to giggle. Whether his first sentence refers to 'The Diddy people', his mother-in-law, or simply includes some renowned catch-phrase —the audience is off.

But speak to even the most famous men of comedy and you will soon discover how carefully their impromptu laughs are prepared . . . how fickle and unpredictable an audience—any audience—can be . . . how even the best-made stories can fall apart at the seams. You will then realize, if you do not already know it, that of all the skills of the public speaker, putting across humour is one of the most difficult of all. For the most experienced of humorists, the path is tough. How much more difficult must it be for the beginner?

On the other hand, the humourless speaker is a menace. There are few occasions when a word of wit is not appreciated, and the longer the speech, the more vital the touch of humour. The more sombre the subject, the more appropriate the tactful, tasteful touch of light relief will be. Humour, then, is a weapon which every speaker should have readily available. Here are some suggestions on how best to put it across.

*　　　*　　　*

The humour must be tailored to the audience and to the occasion. This applies most obviously to the *risqué*, the rude or the plain vulgar. There is never any excuse whatsoever for the use of the obscene. But the element of dirt can sometimes add spice to the meal. When?

Obviously, the stag dinner is the place for the dirty story. Conversely, those who introduce the *risqué* tale into solemn or sombre occasions are inviting contempt. In between come all the rest. You must judge each occasion as best you can. If in doubt—keep it clean.

Similar considerations apply to the dialect story. There is still a place for the saga of the Scotsman, the Irishman and the Jew. But to copy someone else's accent is generally an error. The only speakers who can do it without undue risk are those who belong to the group satirized. Scotsmen, Jews, Irishmen, Negroes

—they all delight in stories about themselves, but usually only when told by themselves. If you enjoy the friendship of Jewish people, for instance, you will soon find that they poke merciless fun at their own foibles. Part of their armour, acquired through centuries of persecution, is the ability to make laughter shine through the tears. No one, in fact, can tell an anti-Semitic story with half the relish of the Jew. But then, masochism is reasonable. *Volenti non fit injuria*—the volunteer cannot complain of injuries brought about of his own free will. We cause no injury to ourselves when we make jokes at our own expense.

Sadism, on the other hand, is always unpleasant, and even a hint may be harmful. Minorities may consider themselves the subject for good humour. But the laughter is often thin when the shafts come from tongues other than their own.

So there are two sides to the coin. First, be tremendously careful not to obtain cheap laughs at the expense of others. Second, many of the best jokes—and those most appreciated—are those about oneself.

'We Welsh . . .' says the speaker with a smile, 'have, through our very name, given birth to an important word in the English language . . .'

'As you all know,' says the speaker in broad Scots, 'I yield to none of my compatriots in the meanness of my approach . . .'

'We foreigners find it very difficult to understand you English. I know that m-i-s-l-e-d spells misled. But when I pronounced t-i-t-l-e-d the same way, everyone laughed at me.'

None of this is great humour. All of it has been heard before. But then, as one famous comic put it: 'There are basically only two jokes—the mother-in-law and the banana skin.' What matters is to make the joke fit the occasion and the audience, and to put it over effectively.

The best way to suit the occasion is to extract the humour from the surroundings and from the people present (for examples, see Part III). But how do you put it across? Here are some hints, culled from some well-known, humorous speakers:

First, you must give every impression of confidence. It is a mistake to say: 'I was going to tell you the story about . . .' and then to tell it, half apologetically. However thin the tale, it requires firmness in the telling. You must believe in the comedy or you will never get your audience to do so.

The confidence must be retained, even in the face of defeat. If a joke falls flat, never mind. Pretend it was not intended as a joke at all—and carry straight on. Alternatively, face up to the situation and say: 'Sorry . . . it wasn't a very good one, was it? Never mind—how about the tale of . . .?' Or: 'Sorry about that —I'll do better next time. But you must admit that after a meal such as we've just had, it is really the height of sadism to expect anyone to attempt to entertain you!'

Timing is all-important. This means that the joke or witticism or humorous thrust must be well placed in relation to the speech, the content of the talk or lecture, the mood of the audience. But it especially means that the joke must be told at the right pace . . . with the correct emphasis . . . with the appropriate pauses. Listen to any first-class comedian at work. Half his effect is achieved by timing. He knows when to wait and when to rush forward. So listen to the experts—and copy them.

Some speakers keep a book of stories, notes of humorous tales which have gone down well and which they would like not to forget. Certainly the jotting down of the punch line on the back of a menu card or in the front of your diary can provide useful ammunition. It may also have the opposite effect—it may help to save you from the gross error of telling an audience the same story that it heard the last time it met. To avoid this fate, you can take some regular attender into your confidence. 'I'm thinking of telling the story of . . .', you say to the chairman. 'Do you know it?' If he says no, then the chances are that you will be safe. If he has heard it, then find out whether it was told at the same gathering. And avoid it, anyway, if you can.

Jokes are for others to laugh at. If you giggle at your own stories the chances are that you will detract from their effect on your audience.

The best stories have a sting in their tail. The laughter should build up. The audience should expect the laughs. But if the first climax brings laughter and turns out to be a false one, giving rise to an unexpected twist, then the story has been a success.

The formal tale also has its place. But the bright phrase, the witty aside, the colourful remark—these are more important. If you cannot think of a suitable, funny story for the occasion, never mind. The odds are that some humorous thought will come to you as you speak. If it does not, at least make sure that your speech is shorter than if you had been able to lighten its darkness with a few shafts of light-hearted laughter.

6 *Quotations*

Your audience have come to hear you. But that is no reason why you should not pepper your speech with apt quotations from the thoughts of others. Quoting, however, is an art of its own. Here are some suggestions on how best to perfect it.

*   *   *

Keep quotations short. To quote at length from memory is a form of 'showing off' which is seldom appreciated. You are not engaged in a stage soliloquy. To read someone else's words at length is seldom an alternative to putting thoughts and ideas into your own words. The reading of speeches—or even lengthy parts of them—is usually an error. And the error is compounded when you are not even reading that which purports to amount to your own original thought.

Quotations are only worth using if they are thoroughly apt. If your audience is flagging, it is sometimes helpful to 'drag in a joke by its ears'. This is a legitimate gambit to reduce strain, but if the joke were apposite, it would be a good deal better. To thrust an inappropriate quotation into your speech merely because you have a fond feeling for it is a great mistake.

By all means attribute the quotation to its true author, if you can. If in doubt, you could try: 'Was it George Bernard Shaw who said . . .?' or 'I think it was Oscar Wilde who once remarked that . . .' or if the attribution is to someone in your lifetime, you can seldom go wrong with: 'I once heard Winston Churchill remark that . . .' Or 'Did you read the saying, attributed to Mr Kruschev, that . . .' Who is to prove you wrong?

Make sure that your speech really is strengthened by putting the statement concerned in quotation marks—and as coming from the particular author. When trying to convince a British audience to adopt an American practice, it is sometimes better to adopt the transatlantic arguments, without stating their origin. Conversely, for any foreigner to express a preference for a candidate in an American election is to impose the kiss of death upon him. By all means use the foreigner's arguments, but if you must put them into quotation marks, try: 'One great American was said to have remarked . . .' Do not quote Satan to condemn sin.

The best quotations of all, of course, are those from the mouths of your opponents. 'Today, Mr Jones condemns amalgamation. But who was it who said, just two years ago—and I quote "Our future depends upon achieving amalgamation. We cannot survive as a small, independent unit"? None other than my friend, Mr Jones!'

Quotations from yourself should be avoided. 'Did I not say, six months ago, that . . .?' Or 'May I repeat what I said at our trade conference last month?' Unless a speaker has previously been accused of inconsistency and must quote from himself to show that he has not changed his mind, this sort of self-quotation is generally regarded as pompous and egotistical. If you have something to say today, say it. Let someone else point out that you are marvellously consistent . . . wise before the event . . . a man whose advice should be taken. The best you can do is to make that insinuation. Quotations are too direct a method by far.

7 Files and ideas

First-class journalists (especially freelances with no access to newspaper files) keep careful files of clippings, cuttings, photographs and ideas which they can later incorporate into articles, features, or books. Speakers should take a leaf out of their file.

Take jokes, for instance (see Chapter 5). There are books of allegedly humorous tales for every occasion, but one sometimes wonders how anyone ever laughed at the bulk of them. But then each of us has his own style . . . his own sense of humour . . . his own preference. Do not be afraid to steal the tales of others. They will be flattered (see Chapter 6). Jot them down and file them. You never know when they may come in handy.

Then there is specialist material, which can be used time and time again. Most popular speakers are invited to talk on their particular specialities. The first time, research must be done . . . facts prepared . . . statistics unearthed . . . notes prepared. But if those notes are carefully filed, next time will be a walk-over, though naturally they would have to be adapted for different audiences (see Part III). But the basic groundwork need not be repeated.

Some speakers favour a filing-cabinet, others one of those newfangled metal boxes with files inside. Still more make do with loose-leaf notebooks for stories and quotations, ideas and suggestions.

The object of it all is to reduce your homework to the minimum. You have no time to repeat any drudgery. So, however boring the keeping of files or notebooks may be, it is well worth some effort in the present if it cuts down work in the future.

9 *Repetition*

A former Duke of Wellington is reputed to have said: 'I dreamed that I was speaking in the House of Lords. I woke up and found that I was.' Repetition and long-windedness may not only demoralize your audience but yourself as well.

On the other hand, it does have its place. 'Brutus is an honourable man . . .' Shakespeare knew how to build a speech upon the repetition of a theme, without ever approaching boredom.

Some of my personal dislikes:

The man who starts his speech by saying: 'Mr Jones has made all the points which I wished to put forward'. A better approach would have been: 'Mr Jones has put forward his case with immense skill, and I commend it to the meeting. However, there are several aspects of his remarks which, I think, require further emphasis.'

'I will not bore you by reploughing the furrows so thoroughly covered by Mr Jones.' Watch out. Boredom is on its way. That sort of introduction, combining mixed metaphor with cliché, is a sure sign of impending audience distress. Leave the meeting if you can.

Then there's the man who repeats his points in the same words. Most well-constructed speeches should begin with a summary of what's coming: a full-blooded exposition of those points in the body of the speech and another brief summary at the end. 'To summarize, then; if we are to achieve success, we must take the following steps. First . . . second . . . third . . . and, above all . . .' But English is a rich language. If you cannot think of similes, consult the invaluable *Roget's Thesaurus*—which should be on the desk or at least in the library of every speaker. And if you must repeat yourself, at least try not to do so in the current and boring clichés, which are merely a sign of speeches made without thought, and so reveal the thoughtlessness of the speaker.

8 Overstatements

Hyperbole—that is, exaggeration for effect—has its place, and is often used by humorists. There is nothing funny about a thin man—but a matchstick man, a creation of skin and bone, a fat head on a puny frame—that's different. About the only time that deliberate exaggeration helps the presentation of a serious case is when that case is thin. 'If something is too silly to say, you can always sing it,' says the operatic librettist. 'If logic and argument are surplus,' says the skilled speaker, 'then it is just possible that if you shout loud enough, exaggerate sufficiently, thump with sufficient force, you may numb the minds of your audience.' This sort of behaviour is the last resort of the advocate and should only be used when *in extremis*.

Otherwise, your exaggerations are likely to boomerang . . . to cause laughter . . . to ruin such a case as you have. Some horrible examples:

Reference to a speech immediately preceding: 'That magnificent and moving oration which we have just heard . . . that tugged at our heartstrings and must now open our purses . . .' The charity goes without money.

'I only saw her passing by, but I shall love her till I die.' Sir Robert Menzies, then Prime Minister of Australia, enthusing at a dinner in honour of the Queen. However well-loved the Queen undoubtedly is, Sir Robert's hyperbole brought only ridicule in its wake.

* * *

Words, like drugs, may be highly beneficial in the correct quantity and dosage. But over-indulgence may cause death. Moderation pays.

10 *The cliché*

One way to while away the speeches of others is to compile a list of clichés. Some examples, culled from a recent company meeting:

'In this day and age . . .'
'Each and every one of us . . .'
'We are escalating towards disaster . . .'
'We must give of our best . . .'
'No politicians are to be trusted . . .'
'We must stem the tide of ill-will . . .'
'The ship of State is heading for the rocks . . .'
'Blood, toil, sweat and tears—that is the only recipe . . .'
'The present system of taxation is destroying us . . .'
'Our expansion plans are going full steam ahead . . .'

There is really no limit to them, is there? And each one is common, hackneyed, trite, and commonplace (see *Roget's Thesaurus*, paragraph 496). Even though the sentiments expressed may be wise, sage, true, received, admitted, recognized (same paragraph), that flexibility of the language which can cloak even the most uninspiring and unoriginal thought with at least the appearance of charm or originality has not been brought into play.

After a particularly monotonous cliché-ridden speech, made by a dull guest in the Cambridge Union, Mr Percy Cradock brought the house down with the following: 'I know that we have all greeted each sentence expressed by Mr — with something of the wretched anticipation felt when one notes the approach of an old but extremely seedy acquaintance.'

Contrast the effect made on the dowdy woman by a new hairstyle, a chic outfit and modern accessories and the moral needs no emphasis. No longer is she seedy. Her familiarity has a new and interesting flavour. She is now worthy of our attention. She is ready for the wooing. And it is no hyperbole to say that the oldest thought in the newest dress can have a rare and surprising appeal. 'There's nothing new to say about this subject' is a cliché. 'Consider the problem from this new angle,' is a worthy start—and if the angle is sufficiently acute, its familiarity may well be forgotten. You may not regard yourself as a bore. What matters is that your listeners should share your view. And a good start to this hopeful process is to learn to recognize clichés in the speeches of others and ruthlessly to eliminate them from your own.

11 *The great I am*

Every speaker should treat the sound of his own voice as a drug to be taken in moderation. The restrained use of the first person singular is worth some careful thought.

There are two possible reasons why you have been asked to speak. Either your audience wanted to hear you or they thought that they ought to. These categories subdivide.

If you have been invited to speak in the hope that you will have something interesting to tell, then you are lucky. But do not push your luck too far by retailing what you are, rather than what you know. Leave it to your introducer to sing your praises. To do so for yourself is to court ridicule. 'Start loving yourself,' Oscar Wilde once remarked, 'and you are in for a lifetime of romance.' Fine. But do not do your courting in public.

If you are asked to give advice, you can usually manage it without ever mentioning yourself directly. If you are requested to tell tales of the trade, you must, of course, draw on your own experience and, indeed, a joke told against yourself can be immensely successful. But you do not need to tell your listeners how good you are. Do so and they will not believe you. Fail to do so and they may think up the idea for themselves.

Naturally, if you have been the rounds of similar businesses, factories, offices or workshops to your own, at home or abroad, and are asked to give your impressions . . . if you wish to express views and to make it clear that they are yours and not those of your organization or, perhaps, of your board or partners . . . if you wish to lighten the darkness of some drab subject with a personal anecdote—then do so. 'I once met . . . in Birmingham,'; 'I was told the tale of . . .'; 'these are my views, I repeat, and if they turn out to be wrong, you will know where to place the responsibility . . .' All fair game.

But 'when I last saw the Prime Minister . . .'; or 'now, I don't like to drop names, but when I was spending a week-end recently with Lord and Lady Blank in their country estate . . .'. Both are unforgivable.

Remember the story of the famous general whose first-person anecdotage was accepted because of his undoubted greatness? He was telling an audience about his battle tactics. 'I could not decide what to do next,' he said. 'I thought to myself: "My God, what is to be done now?" "General," came the answer, "You decide. I have every confidence in you." So I did.'

Of course, people like to be given the inside information (for traps, see Chapter 13 on how to handle the Press). It is all a question of sensibly putting on a cloak of apparent modesty.

All this becomes even more important when you are the Guest of Honour—which is not necessarily the same as the honoured guest. Maybe your hosts want your money . . . your support . . . your services . . . your backing. Maybe they are simply hoping to lubricate you sufficiently to obtain some useful information which, in a less cordial or obligated moment, you might never give. Whatever the reason, you are on show. So play up to it. Be grateful that—whatever the reason—you are to be honoured and not reviled. Help to keep it that way by making your speech extremely modest. Or try the favourite of Sir Barnett Janner, M.P.: 'After all those kind words, Mr Chairman, I can hardly wait to hear myself speak!'

'It is extremely good of you to honour me in this way,' you might continue. 'I fully appreciate that your intention is, through me, to honour my company . . . my organization . . . my entire Board . . .' (or as the case may be). 'We are all deeply grateful to you.'

In the body of the speech, tell them about the work your organization is doing. Give them as much inside information as you decently can. If you are being honoured for long service, then reminisce—and mention as many individuals amongst your audience as you can. 'Now Bill Black over there . . . he'll remember when we were both involved in an embarrassing disaster in 1967 . . . Sir Michael Brown—whom we are all very pleased to see amongst us—shared many an exploit . . . Richard Jones, whose sobriety is a proud tribute to the breathalyser . . .' and so on.

Everyone mentioned is flattered—assuming that he receives an honourable mention. You have achieved the all-important, informal touch. Your audience are your friends. The ice is completely shattered, and you are shown to be a man of the people and not the complete egotist everyone had thought you to be. And if they are after something which you are not prepared to give, try this line: 'You are indeed lucky to have in your active ranks tonight and always, Reginald Property . . . Mr James Industry . . . and that lady, famous for her good deeds, Mrs Jewel.' The guest who gives honour will receive it.

'I now must close . . .' (one hopes because of the time of the clock and not the time you have taken in your speech)—'but, before doing so, I would like to thank you once again, most sincerely, for the great kindness and generosity you have shown to me. I have thoroughly enjoyed being with you. I hope that we shall meet again many times, always on happy occasions. And

may this organization/company/institute (etc.) flourish for
many years to come under your leadership, Mr Chairman.'

A resounding ending to a good speech. Your hearers will tell
you so—and mean it.

12 *The spoken word*

The old, pedantic rules for writing have largely been discarded
in favour of freedom of expression. Freedom of speech has
followed in its wake. Sentences without verbs . . . split infinitives
. . . they offend the ears of some but are generally forgiven. Still,
here are some general rules which may prove helpful.

*   *   *

The most common grammatical error of all arises in the use
of the first person. 'Between you and I' is wrong. So is 'Dr Brown
and me were most impressed with our welcome' and 'You and
me must give some careful thought to this problem.' If this
sort of problem worries you, discuss it with a friend whose
grammar is impeccable.

Swear words and obscenities are best excluded, even from the
stag-dinner oration. There will always be those who are offended.
But slang and modern idiom are to be expected. If in doubt,
you can always put them 'in quotes', so to speak.

If in doubt about the precise meaning of a word, either avoid
it or look it up beforehand in a dictionary. If given the choice
between two words, one long and one short, choose the shorter.
Good old Anglo-Saxon monosyllables are usually the most
effective.

Sentences, too, should be kept short. Quite apart from your audience losing the thread, you may do so. 'Now, where was I?' is a dreadful admission of a speaker's failure.

Avoid precise statistics if you can. Apart from the possibility of being found out, the effect of an understandable approximation is much greater than the spelling out of some lengthy figure. Clichés should be 'conspicuous by their absence'. You should 'leave no avenue explored' in your attempt to avoid phrases of this sort. (See Chapter 10.)

There are occasions upon which it is necessary to use material which is full of sound and fury but signifies nothing. The higher you get in the Government of a country or of an organization, the more frequent those occasions become. But in general, direct speech is better than indirect, the active voice better than the passive, the straightforward greatly to be preferred to the insinuation.

*13 Dealing with the Press**

Publicity is the life-blood of any trade. 'I don't care what they say about me,' said one famous magnate, 'just so long as they say something.' 'There's no such thing as bad publicity,' said another. Exaggerations, both. Still, if things go well with you, your greatest difficulty may be to get the Press to come at all. Once there, you must know how to deal with them.

The Press may come in many guises. They may be both wanted and invited. Alternatively, they may be unwanted—and represented by your own members or colleagues with a taste for

* See also Chapters 42 and 60.

the pen or for the payment that the Press offers for appropriate tit-bits. The chances of an important and interesting meeting really being private are fairly remote. Someone is likely to 'leak'. So choose your words accordingly.

Unfortunately, there are few speeches which read as well as they sound (or vice versa). The witty jest which provokes friendly laughter may read like a jibe. The sincere appeal may sound good but look limp in print. The flamboyant utterance which rouses or enthuses the audience may land you in deep waters when it appears in the local paper.

'I didn't say that,' exclaims the scandalized speaker. The reporter refers to his notebook. 'Sorry,' he says. 'I have it all down.'

'You took it out of context.' (Always the next ploy.) 'The context is your entire speech. Anyway, the sub-editor did a job on it. It's what you said, isn't it?'

You are powerless. Condemned out of your own mouth.

Of course, if there is some gross mis-statement or unfair representation of your words, you could report the paper to the Press Council. If your complaint is considered to be well-founded, the newspaper will be honour bound to publish the finding in its own columns. And no doubt you will get an appropriate apology. But far more often, it is the speaker who is in the wrong. Reporters are only human. They make mistakes. But it is far rarer for them to get carried away by enthusiasms of the moment than it is for those whom they are paid to report.

That is the important point. Press men earn their living by supplying material for the Press. They follow a code of conduct which helps them to obtain background information, inside stories and retain goodwill. Tell them something 'off the record' and it is highly unlikely that your trust will be betrayed. But do not try to get them to conceal that which the public should know.

'I must now deal with a most serious matter,' says the speaker. 'I know that our friends of the Press are present and I must ask them to treat what I am about to say as confidential.' The chances are that they will.

'We have just heard from our chairman. What he said was

entirely confidential and must not in any circumstances be reported.'

Why not? What right have you to impose a censorship on the Press? If what the chairman said was intended only for private ears, it should have been left for a private occasion.

Conversely, 'What I have just said is of the greatest public interest. I trust that our friends of the Press will give it full publicity.'

They may. It all depends on whether their assessment of the interest of your words matches your own.

The private interview with the Press man needs careful handling, too. Accuracy is essential. Consider some common pit-falls.

'Do you think that this industry is heading for disaster?' you are asked.

You think. 'Well,' you say, hesitatingly, 'I suppose that in one sense you could say that.' Next day's headlines: JAMES CAXTON SAYS: 'INDUSTRY HEADING FOR DISASTER'.

Or: 'Would you say that the industry is heading for disaster?'

'Oh sure,' you answer, your voice thick with sarcasm. 'With exports such as we have recently achieved, I would say disaster is just around the corner, wouldn't you?' And you both have a good laugh about it.

'DISASTER JUST AROUND THE CORNER,' SAYS WILLIAM HICKS.

Extreme examples, of course, but none the less a warning to choose your words with care. After they have appeared in the Press, it helps little to write saying you have been misquoted . . . that you meant something else . . . that the report was inaccurate . . . Some people may believe you, of course.

How about those items, then, that the Press get hold of but you would prefer to have kept out? At worst, the wife of a senior executive has been caught shop-lifting . . . the company secretary is in matrimonial distress . . . the senior partner was drunk and disorderly. Whether you like it or not (and you do not) the Press will be there at the trial. What to do?

Send along a Queen's Counsel to defend the accused on the minor, magistrates' court charge and you are bound to alert the watch-dogs. Put in a plea of mitigation, say how vital it is for the accused to have his car because he is such an important company official, and you are begging to be reported. But just keep as mum as possible and allow the proceedings to slide through along with the rest of the queue and, with a little bit of luck, no one may think the matter worth reporting. But the man who tries to bribe or to threaten a reporter into silence is almost certain to be fully reported. Cajolery and an appeal to the better feelings of the Press man might succeed—but if the story is a really good one, the odds are heavily against you. Silence is undoubtedly your best hope, in most cases.

Of course, the Press may be put on its honour if entrusted with your private secrets, as we have seen. But if the secrets really are not yours . . . if they have come into the public eye . . . if they are not, in fact, secret—then it is luck rather than good judgment which will keep them off the front page. The laws of defamation are unlikely to do so—as we shall now see.

14 Defamation—the laws of libel and slander

It is defamatory to publish anything about another person which would tend to 'lower him in the eyes of right-thinking people'. You must not bring others into 'hatred, ridicule or contempt'. To defame someone in writing or some other permanent form (including, incidentally, a statement made on television) is a libel. To speak ill of another is slander. The public speaker— even when he thinks that he is talking in semi-private, as in a meeting of his Board or any other committee—must beware of both.

The fact that a statement is true does not prevent it from being defamatory. But no one is entitled to a good name which he has not earned. So, if sued for a defamatory statement which you can prove to be true, you may plead 'justification'. But the effect of a plea of justification is to repeat again—and even more loudly and publicly—the very same defamatory statement that you made before. Hence if a plea of justification fails, your offence has been severely aggravated. The damages awarded against you will be greatly increased.

A much more helpful defence for most businessmen on many occasions is that of 'qualified privilege'. The law recognizes that certain statements must be made, for the public good. People must be entitled to speak their minds. Hence 'privilege'.

No action in defamation will lie in respect of any statement made in a court of law by anyone, whether it be judge, juryman, witness, or counsel. Absolute privilege also attaches to all state-ments made in Parliament. Our legislators must be able to speak without fear of legal reprisal. However malicious, untrue or un-justified a statement in court or Parliament may be, it can never give rise to a defamation action.

Similar privilege attaches to occasions upon which the law recognizes that the maker of the statement has a public or private duty to make it and the hearer a direct interest in re-ceiving it. For instance, references are necessary if the wheels of business are to be kept turning. So the giver of a reference is protected. He is under a moral duty to speak his mind to the inquirer (although, note, he is under no legal duty whatsoever to supply the reference). The recipient of the reference obviously has an interest in knowing its contents. The occasion is 'privileged'.

Or suppose that you have to discuss at a board meeting the possible sacking of a member of staff. It is alleged that he was dishonest . . . slovenly . . . disobedient . . . stupid . . . in a word, unfit to be in your company. Every time anyone speaks ill of him, he is defamed. But clearly, this sort of discussion must be allowed to take place. It is no mere idle gossip. It is essential company business. The occasion is 'privileged'.

But whilst the privilege of courts and Parliament is 'absolute', that of the businessman speaking to his colleagues or supplying a reference is 'qualified'. The qualification? That if it turns out that the statement was made out of 'malice', the privilege evaporates. 'Malice' simply means some wrongful motive. If it can be shown that the object of making the statement was to harm the person defamed rather than to assist the Board in coming to a sensible conclusion, or the prospective employer to decide whether or not to employ the man, the privilege goes. The law is not designed as a shield to guard the spiteful.

Normally, however, you can speak your mind without too much worry, provided you do so at a private gathering of people with similar business interests. The larger the gathering and the less obvious the community of interest, the more risky the defamatory statement becomes. If in doubt, consult your solicitor. Or bring him to the meeting and let him make the statement for you, if he sees fit. He will be acting as your agent, but the chances of any defamation action being brought against him are remote in the extreme.

So what other defences remain to the speaker of evil words? 'Fair comment on a matter of public interest.' In a country where free speech is treasured, people must be allowed to comment on matters of general concern.

Note, first, that what you say must be a statement of opinion and not of alleged fact. If the words complained of were partly opinion and partly fact, then in so far as they consisted of fact, they must be substantially correct. Comment to your heart's content, but do not mis-state facts.

The comment must be 'fair'. But this does not mean that your audience or the person named must consider it reasonable. In practice, this word provides little restraint upon your comment. Provided you are not simply using the occasion to forward a private grudge rather than to comment on a matter of public interest, you have nothing to worry about. But I repeat: The Englishman's right to comment must not be confused with his continued liability in damages if he confuses fact with fiction and, under the guise of comment, propagates false statements about his enemies.

The speaker, then, should watch his words, whenever he is speaking evil. Remember the three little monkeys? The one with his hands clapped firmly over his mouth is the most intelligent of all. Speak no evil and you need fear no action in slander.

All this works, as usual with the law, also in reverse. If you are at the receiving end of unkind words, apply these principles and you will know whether, in theory at least, you might have a good action in defamation against the speaker. But do not be surprised if you are advised by your lawyer not to sue, even though an action may lie. Defamation proceedings tend to be perilous in the extreme. Even if you win, you are in for a good deal of worry, aggravation and probably expense into the bargain. While orders for costs are customarily made in favour of the winners, these rarely cover all the costs incurred. There is usually a balance over which has to be paid by the winning litigant to his own lawyers, in any event. So litigation is a luxury. Nor can defamation proceedings ever be brought with the help of Legal Aid. Together with actions for breach of promise, they lie at the suit of the litigant at his own potential risk and expense.

Then, of course, your action may go wrong. The lesson of Oscar Wilde should be read by all potential plaintiffs in defamation actions.

Then there was the recent case of the leading plastic surgeon who was defamed in print by an erstwhile colleague. He sued. Now, juries have almost entirely disappeared from the civil courts, but they still remain in defamation proceedings. In the plastic surgeon's case, the first jury failed to agree. The case had to be retried. The second jury failed to agree. Once again, the worry, nervous strain and expense recommenced. Only on the third round did the plaintiff win. It was a handsome victory but the cost in frayed nerves and sleepless nights was extreme and the financial risk quite staggering.

So look well before you leap into proceedings arising out of the evil words of some other speaker. And hope that when you are guilty of defamation, the person referred to will, like yourself, have taken this chapter to heart.

Still, those who speak in public cannot be too careful about their words. As we shall now see.

15 *Personal attacks**

The word 'gentleman' has been defined as meaning 'one who is never unintentionally discourteous'. But just as the mature speaker never unintentionally loses his temper, so he does his utmost to cause offence only by design.

Outside the realm of politics, most wounds are both regrettable and regretted. 'The moving finger writes; and, having writ, moves on: Nor all thy piety nor wit shall lure it back to cancel half a line, nor all thy tears wash out a word of it.' With one, off-guard moment, you may acquire an unnecessary enemy for life. Regret it as much as you wish. The uttered word cannot be erased. So be careful.

Humour and wit are vital to the speaker (see Chapter 5). But many a jest, however kindly meant, has been taken amiss. There is all the difference in the world between pulling someone's leg in private and tweaking his sensitive tail in public. The same joke which went down splendidly at the dinner table may be a disaster when told from the platform.

No section of the public is more concerned with its own dignity than the men of commerce. Lawyers are reputed to be pompous. But they recognize as part of their trade the bitter court battle—which has no reference to their personal friendship outside the court. Barristers from the same chambers fight as

* See also Chapter 29 on Rudeness.

bitterly as need be for their clients. The personal jest is seldom resented.

But the businessman whom you attack in public is unlikely to wish to speak to you in private.

The seasoned politician revels in the 'cut and thrust' of debate. In most cases, he is able to dissociate the nature of an opponent from his public words.

But there is no such code in the world of business.

It follows that (quite apart from the laws of defamation—see Chapter 14) it is as well to keep the discussion at the level of ideas, rather than personalities. If you do attack your opponent, be sure of your ground. Make certain that his discomfiture is intended—and that it has a reasonable chance of leading to the results you seek. The thoughtless, careless, unprepared and vicious outburst in public can wreck a friendship, a partnership, a board, a project. Whether you are speaking at a comparatively small meeting or a mighty gathering, be careful. You are not alone. But if your attack is ill-chosen, you soon may be.

On the other hand, if you must attack a personality, then prepare your case with special regard to documentation. Letters, quotations, firm facts—these are what should accompany your theme. The more bitter your resentment, the quieter and more apparently reasonable your tone should appear. If you lose control of yourself, you will probably lose control of both the situation and the organization, in due course.

It is also a good idea to find out in advance whether your words are likely to be well received. There is no worse time to be shouted down than during a personal attack.

The chances are that if you must tell a man what you think of him, it is better to do so—and not to tell others.

If you are satisfied that rudeness is in season, then make full use of the power of ridicule. Shortly after the last Great War, there were bitter arguments as to whether the Fascist movement should be banned—'after all, have we not just finished a war against it? They would not give us our freedom, if they had their way—so why should we give them theirs?' But the 'leave them alone and let us hope they die of attrition' group won the day. They poured scorn, ridicule as well as contempt upon Hitler's British imitators. And so far at least, the recipe has worked.

But if the time does come for a personal vendetta, then the time and place must be most assiduously selected. By launching an attack, you invite a counter-attack. By mentioning the name of your opponent, you give him not only the publicity that he probably seeks but—in the eyes of those who believe in fair play—a moral right to reply. Instead of being in sole occupation of the platform, you may have to surrender it to an opponent who would be better off to lurk unseen.

16 Negligence—and those who speak without due care

To drive without due care is an offence dealt with by a magistrates' court. If someone else suffers damage as a result of a careless statement, it may lead to trouble all round. That was one effect of a recent, important decision of the House of Lords, sitting in its judicial capacity.

The story? A well-known merchant bank was asked for a reference. The inquirers wished to know whether a certain company was worthy of credit. The bank supplied the information; and when this turned out to be quite incorrect the inquirers lost their money. They sued the bank, claiming that although they (the inquirers) were not customers and the information was supplied gratuitously, the bank still 'owed them a duty of care' —that is, was under a duty to them to exercise such care as was reasonable in all the circumstances to ensure that the information given was correct.

'Nonsense,' retorted the bank. 'We supplied the service at no charge and you cannot expect us to have the same liability to you as we would have had, if you were a customer or we had charged you. And anyway,' they added, 'there was a disclaimer on the reference saying that it was given "without responsibility" on the part of the bank or its officers.' And they denied negligence.

The trial judge held that they had been negligent but that the effect of the disclaimer was to let them off the hook. They were under a duty of care, even though the service was given gratuitously. This decision was eventually upheld by the House of Lords.

The basic principle was established long ago. We each owe a duty of care to our 'neighbour', and a 'neighbour', in this sense, is any person whom we ought reasonably to anticipate would be likely to be affected by our negligent act. If, then, you are a manufacturer, you have a liability in contract to the people who buy your goods. If the goods are faulty, then you are in breach of contract. If you are negligent and they suffer injury, loss or damage, then you may be held liable.

But your responsibility does not end there. It extends to 'the ultimate consumer'. Suppose that you manufacture drink. It must be obvious to you that the person who is likely to drink it is not the wholesaler or retailer to whom you actually sell the stuff. The man behind the bar may drink some of his brew, but if he drinks it all there will be no profits. The 'ultimate consumer'—the customer of the retailer or caterer—is the man who will be poisoned if the drink is defective. He is the 'neighbour' of the manufacturer.

So there is a liability in the law of negligence not only to those whom you know but even to complete strangers.

'And the bank,' said the House of Lords, in effect, 'must be taken to have realized that the reference was asked for with a purpose in mind. The intention was that the reference be acted upon. So the bank ought to have realized that if the reference was incorrect, the result might well be that the recipient would suffer damage. So the bank "owed a duty of care" to that recipient, even though the service was given gratuitously.' The milk of human kindness may prove a very costly commodity.

So negligence had been found against the bank and a duty of care was owed. The damage was also proved. That left the disclaimer. The bank had given the reference upon the explicit and clear understanding that it was not to be held responsible for the accuracy of the document. The recipient could not go behind that disclaimer which was fully effective to protect the bank. As a result, the House of Lords did not have to consider the question of whether the defendants had been guilty of negligence. The bank escaped because of its disclaimer.

Ever since that case, all sorts of people have shivered slightly in their shoes—and rushed off to insurance brokers to get cover. The giver of every sort of reference must take care not only to avoid defamation in circumstances in which malice may be imputed to them (see Chapter 14) but must be careful to see that, if asked for a reference for one Peter Smith, he does not provide it in respect of another. He owes a 'duty of care' to the recipient.

Now suppose that you are making a speech. You are supplying information or advice. You owe a duty to your audience to be accurate. You are not guaranteeing complete accuracy in every word. The law only requires of you that you take such care as is reasonable in all the circumstances to ensure that what you say is correct. You will be expected to be as careful and accurate as an average, reasonably skilful speaker, dealing with your area of country. But you do owe a duty of care to your audience. You could, of course, start your speech by saying: 'Everything that I say to you is without responsibility on my part.' The audience will then be in the same position as the man who accepts a lift in a car with a sign up inside: 'Passengers carried entirely at their own risk.' But normally, you must exercise care because if you do not and as a result damage is suffered, you may be held liable in law. If you are obliging your audience by speaking . . . doing an unpaid kindness . . . doling out free information out of the goodness of your heart . . . the result may strike you as distinctly unfair.

Of course, it is not enough to prove that you were negligent in giving the advice or information concerned. To obtain damages against you, your hearers would have to prove two other matters. First, they must show that the statement concerned was acted upon. Second, they must prove that they suffered damage foreseeably arising from the negligence.

Infallibility being a divine attribute, everyone makes mistakes. But happily, most of them lead nowhere. We ourselves may even benefit from them—one wit observed that the great advantage of making a mistake is that next time you may recognize it. If others do the recognizing, then that is unfortunate. But it is only if they do not realize that you have been in error and actually take action as a result of your mistake that they will be able to claim a legal remedy.

Suppose, for instance, that you make a misleading statement in a speech to a trade gathering. As a result, one of your hearers consults his Board, his solicitor, his accountant, his management consultant and then—bolstered by the expert approval—takes action along the lines you have suggested. The chances are that he could not blame you. There were too many intervening people, facts and ideas.

Alternatively, suppose you make some provocative statement. It may never enter your head that anyone would be stupid enough to act upon it without further research or inquiry. But then maybe you were being obtuse. The question is: Would the 'reasonable man' have expected you to have foreseen that your hearer would act upon your words? Should you reasonably have prophesied, had you applied your mind to the situation, that your words would give rise to someone else's action? If not, then your mistake will lead nowhere—at least so far as you are concerned.

Assume, now, that your hearer can overcome both these hurdles. He has still not reached the end of the trail. He must show that the damage was not too remote. Take an example from an ordinary road traffic accident. Your employee caused it through his careless driving. If the man was driving in the course of his employment, you are as responsible as if you had yourself been at the wheel. Therefore you would have to compensate anyone who suffered injury, loss or damage as a result—provided that this was foreseeable.

So the cost of repairing the other vehicle . . . or reimbursing the injured man for his lost wages . . . paying damages in respect of his personal injuries—all these can be laid at your door.

But suppose, on the other hand, that the other driver had missed an important appointment and hence a potentially profitable contract. That will be his misfortune. The damage was 'too remote'.

All this involves some very complicated legal considerations. If by any chance your speech-making leads to the threat of legal prosecution, the sooner you get to your solicitor, the better. Meanwhile, just treat this chapter as a warning—and take care. Even if you are not paid for making your speech, you still owe a duty to your audience. Bore them and they get no recompense—except to take their revenge either by returning the compliment or by not renewing your invitation ever again. But cause them actual loss or damage as a foreseeable result of some careless misstatement and the sound of your own voice may be a very expensive product indeed.

17 Blasphemy, sedition, injurious falsehood and other spoken traps

There are various other respects in which the law interferes with freedom of speech. They are all comparatively uncommon in practice, but still require a weather eye from the speaker. So here is a miscellany of civil and criminal consequences which can arise out of use of the wrong word.

*　　*　　*

It is a serious offence 'to speak or otherwise to publish any matter blaspheming God'. You must not 'deny His existence or providence or contumeliously reproach Jesus Christ, or vilify or bring into disbelief or contempt or ridicule Christianity in general or any doctrine of the Christian religion, or the Bible, or the Book of Common Prayer'. But it is no longer a crime merely to 'propagate doctrines hostile to the Christian faith'. The question is—how do you do so? You must not 'exasperate the feelings of others' through any element of 'ridicule, irreverence or vilification'. You must not cause a breach of the peace.

Note that you may reproach Buddha, Mohammed, Abraham, Isaac or Jacob . . . Moses, Vishnu, the Gods of the Medes or the Persians . . . and the law will (unless you are provoking a breach of the peace or anything contrary to *The Race Relations Act, 1965*) do nothing. But then it does nothing, in practice, about blasphemy either. *The Blasphemy Act, 1697,* is still technically on the Statute Book . . . 'if any person or persons having an education in or at any time having made profession of the Christian religion within this realm shall by writing printing teaching or advised speaking . . . maintain or assert there are more Gods than one or shall deny the Christian religion to be true or the Holy Scriptures of the Old and New Testament to be of divine authority . . . and shall be convicted thereof, he shall be stripped of his public offices and if convicted again, he shall cease to be entitled to be guardian of a child, executor or administrator of any person, holder of any office, civil or military or beneficently ecclesiastical for ever within this realm . . .' He may also be imprisoned for up to three years. This curiosity of the law was unearthed, of course, in the recent *Gay News* case.

The offence of sedition embraces 'all those practices, whether by word, writing or deed, which fall short of high treason but directly tend to have for that object to excite dissatisfaction or discontent . . . to create public disturbance, or to lead to civil war . . . to bring into hatred or contempt the sovereign or the government, the constitution or the laws of the realm . . . to excite ill-will between different classes of the sovereign's subjects . . . to incite people forcibly to obstruct the execution of the law . . .' and so on, and so on.

In theory, this offence may put a heavy rein on free, political discussion. But in practice, it, too, is almost as dead as the proverbial dodo.

Not so perjury. If any person who is 'lawfully sworn as a witness or as an interpreter in a judicial proceeding wilfully makes a statement material in that proceeding, which he knows to be false or does not believe to be true . . .' he is a perjurer and may be imprisoned for up to seven years or fined an unlimited amount—or both. So when appearing before any 'tribunal, court or person having by law power to hear, examine and receive evidence on oath', mind how you speak (and see also Chapter 44 on witness-boxing).

Although there are prosecutions for perjury, bearing in mind the number of perjurers, it is obvious that the fear of committing this offence has about as little effect on the dishonest witness as any terror of purgatory, caused by flouting the witnesses' oath.

Now for some civil results of uncivil words.

As we have seen in Chapter 14, defamation may lead to trouble. But has it occurred to you that to speak ill of a person's goods may be defamatory of his person? Suppose, for instance, that you say: 'Jones is turning out really shoddy stuff these days and selling it at a very high price.' You are hardly heaping compliments on Jones's goods. You are saying, in effect: 'That man Jones is a rogue—he is selling low-quality goods at a high price.'

But quite apart from libel and slander, words may themselves give 'a cause of action' if they cause damage to a person 'in the conduct of his affairs' or are calculated to cause him pecuniary loss.

Suppose, first, that any sort of property is up for sale. A man 'without lawful motive' untruly alleges that the property is charged or that there are liabilities upon it or that the vendor is not in a position to sell. This is 'slander of title'.

Again, to say of someone that he is selling goods in infringement of copyright or patent, you may be alleging 'slander of title'. But nowadays, there are various statutory remedies available to those accused of this sort of behaviour (as by Section 65 of *The Patents Act, 1949*—which says that a person who is threatened with proceedings for infringement of the patent may bring an action for declaration that the threats are unjustifiable, and may also claim an injunction and—if he has suffered any— damages as well.)

Again, falsely and maliciously to disparage the quality of a man's goods may give rise to a cause of action—if the disparage-ment prevents their sale. By all means indulge in 'mere trade puffery', but 'knocking' may lead to trouble.

So where a false statement is made maliciously (out of a desire to injure and without lawful authority) and produces as its direct consequence 'damage which is capable of legal estimation', an action may lie for slander of title, slander of goods 'or other malicious falsehood.'

Finally, just a note on 'malice'. 'Maliciously' has been defined as meaning 'without just cause or excuse'. Unlawfully and in-tentionally to do 'without just excuse or occasion' an action which causes damage may lead to trouble. But it is certainly malicious to act out of some improper or dishonest motive or with the intention of causing injury. Where there is 'a distinct intention to injure the plaintiff apart from honest defence of the de-fendant's own property', an action may lie, without there being any defamation as such. (For 'malice' as affecting the defence of 'qualified privilege' see Chapter 14).

What it really comes to is that if you improperly or dishonestly attack the title or property or products of your competitors, they may have a good claim against you. The law approves of com-petition but frowns upon the more unpleasant forms of 'knock-ing' of the goods and property of others.

Part II
The arts of delivery

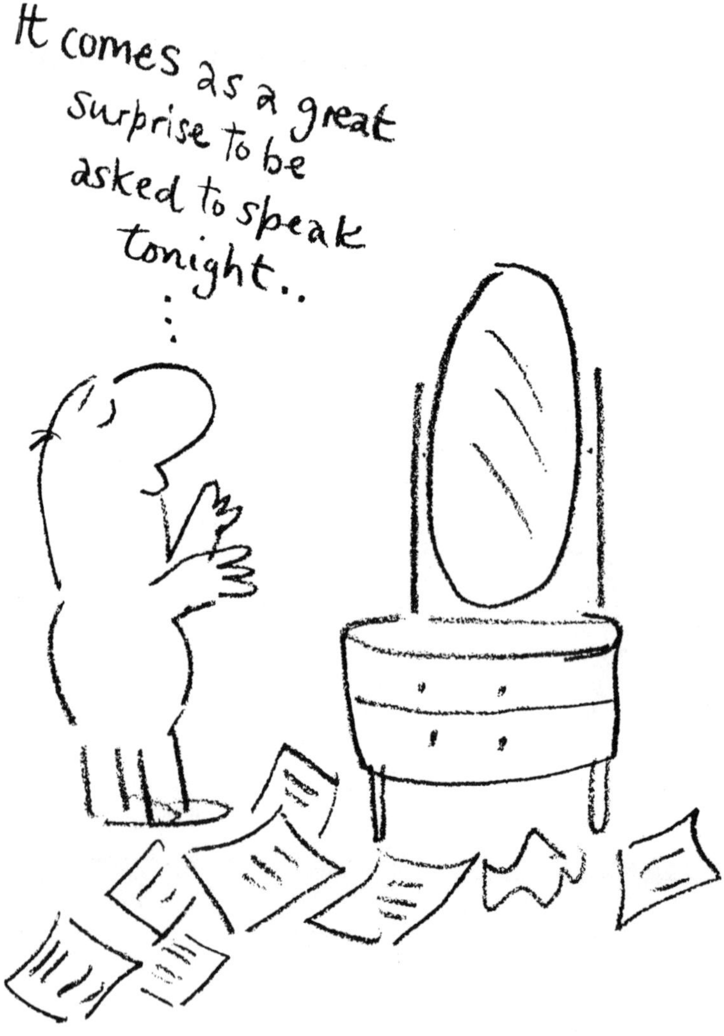
It comes as a great surprise to be asked to speak tonight...

18 Advance organization

In Italy, opera singers employ a claque. They have to. They pay the organizers who then ensure that the star receives the appropriate (or even inappropriate) applause, at the right times. If any star sees fit not to pay up, then (as one of them recently remarked), 'they are quite capable of whistling instead'.

Those who speak in public may also have a claque—paid or unpaid. And if the opportunity arises, no harm is done by ensuring that you get off to a good start or that your words appear to be treated with such delight that (with luck) your opponents may not like to speak out. People are like the proverbial sheep, particularly in public. They like to be on the winning side. Few have the courage to speak their minds openly in the face of a vociferous majority. 'What's the good of it?' they say—not realizing that if they only spoke out, they might well win the day. And they might discover that the noise-makers were in fact nothing more than a loud-mouthed minority.

The most inoffensive type of claque work is easily organized. 'For heaven's sake show me some support,' you say to your friends. 'If you do not give me some loud "Hear Hears", I shall stop trying. I refuse to be shot at on my own.'

Alternatively: 'This is going to be a very difficult audience to warm up. If you would be kind enough to start the clapping when I am called upon to speak, I shall remember you in my will!' (Have you ever noticed that it only takes one or two people to clap the speaker and the rest join in—but if no one starts, he goes on 'cold'?).

Again: 'I am going to tell them the story about the . . . For heaven's sake laugh!'

Of course, you may carry your claque along with you because they are under some obligation. Maybe you employ them . . . are the kind benefactor on whom they rely . . . have patronage in your gift. In that case, no preparation should be needed. Wise barristers soon learn to laugh at the judge's jokes—and whenever possible to produce any of their own ideas in the guise of words of wisdom dropped by Their Lordships.

But if you are on strange ground or amongst an unfamiliar audience, do not be afraid to ask your friends to give you the appropriate leg-up. One day you may be able to return the compliment.

Of course, advance 'softening up' of an audience may often go far deeper than this. If you have a case to put forward, you should do your best to sound out your audience in advance. If you have a resolution to propose, make sure that someone will be prepared to second it. The proposer without support is a miserable fellow and, in most cases, would have been better off to keep silent. A good speaker not only prepares his case, but also his audience.

Of course, none of this preparation should show. One reason why inexperienced speakers often take too little care in the preparation of their material is that they have seen how apparently easy the experienced speaker makes it all seem. Be not deceived. In general, the higher the polish, the greater the elbow grease . . . the more relaxed and effortless the style, the more careful has been the preparation.

Of course, there are natural speakers who need to take less care than the rest. But follow one of them round. Note how his performance varies. The odds are that when he stumbles, repeats himself, goes on for too long, breaks the basic rules of good speaking and starts to bore his audience—then he has not prepared his speech.

The better the preparation of the material and of its reception, the less it will show. The more it shows, the less its effect. In fact, if audience preparation shows at all, the insincerity of the claque may rub off on your speech. And that could be a disaster.

So choose your supporters with as much care as your words. But do not be too proud to prepare both with equal attention.

*   *   *

Incidentally, if you are the chairman, do make your preparations with special care. If there is to be a question time, prime someone to break the ice and to ask the first question—otherwise the silence may be unreal and embarrassing and ruin the evening. If you have to appear neutral but would like to espouse a particular viewpoint, make sure you get the best proponent possible to be ready with his speech at an early stage—and someone else available to do a later mopping-up operation. If preparing a team, the basis used by most athletes for relays could be helpful. The anchor man—your best—goes last. The next best goes first. The third does the third leg. And the worst goes second. You may want to put your anchor man first, of course—particularly if he has a right of reply (see Chapter 24).

If you are not the chairman, but are particularly interested in a particular topic or anxious to speak on it (or if you have to leave early or arrive late—see Chapter 77) do get the arrangements set up in advance. Most chairmen will oblige. They will probably be glad to have advance notice of your intentions, so that they can plan operations accordingly.

There is nothing like a pre-arranged plan to produce a happy result—provided the pre-arrangement is done with care and common sense.

19 Practice—and nerves

The more practice you get in public speaking, the better. But you will never chase away the butterflies for ever. 'Nerves' are part of the equipment of every public speaker.

The finest athletes are liable to feel decrepit and wobbly before their big event. But the moment that they line up at the start, or are in position for the game to begin, their nerves fall away. Nature has done its job. Adrenalin has been pumped through the body. The athlete is keyed up and ready to give of his very best.

The same process precedes the making of an important speech. Its importance may have nothing to do with the size of the audience (see, for example, Chapter 42 on Interviews). It may assume special gravity because it concerns your reputation or your future—or because you are dealing with a new and unfamiliar audience. There are very few of us who escape that nasty feeling in the pit of the stomach before some big speech.

So the beginner can comfort himself with the thought that even those who appear to have the most confidence and experience may well be feeling much like himself. Of course, they will not show it. The skilled man will not twist his hat, chew his finger-nails or tear up bits of paper. Part of his art is to dissemble his feelings. To some extent, the public speaker is an actor—but one who must normally write his own scripts.

Far from worrying about your 'nerves', you should be grateful for them. They are causing the adrenalin to build up and to prepare you for your ordeal. If you have no nerves . .. no feeling of apprehension . . . no pre-speech worries—then the odds are that you will not give of your best.

So banish those terrifying fears that your throat will dry up, your voice crack, your mind go blank. Provided you have prepared your speech ... that you have your notes handy (see Chapter 3) ... that you know what you are to be talking about

—all should be well. Under no circumstances must you panic, or all will be lost.

The more practice you get, the more your basic confidence will grow. If you are at a meeting, steel yourself. Ask questions of the speaker. If you are offered the chance of proposing the vote of thanks, accept. If a small group wishes you to address it, agree to do so. If you have been dealing with some new and interesting project . . . if you have gone on a lengthy and unusual journey . . . if you have something out of the ordinary to say— then let this be known. The chances are that your club, friendly society, pet charity, political group, trade organization or other body which you have previously merely belonged to, will be only too delighted to invite you to speak to its members or some section of them.

Or maybe you have a social function of your own: a dinner party, a cocktail party, or a company lunch. This time, stand up and say those few words of welcome, of thanks, of genuine greeting. If the speech is to be of any length, then (whatever the social occasion) the rules in Chapter 33 (on After-Dinner Speaking) will provide you with some useful guides. Remember: the higher you rise (or would wish to rise) in any field, the more vital it is that you should be able to express yourself on your feet. The only way to gain experience is to get up on those feet and, as the Americans put it, to 'sound off'. You will then cease to be afraid of becoming the centre of public attention; you will get used to the sound of your own voice, raised in public. You will stop worrying about 'making a fool of yourself'. And you will eventually learn how you can even cash in on your own mistakes.

So speak. The odds are that, however much you were previously kicking yourself for having agreed to do so, your nervousness will fall away when your words come through, loud and clear, and you see that your audience is listening to them. To borrow the words of President Roosevelt, you have nothing to fear but fear itself.

20 Handling an audience

Many an outstanding speaker does not talk to his audience at all. He looks around for some friendly face, and even amongst the most hostile gathering, there is usually someone from whom he can extract a friendly or tolerant smile. He then talks to that person. The speaker who looks over the top of his audience, out into space, seems to be indulging in soliloquy. But even he is better than the man who keeps his head lowered and mumbles into his notes.

Audiences are people. They want to be entertained. In most cases, they have come to the gathering, whatever it may be, because they are interested—if not in what you are going to say, then in what the meeting is to undertake. You keep their interest by talking to them—and not over their heads, literally or metaphorically. Look at them. Speak to them.

If asked to address a particular gathering, try to find out the sort of people to whom you will be talking. By all means inquire what the size of the audience is expected to be. Your preparation may differ considerably according to the number of your listeners. But even more important, try to find out whether they are skilled or unskilled, simple or learned, well versed in your topic or new to it, likely to be friendly or hostile.

After all, if you are attempting to put through a business deal, in private, you would not give the same 'spiel' to everyone. You would try to tailor your talk to the nature, personality, interests and sensitivity of your hearer. 'That's only common sense,' you say. Well, if more public speakers would apply that same sense to their audiences, the market for public speaking would not be spoiled as it is. People would turn up to meetings, instead of preferring their television sets. And speakers would be a great deal more successful than they are.

Whatever and whomever your audience may be, you must watch them while you speak. You can easily see whether they are concentrating or shifting around in their seats. If you have held them still for some time, then stop. Pause. Take a sip from your glass of water. Fiddle through your notes. Give your audience the chance to shift about and then to resettle. No one can concentrate for any lengthy period of time without a break.

If, on the other hand, your audience is restless when you do not intend it to be so, you must restore your hold upon it. If you have been pretty serious, then throw in a joke, a story, an anecdote. If you have been speaking at high volume, then switch to a confidential tone. If nothing works, then wind up—either permanently or for an extended question time. There is no more important rule for the public speaker than to keep a hawk-like watch on his listeners. It is different, of course, if you are talking to yourself—and if you ignore this rule, you soon will be.

POSTSCRIPT—LOOKING THEM IN THE EYE

As we have already seen, one of the speaker's problems is where to look. Facing your audience and looking them in the eye is a problem. But why should it be? Know the reason and the problem becomes easier to beat. Consider, then, one paragraph in that most revealing of recent books, *The Naked Ape* by Dr Desmond Morris:

'A professional lecturer takes some time to train himself to look directly at the members of his audience, instead of over their heads, down at his rostrum, or out towards the side or back of the hall. Even though he is in such a dominant position, there are so many of them, all staring (from the safety of their seats), that he experiences a basic and initially uncontrollable fear of them. Only after a great deal of practice can he overcome this. The simple, aggressive, physical act of being stared at by a large group of people is also the cause of the fluttering "butterflies" in the actor's stomach before he makes his entrance on to the stage. He has all his intellectual worries about the qualities of his performance and its reception, of course, but the massed

threat-stare is an additional and more fundamental hazard
for him.'

There it is. We fear those who stare at us. But if you want to
lift your head above the crowd, you must expect people to stare
at it. Learn to stare right back.

21 *Your friend, the microphone?**

In the old days, you had to speak to be heard. (For details, see
Chapter 22 on Voice Production.) Nowadays, a whisper will do.
The microphone has definitely arrived. What matters is to know
how to use it. Well employed, it is a trusty ally. Over-employed
or mis-used and it will blast away your audiences for ever.

A voice was a pre-requisite for a singer. No more. With the
aid of the 'mike', the men of alleged music can make their for-
tunes without, in many cases, enough power in their lungs to fill
a telephone box. Alternatively, they may belt out the tune—but
the nuances and expressions which the opera singer spends years
learning to create are absent. The effects which brighten so many
otherwise even more miserable music moments are created by
the microphone—through the tricks of the trade.

Now, not every businessman required to speak in public is
blessed with the voice of a Churchill. Some of us have voices
which refuse to be produced. Never mind. We can learn a good
deal from the pop singers.

First, make sure that your mike is switched on. Tap it with an

---

* See also Chapter 37 on Microphone in the Open Air and Chapter 44
on Radio and TV techniques.

inquiring finger. The sound of the tap should reverberate. And you should hear it. Nothing is more embarrassing than to talk into a microphone which is dead when you think it is alive but your audience knows that it is not.

Next, adjust the microphone to your height. Whether it is a standing or a table model, the chances are that there is a turning ring near the centre which—with a bit of luck and some reasonable wrist power—should enable you to fix the microphone at just below the level of your mouth. The top of the speaking part of the instrument, then, should be almost level with your lips. You may, of course, be lucky and be given one of those marvellous, modern gadgets you simply hang around your neck. Then you have no worries at all—assuming that it works. But otherwise, adjust for level.

In the artillery, there's a routine. You line up your gun as follows: roughly for elevation; roughly for line; cross-level; accurately for line; accurately for elevation. Hours of incredibly boring drill drum this routine into the mind—so that even years later, the odds are that the order is approximately accurate. There should be a similar routine for the mike-user. Roughly for height; roughly for position; volume; accurately for position; trial words.

So position the microphone in front of you, even if this means keeping people waiting while you adjust the cord or, if at a table, whilst it gets lifted over the wine and whisky. With the position and the level right and the mike switched on, you now check for volume.

You should be able to stand (or, in some cases, to sit) comfortably and perhaps six inches away from the microphone and still have your voice come through loud, clear and undistorted. If there is a scream, a whistle or a shriek, then it is on too loud. If there is a whisper, it is on too soft. If your voice sounds as if it were coming from outer space, with a Martian echo or an eerie ululation, then something needs adjusting.

This, of course, is not an engineer's summary. It is simply the result of years of acquaintanceship with microphones. So get hold of the mike, position it, and speak out. If the sound is wrong, then stop and have it adjusted before you launch into your speech.

'Fellow directors . . . ' Silence. Lift up your voice: 'Will some-one kindly switch on this mechanical marvel?' Laughter. With a bit of luck, the engineer scurries around and flips the appropriate switch. 'Thank you.' Screams and whistles from the machine. More laughter. 'There's no need to overdo it.' The engineer tries again. 'Fellow directors . . .' Silence. 'Are you receiving me?' you say, smilingly tapping the dreaded instrument. 'Do you hear me at the back?' Loud cries of 'No, no' and more laughter. But note: They are laughing with and not at you. You have command of the situation. You are waiting until the conditions are as you wish them to be before you start speaking.

With luck and perseverance, the microphone will be put into proper order. If it is not—or if reception is intermittent or un-pleasant—then you must make up your mind as to whether or not your voice will carry. Is it better to risk being unheard than to submit your audience to squeals and screeches from the machine? Will you succeed in interesting your audience, when the microphone is playing up? Have you, perhaps, a genius in the place who can adjust the amplifier, the loudspeaker, or some other unmentionable or unpronounceable part of this gadget? Think on your feet—fast.

'I shall do without the microphone,' you belt out. 'And I hope that you will all hear me.' Applause.

'Alternatively: 'I apologize for the inefficiency of this modern marvel. I think I had better submit you to the occasional grunt and growl, so that at least I may have the pleasure of letting you hear what I have prepared to say!' Hear, hear!

One way or another, you are off—even if it is to a late and unhappy start. But your audience have seen that you have complete confidence. More good speeches are ruined because the speaker is not prepared to take his time and make his preparations with the microphone than for almost any other reason.

Once you are speaking into the mike, remember that (usually) you are limited in your movement (see also Chapter 21). When you shift away from the mouthpiece, the volume falls. Turn your head either way and your words may be addressed to the entire hall but heard only by those at your feet. Find your distance from the machine and stay there. Within limits, you can relax. But move outside those limits and a lot is lost. Hence, of course, the special virtue of the hanging mike. Use one of them and (assuming, as before, that it is properly adjusted) you can move wherever the cord will allow.

For this reason, the hanging mike is infinitely to be preferred to the standing variety, whenever there is to be a lecture or other long speech which may require the speaker to move to blackboards . . . to wield a pointer at slides or diagrams . . . to alter his position. The man who speaks into a standing microphone, then rushes across the stage to point silently to some screen and then back to the microphone once more, is asking for trouble. He is also, of course, breaking his thread of speech and the audience's thread of thought. The good speech has continuity. The attention of the audience remains with the words spoken or, at the least, with the speaker's thoughts and not with his movements.

Experience will show each speaker how best he may make use of the microphone. But most of the above rules apply to us all. Make the mike your ally. Never panic when it goes wrong. Be prepared to fall back on your own voice power, if you have to—so that you are really not afraid of the microphone not working. Take your time when you start. Make friends with the engineer so that he is particularly careful to have the gadget fixed to your convenience, your height, your voice. And you have a trusty friend that King Henry V, Elizabeth I, Mark Antony and Julius Caesar would have welcomed. Come to think of it, how did any of those great speeches ever get heard by more than a fraction of the alleged multitudes ready to receive them?

22 Voice production

We may not all be opera singers, but we must make the best of such voice as we have. With luck, this happens naturally. Even the maximum of training, coaching or attention would prove useless without a basic flair for speech. But the unheard word would be better to remain unheard.

Basically, we are told, the chest is a sound-box. The voice should reverberate and carry, in the same way as a stringed instrument acquires its volume through the resonance of its sound chamber. The human voice, then, is an instrument and may be used properly or otherwise.

Try saying the word 'war'. First, talk through your nose. A puny sound. Then, speak the word from the front of your mouth. That's a little better. Now take a deep breath and expound the word until you can feel the vibration in your chest.

'If war comes again,' says the speaker, 'then it must mean disaster for us all.' 'War' is a word which receives no special attention and produces little drama.

'Disaster . . . faces us all . . .' says the orator. 'We are standing . . . perilously close . . . to the menacing brink . . . of . . . WAR!' Now, this may produce a 'ham' effect, but if the well-produced, deep and resonant sound is used from time to time to vary the more general conversational tone of the speech, it can be immensely effective.

The opposite also applies. To get and to hold the attention of an audience it is not necessary always to shout at them. The dramatic effect of a whisper can be intense. 'What greater menace is there than . . . the industrial spy?' Proclaim the last three words and they have an untrue ring. But whisper them and you can give them a snake-like quality.

But above all, however much you change the volume and tone of your speech, you must be heard. Speak to the rather deaf-looking lady in the back row. If she can hear you, you need not worry about the gentleman in the front. Be particularly careful not to drop your voice at the ends of sentences. The final few words should generally be spoken even more loudly and clearly than the rest—it is the inexperienced speaker who drops his last few words into his beard.

Assuming that you can be heard, what really matters is to avoid monotony. Vary your tone . . . the speed at which you speak . . . the volume of your words. Your job is to keep the attention of your audience. While to do so you must produce your voice with reasonable skill, the odds are that the less you actually think about voice production while on your feet, the better. Concentrate instead upon what you are saying . . . upon letting your audience hear it . . . and upon keeping their attention focused always upon you.

23 Persuading—the art of advocacy

Barristers, said Dean Swift, are men 'bred up in the art of proving that white is black and black is white, according as they are paid'. He left out of account, of course, the ethics of the Bar, which often requires its members to keep faith with the court by acting (and speaking) against the interests of their clients. Advocacy is one thing, deception another. Still, the Swift aphorism is too good to forget. And even the businessman may often be forced to propound or to defend in public, policies or decisions which, in private, he abhors.

It is not only the Cabinet that must stand by its majority decisions. The same normally applies to the Board of a company, the partners of a firm or the committee of an organization.

Either you accept democracy—allow your views to be overruled when the majority of your colleagues are against them—or you resign. If you remain in office, then you must stand by your colleagues. And this may mean engaging in their public defence.

So the advocate may not only have to propound views which are unpopular with his audience, but even those which find little favour with himself. Businessmen customarily attack lawyers and politicians as sophists and word twisters. But just listen to that executive, trying to make the creditors' meeting 'see sense' . . . the chairman attempting to extract himself (and possibly the company secretary) from trouble . . . the sales director, drilling his sales force about an unpopular (and perhaps not very satisfactory) product. There is really no end to the categories of persuasion in which the modern businessman has to indulge.

There is little art in persuading the convinced, preaching to the converted or keeping your team behind you when they all agree with your views or policies. To enthuse is, of course, important. But to argue a difficult case—or even one that seems on the face of it to be impossible—is a very much greater task. And here the businessman may take many a leaf from the brief of the skilful barrister.

Start with the quiet, sincere but firm approach. Call it 'the soft sell' if you like, but the studied lack of histrionics lies at the root of the modern persuader's art. Gone are the days of the ranter, the arm waver, the loud shouter (see Chapter 27). The theatrical tugger at the strings of the heart may still have his place in the revivalist meeting or the Welsh chapel, but he is a stranger to the court of law—and should be equally so to the company or organizational meeting.

The more your audience starts against you, the greater the importance of moderation—especially in your opening. Here are some well-tried gambits for the man in a minority:

'I fully appreciate the difficulty of my task in convincing you that . . . But I hope and believe that if you will be good enough to give my case a fair and full hearing, you will be as convinced as I am that . . .'

'Mr Black, who has just addressed you, is a skilled and experienced advocate and has presented the case against: with skill and eloquence. But there is another side to the picture and, before coming to a decision, I am certain that you would wish both sides of the story should be fully ventilated . . .'

'I am sure that many of us were extremely sorry to hear the vehemence and, in some cases, even the venom—with which the case for—has been put before this meeting. Whilst many of the points made have at least apparent validity, when you go a little beneath the surface, all is not quite as some of my friends have suggested. There are some very important points to be made to the contrary and I am sure that this committee/organization/ meeting would not wish to take any decision on such a very important matter without having had both points of view put before it. I shall do so, as briefly as possible: but I would be grateful for your indulgence, Mr Chairman, if I take a little longer than usual because one really does have to go into the case against—in some depth in order to establish its essential correctness . . .'

'This is a small committee of busy people and I really do think that we should expend no more time and energy in surplus pursuit of Mr X. He has made serious mistakes and is in the process of paying for them. Let us look to the future. And would it not be helpful to start with some of the achievements of Mr X. In many ways—some would say in most ways—he let us down badly. But he has laid certain foundations for our future success. First . . . Second . . . Third . . . Fourth . . . Fifth . . . Sixth . . .' By the time you are finished, Mr X appears to be quite a splendid character, does he not? But if you had started with his virtues, you would have lost all hope of winning your case.

*　　*　　*

Here, now, are some notorious traps to be avoided:

'Does anyone really think Mr Y has cheated the company?' Cries of 'Certainly . . .'

'Could it conceivably be in the long-term interest of this organization to follow the line proposed by Mr Blank?' Shouts of: 'Of course'.

'Does anyone really think that I do not know my job after all these years?' Loud cries of 'Yes'—and laughter.

Avoid the rhetorical question.

'I am . . . a man . . .' pause: shouts of 'No, no,' . . .

The Pause is a useful weapon—but watch where you place it (see Chapter 25).

'You may think that the statements you have just heard from Mr Z are about as untrue, misleading, ill-conceived and plain stupid as one could ever envisage.' This sort of attack—especially by someone in a minority—can only lead to vituperation, venom and defeat. Softly, softly, catchee monkee . . . as the Chinese are reputed to put it.

'I am furious . . .' Then do not show it.

'I could weep when I hear such extravagant attacks.' They all know that tears are not in your line—so away with the crocodiles.

*　　*　　*

Another move which is nearly always an error is to walk out of a meeting in high dudgeon. There are occasions when there is no decent alternative left to you. If decisions are taken which you regard as illegal, dishonest or so contrary to the welfare of the body concerned that you disassociate yourself publicly from them, then you may have no alternative. But otherwise, stay put and fight. Your chances of winning from without are far less than of working your colleagues or audience around to your way of thinking, from within. If you leave, remember that it is highly unlikely that you will be invited back. The dramatic exit is necessary for the diplomat whose country is publicly attacked in his presence. But it is seldom the answer for the orator spurned.

The threat of resignation is, of course, a powerful and a valid weapon. But it must not be misused or over-employed. Before it is used at all, you must consider whether it has any persuasive power. If your colleagues or the meeting would be happy to see you go, then you should rarely offer to provide satisfaction.

'If this decision is to be made, then I hope that it will not be taken amiss if I say that I shall have no alternative other than to reconsider my membership.' Fairly put. 'I have worked for this organization for many years and am anxious to continue to do so in the future. I would not wish to sever my ties nor to be forced into such a position that I would have no alternative other than to do so. I do beg you to reconsider. Or at least, please do give me a fair hearing for the other point of view. I would put it like this . . .' The chances of your not getting a fair hearing are remote.

On the other hand, avoid: 'If you do not change your minds, then I shall resign.' You are inviting the retort: 'Go right ahead'.

24 *The reply*

The debater who contents himself with making his own speech, without reference to those which have gone before, does not know his job. And many discussions—in public and private meetings of companies and organizations of all sorts—are really debates. The skilled speaker must study the art of making a reply.

The proposer of a motion or resolution is normally accorded the 'right of reply'. He opens the debate or discussion, and before the vote is taken, he has the privilege of closing it. His speech should not be a mere repetition of his original effort. He should deal—courteously, clearly and firmly—with the speeches which have intervened.

First, he should thank those who have spoken in favour of the resolution. Directly or by implication he should congratulate them on their perspicacity. 'I was not surprised to have the warm support of that experienced businessman, Mr Brown—but I was grateful for it none the less . . . Mr Green is highly experienced in the trade and I do hope that everyone here will give his words due weight . . . Mr White comes to us from an entirely different side of the trade. It is therefore all the more significant that he approves of this resolution . . .' 'Mr Green is, as you will all know, an extremely skilled and public-spirited lawyer. We must all be grateful to him for the careful analysis he gave to our problems—and for the legal light which he cast upon the dangers of the course of action espoused by those who oppose this resolution . . .'

Then demolish your enemies. 'I am sorry that Mr Diamond has not appreciated the warnings given by Mr Black . . .' 'If Mr Stone had really considered the argument that . . . I feel sure he would have come to a different conclusion . . .' 'Mr Ruby is, I fear, just plain wrong. The facts are not as he has suggested. The true position is . . .'

Then sum up your arguments once again, in a few sentences (see Chapter 2 on Perorations). Commend your resolution to the meeting. Then hope for the best.

Do not be afraid to use notes when replying. No one will expect you to remember all that has been said without keeping jottings. Once again, the card system may be very helpful (see Chapter 3). You can, if you like, deal with the questioners or opponents in turn. But you would probably be better off to rearrange the comments and criticisms to suit your argument. Remember that a reply is a speech like any other. It needs a good opening; a sound body; and a proper end.

Some suggested openings:

'Thank you, Mr Chairman, for permitting me to reply to some of the points raised . . . .'

'Mr Chairman, I suggest that nothing that has been said against the resolution has in any way destroyed its essential validity . . .'

'We must all be grateful to those who have taken part in this debate. Even those who oppose the resolution do so with the interests of the company at heart. But as, I think, we have seen from the speeches of Mr Brown, Mr White and Mr Black, its opponents have not really grasped the importance of the course of action suggested—and the risks of following any alternative . . .'

'The differences between us, Mr Chairman, have been fully aired. Every possible alternative has been thrashed over. But, at the end of the day, are we not still left with only one real possibility? The resolution must be passed.'

*   *   *

The making and answering of toasts is the subject of Chapter 33, but some of the above rules also apply to many responses to toasts. Do not ignore the speeches that have gone before. Do deal with any points of criticism or suggestion raised by previous speakers. Do not fear to use notes to remind you of the words of others. And do make certain that your speech is properly constructed. You have one great advantage over the man replying to a debate. His speech must not only appear extempore but must actually be so. Yours may be carefully prepared.

25 *The pause*

Churchill used the pause more than any other great orator. It is this interval between words, phrases or sentences that keeps the audience expectantly waiting for the next thought. Whilst the 'er' is normally the sign of a bad and aggravating speaker, and should be avoided like the plague—if you are a good enough orator, you can even use that irritating habit to good effect. 'We . . . er . . . have no intention of allowing that . . . er . . . maniac to control our lives.' Each pause and each 'er' merely whet the audience's appetite for Churchill's next slashing attack on the Nazis.

But for those of us who are not Churchills the pause without the 'er' is to be recommended. If you cannot think what to say, never mind—say nothing. So long as the audience thinks you are searching for the *mot juste*, even though you know you have a blank mind, all is well. 'Er' not. Stand firm. Look fierce. Look around. And when you are ready with your next pearl, drop it.

At the start of a speech, talk or intervention, you must be silent until you have the attention of your audience. If you are interrupted—whether by a drop of a window, the shrill of a jet passing overhead or the intervention of a colleague or interrupter—wait for silence before you proceed. To pause is not the sign of indecision or weakness. It is the speaker's greatest potential weapon—and the one that most speakers use far too little.

The pause before an important word is a superb trick, provided that it is not used too often. 'Ladies and gentlemen, if we do not now take the steps I have suggested, I foresee only one result.' Pause. Look round. Wait. 'Absolute disaster for the company.'

'We all remember the terrible days of . . .' pause. You are only using an extension of the suspense motivation, employed at the end of each properly constructed instalment of a radio play . . . the end of the chapter of a tightly written crime story . . . you are keeping your audience on its toes.

'After hearing all the views of this committee, I have come to my decision. I think that we have no alternative other than . . . to . . .' Wait for it . . . keep them waiting . . .

Of course, the pause must not be too long. Just as brevity of a wait may show lack of confidence and cause the pause to lose half its effect, so too great a length may be regarded by the audience as 'pure ham'. To over-dramatize is as bad as to under-

play. Only experience can teach the speaker how long to pause
Only practice can show the maximum period for the best effect,
But if in doubt, pause longer. Under stress, time tends to pass
slowly. Prepare an important speech and rehearse it more or less
word for word and time yourself on a stop-watch. Then make the
same speech on the important occasion and get someone to time
you. Ten to one you get through it quicker under stress. (Only
when you must expect and deal with interruptions . . . including,
one hopes, applause . . . will the converse apply, of course.)

While gaining that experience, then, consider the most
common occasions for pauses.

1 THE OPENING Make sure that your audience have settled
   down and are ready to hear you—whether you are making
   a major oration at a rally or a minor intervention at a Board
   meeting.
2 IN MID SENTENCE To emphasize a really important point.
3 AFTER AN INTERRUPTION OF ANY SORT Once again, your
   audience must be settled in to hear what you have to say.
4 BEFORE YOUR LAST FEW WORDS 'And now, ladies and
   gentlemen, I beg you once more to support your Board . . .'
   pause 'so as to ensure . . .' pause '. . . that this great organization . . .' pause '. . . will continue to flourish.' Pause. Look
   around at those from whom you expect applause. And then
   sit down.

Which brings us to the final hint. Applause is a very helpful
(not to say invigorating) leg-up for any speaker. If you did not
want it, you would not speak. We all like to be liked. We all wish
our words to be accepted. The 'hear hear' or clapping is as grati-
fying to the speaker as the groan is a misery. It is essential to
anticipate and to deal with the cheers—and to fish for and to
pause after them.

It is rare that a pause should be used against the groaner. By
all means look round and glare at the man who has the temerity
to jeer at you. But then leap back at him with both feet. 'People
who have the interests of the company at heart and want to see
this venture succeed will not assist by that sort of behaviour . . .'

Or: 'I do not think that you, sir, are assisting your cause by behaving in that manner.' Or, if kindness seems to be the best way to deal with the situation: 'I am sorry that you should see fit to jeer, sir. If you would be good enough to wait a little, you will hear the reasons for my last remarks. And you will see that they are correct.' Then pause. Allow the effect of the jeer to die away. But do not pause so long that the interrupter is encouraged to have another go. The borderline between the effective and the defective pause is a narrow one. Each case must be judged on its own facts. But far more people rush forward in haste than regret the (apparently) confident wait for silence, attention . . . effect.

The pause is even more vital—and less of a risk—when fishing for cheers. If you are nervous, follow the sound theatrical first-night tradition of organizing your own claque. Tell them that when you refer to Mr Jones and his great service to the company, they must immediately clap. 'Be a good chap and cheer loudly when I finish the sentence about . . .' It only takes one or two people to get the applause moving. 'When old Smith gets up to speak, for heaven's sake help me to give him a good reception . . .' A fair gambit. So is: 'We must give the impression of vast enthusiasm for the new project. So when I say how confident I am that it will be a success . . .' pause '. . . clap!' (The pause gambit is even useful in ordinary speech.)

An audience generally likes to know when applause is expected. 'We are all pleased to welcome our guest of honour from abroad, Monsieur Jaune.' Pause and you will get a clap. Rush on and you will not.

'Here, ladies and gentlemen, is the first sample of our new product. I present it to you . . .' pause '. . . with pride . . .' Pause '. . . I trust that you will sell it, to your profit and that of the company . . .' Pause. Look round. Someone will probably say 'hear hear . . .' if only to please you.

One possible approach if no one applauds is to attack them for their silence. 'Gentlemen, the success of each of you, as well as that of the company, depends upon the way you push this product. So I trust that your silence is no indication of any lack of enthusiasm. I invite you . . .' pause '. . . to greet with pleasure this new success from our research department.'

If that does not do the trick . . . if you cannot drag up the applause you want, then never mind. Move on. Change your tack. Alter your approach. Try again. But do not rush. Wait. Control your audience. Do not be afraid of the pause. The old saying, 'silence is golden', has no more vital and accurate application than in the world of the spoken word. Silence is sometimes a weapon as valuable as speech itself.

26 Interruptions

Sometimes speakers welcome interruptions—in the right places. Apart from giving the speaker the chance to show his mettle, the heckler can rouse the audience and put them on the speaker's side . . . the unexpected break can bring variety to a dull occasion and spark off an easy flood of laughter . . . and sometimes, the interruption can make a point better than the speaker could do on his own. But you have to be alert to reap the benefit. If you are tied to a script, written or memorized, you may be thrown off your balance. If you cannot think on your feet, you are better off sitting down.

First, take the heckler. The shareholder comes to a company meeting to criticize. He shouts interruptions at you. How do you deal with him?

You must maintain your dignity. Quiet but firm appeals for a fair hearing usually bring applause. 'I appreciate that the gentleman has a point of view to express and he will be given every opportunity to do so. Meanwhile, I would ask him to have the courtesy to listen.' Alternatively: 'If, sir, you would be good enough to listen to what the Board has achieved in the present difficult circumstances, you might learn something to your benefit.'

If the moment has come to be rude, try: 'If you would listen to me, sir, instead of to yourself, you may be doing yourself a favour, as well as the rest of us.' Or: 'For heaven's sake have the courtesy to be quiet.'

Naturally, if the meeting gets too rowdy and you cannot control it—or, to be more precise, the chairman cannot deal with the interrupters, in the atmosphere which you created or in which you are speaking—then the chairman may have to call on the stewards to evict the interrupters. He is not bound to let your meeting be wrecked (see Chapter 75).

Still, it is rare that a wide-awake speaker cannot keep his audience in reasonably good humour—or at least obtain a hearing, literally as well as metaphorically, without the use of force.

Some interruptions are healthy and helpful—whether or not they were intended to be so. The humorist's outcries can often be turned against himself—assuming that the man on the platform is alert. The scream of a jet engine overhead may drown you for the moment, but give you the opportunity to draw some moral about the point you are making. Even a friendly remark addressed to a member of your audience arriving late may save you both from embarrassment, as well as giving you the opportunity you may in any event need to sort yourself out . . . to vary the pace of your talk . . . to give your audience the chance to relax for a moment, to shift about in their seats and to prepare for the rest of your speech.

What is required, of course, is self-confidence from the speaker. He must pretend to be in complete command of the situation— and will probably discover that in fact he is. The more you feel like panicking . . . the more likely you are to lose control . . . the more you must smile, pause and give the appearance of absolute 'unflappability'. The rowdier the meeting . . . the more disconcerting the interruption . . . the more aggravating the break in your train of thought—the more important it is for you to demonstrate to your audience that you are not to be thrown off your guard. When they see that you are determined to remain in control, the chances are that they will help you to do so.

Go to any first-class political meeting—if you can find one these days—and watch the skilled politician at work. Listen to how he prompts his audience to get cross with hecklers . . . to tell them to 'Shut up' . . . to demand from others in the audience that they give the speaker a fair hearing. Half the good political speaker's work is done for him when he has a few inefficient hecklers in his audience. They rouse supporters, bring the uncommitted to the speaker's side and enliven what might otherwise be a dreary occasion.

The more spontaneous the reply, the wittier the retort, the speedier the counter-attack, the more effective the speaker and his speech. A weak riposte now is better than that brilliant barb which you afterwards wish you had thought of at the time.

So do not be put off your stroke by the interruption. Make use of it.

27 *Passion*

There are certain matters about which we all feel particularly strongly. It may be something affecting one's personal integrity . . . one's family . . . the entire basis of one's work. It may be a personality . . . an idea . . . a scheme. If our passions are shared by others—all others—then they will have no real place in a public speech. But if we have to fight for our ideas and ideals, they are likely to be the subject of motions and emotions, resolutions (in both senses of that word), speeches and harangues. So in case you have to introduce passion into your public words, here are a few suggestions.

*   *   *

Passions must be controlled. The speaker who loses control over himself will fail to handle his audience. Unless your mind is clear, you cannot put on your best performance. Passion clouds the mind.

Studied calm is a powerful weapon. Your audience will be well aware from your demeanour that you feel deeply. But if you make it clear that your mind is guiding your heart, you are far more likely to influence the ideas, votes or pocket-books of your listeners in the direction you require.

You may wish your audience to feel sorrow with you, but you do not want them to feel pity for you. Just as you may seek to have them laugh with you, if they laugh at you all may be lost. So direct your words at your theme—but not at your own feelings. Finish off, if you like, with a thundering peroration— or an icy blast—indicating your own views and calling for support. But do not let your feelings prevent you from making a good, well-constructed, carefully thought out and well-presented speech. Crying does not pay. Passionate eloquence may have its place in the pulpit but it seldom produces results at a company meeting, organizational gathering or public conference.

If you must let off steam, do it at home.

28 Stance and gesture

Most speakers hope to put across ideas. Even if engaged in pure entertainment, you still require the attention of your audience. And it is the words that should be having their effect. So nearly all physical movement is a distraction, to be avoided where possible.

We all know the man who strides up and down while talking, like the American lawyer in the television court-room scenes. In England, lawyers stand still. Their speeches are the better for it.

Comedians doing a tumbling act must gyrate and mime. Not so the man who relies upon the words. Consider the mastery of such as Bob Hope, who stands still and pours wit into the ears of his audience.

The more motionless you stand, then, the greater the chance of your speech reaching the minds of your audience.

But what to do with your hands? The more inexperienced the speaker, the more difficult he finds it to dispose of his hands.

If you have a rostrum or music stand before you, then grip the edge. If you are standing by a table, then you can keep your hands down in front of you. If you stand on your own, then you could do much worse than to put your hands behind your back, *à la* Duke of Edinburgh. What matters is that you should be erect and still.

What of gestures?

These should be sparing. The rarer and the more restrained the movement, the greater its effect. The days of the ranting, tub-thumping, rabble-rousing arm waver are gone. The business-man who 'hams' is regarded (not always rightly) as an insincere show-off. A contemptuous shrug . . . an occasional, accusing finger . . . a reference to the heavens and a hand pointing to the sky . . . these all have their place in the skilled speaker's repertoire. Those who use spectacles may find them quite useful weapons. To emphasize a point, remove them gently from your nose. Hold them still in your hand. Bend forward and glare at your audience. Make your point and then replace your glasses and return to your theme. Even the occasional jab with the closed spectacles can be dramatic and useful. Speakers with spectacles need not be shy. Many excellent speakers who could do without their glasses, even for seeing their notes, deliberately wear them. So do not be afraid of your poor eyesight. Like many other defects, it can be turned to good account.

But generally, the speaker should use his tongue, his face and his mind—not his feet or his fingers. Otherwise his audience may take to their heels.

29 *Rudeness—and water off a duck's back**

To turn the other cheek is often a desperately difficult proposition. There are those who recommend it as being good for the soul. But for the businessman who speaks in public, to demonstrate the self-control that this sort of reaction to rudeness inevitably demands is almost always also a good gambit. To lower yourself to your opponent's level rarely achieves the desired results.

Your object, after all, is to win your case—to convince your audience of your rectitude . . . of the usefulness of your activities . . . of the excellence of the way in which you are running the business—or, conversely, of the errors of your opponents.

* See also Chapter 15 on Personal Attacks.

The sharp intellect is a far better weapon than the rough tongue. When the theme is laced with incivility, the audience is likely to suspect a lack of factual backing or to deplore a lack of self-control—or both.

If ever you have a half-hour to spare and are in the vicinity of a court of law, watch how lawyer advocates do their job. They must 'handle the judge'. As one distinguished practitioner put it: 'What matters at the Bar is not whether you know your law but whether you understand your judges.' So spare a moment to watch the professionals—good, bad and indifferent—earning their living through advocacy.

Try, in particular, to find a judge or a magistrate who is known to be 'difficult'. Happily, the vast majority of men and women on the Bench, at all levels, are courteous and, in general, kindly. But there are exceptions—most of them well known to the profession. And even the best of men may be suffering from ulcer, backache or matrimonial troubles. So see how lawyers politely but firmly stand up to the rigours of the unfriendly judge. Quietly, firmly and respectfully—and sometimes with considerable courage—they refuse either to be browbeaten into premature silence or provoked into unseemly loss of temper. They well know that their client's chance of winning his case is rarely helped if they lose their self-control—or even appear to do so.

There are, of course, famous exceptions. Legal memoirs and reminiscences are full of tales of the brilliant barristerial repartee . . . of Sir Patrick Hastings putting the judge in his place . . . of F. E. Smith carrying his client to victory on the shoulders of a deadly rebuke directed at a disagreeable judge. Like good wines, these tales tend to mellow and improve with age.

But for the average public speaker—whether he be the company director, trying to talk sense into the heads of his Board in revolt . . . the salaried director or company secretary, dealing with the irascible chairman or managing director who is seeing fit to dress him down at a Board meeting . . . or an angry shareholder, making loud-mouthed, unwarranted and personal attacks against the company at its Annual General Meeting—the 'other cheek' policy is seldom out of place.

'I am extremely sorry that Mr Jones has seen fit to deal with this serious matter in such a vituperative fashion . . .'

'If Mr Jones would be good enough to listen to what the Board has achieved, I think he will regret the manner in which he has seen fit to refer to it . . .'

'We are all here for a common purpose—to advance the welfare of the business. The sort of remarks which have just been made are likely to send it into retreat. They can only give comfort to our competitors . . .'

'We will answer each criticism, in turn. We will ignore the personal and regrettably offensive manner in which some of these attacks have been made. If Mr Black really is, as he says, concerned for the welfare of this organization, I trust that when he has heard the case for the steps which he has so bitterly criticized, he will not only have the good grace to withdraw those criticisms, but also to apologize to those whom he has inevitably hurt by his unkind remarks. I hope that such was not his intention. He is, as we all know, a kindly man, and we all appreciate what he has done for the company. We know how deeply involved he is, emotionally and otherwise, in its success . . . and no one will bear him the least ill-will because he has spoken his mind . . . But . . .'

'We all appreciate, I know, the customary frankness with which Mr White has dealt with this resolution. We do not appreciate, however, the personal insinuations he has made—which can only detract from the genuineness of his case and the real concern with which he and those who support him—and, indeed, many of us on your board—view the circumstances he discussed . . .'

*   *   *

There is a basic psychological truth that hostility breeds hostility, and an aggressive approach nearly always invites a like response. The converse often applies. Surprise your critics with your moderation, understanding, sensitivity and those views may mellow. It is, in any event, an approach far more likely to succeed than the frontal attack.

What is more, once you have let rip with your hostility, not only has the reasonable possibility of future friendly relations been gravely affected, but you have even discounted the off-chance that the critic was really on your side all the time. Any experienced politician will tell you that some apparently hostile questions are asked at meetings so as to obtain an answer for the benefit of those whom the questioner wishes to convince, and not for the questioner's benefit at all. 'All right, don't listen to me . . . We'll ask old White . . . He'll tell you a thing or two . . .' Blast the questioner for being an idiot and you have obliterated a friend and confirmed a foe in his enmity.

If you must lose your temper, then at least do so with deliberation. Choose your moment and your words with equal care. Absorb the chapter on defamation (Chapter 14). Consider the rules on disorders (Chapter 76). And then—if you must tear into your opponent—do it properly.

A judge once said to F. E. Smith: 'What you are saying to me is going in one ear and out the other.' To which F. E. Smith replied: 'That, my Lord, does not cause me any surprise, having regard to that which lies in between.'

But most of us think of the best repartee when the occasion is past. While swift retorts often produce acclaim far beyond their merit, the rude, unkind, offensive or angry outburst . . . the facetious, sarcastic, ironic or spiteful suggestion—these breed contempt, derision, stony silence—and defeat. And not for the individual towards whom the words are directed.

30 In a tight corner

Metaphorically speaking, we tend to draw our allusions, in time of trouble, from the worlds of fencing or boxing. A cutting remark ... a debating thrust ... out for the count ... to hit below the belt ... in a tight corner ... and so on ...

Well, if you are in difficulties, you must choose your words with especial care. To emerge unscathed, you have three alternatives. You can throw in the sponge ... trade blow for blow ... or duck smartly under your opponent's fist, and make nimbly away.

You are proposing a toast to the bride and groom? The bride's father is dead? The groom's parents are divorced? What do you do?

You can surrender by making no mention of the parents. This is abject cowardice, and generally regarded as such.

You may neatly duck the situation by a few, carefully chosen sentences: 'The bride's father ... we wish he were not here only in spirit ... but he would have been proud and happy today ... How pleased we are that our groom's parents are both so well and handsome—and here together for the celebration ...'

Finally, you can take the bull by the horns (to take an analogy from a sport of another kind). You can start with the sort of comment given above—and then extend it into the appropriate elegy. 'Let us face it, ladies and gentlemen—no occasion is completely perfect, no life without its problems. How sad we are that the bride's father is not here ... but we admire her mother doubly for the fortitude with which she bore her loss and especially for the courageous and splendid way in which she brought up the bride ... the extent of her triumph is revealed by the radiance of our bride today ... We know, too, that our groom's parents, alas, have not been without their differences. But today, as always, they put the happiness of their son above all else—and they sit together with him, united in their joy at his happiness and good fortune...'

There are plenty of equivalent situations in business. The surrender is achieved by an apology. The counter-attack is explained in Chapter 29 (Rudeness). And the form of ducking away from trouble, to be adopted in any particular circumstances, will depend upon those circumstances themselves. Here are some useful, opening gambits:

We fully appreciate the circumstances which have led to your anger and disappointment. But there is another side to the story and we do hope that you will give it your earnest consideration...

You are quite right, on the face of it—but...

I do see your point of view—but am sure that you will give consideration to mine...

Yes, we made a mistake—but in all good faith. The situation nevertheless remains that...

We see your viewpoint. Now please do consider our's...

You have set out your case quite admirably. It is only courteous, then, for me to set out as fully as possible the situation as we see it...

We genuinely feel that your complaint is based on a misunderstanding. We do see that... but would urge you to consider...

Yes, you are right. But...

No, we do not agree with you. But nevertheless...

*   *   *

Have you noticed that the man who uses words as weapons employs very similar tactics to those of the fencer or boxer? You give way a little, so as to attack a lot. You retreat gently, so as to counterattack with firmness. You at least pretend to see the other man's viewpoint, so that he will be prepared to consider your's. Alternatively, you politely disagree—and then show your magnanimity and/or good sense or good will by then offering a compromise or giving in on some point, however small.

The French put it well: 'Il faut reculer pour mieux sauter'— You must withdraw, the better to leap forward. As with weapons of war, so with words of forensic skill, written or spoken. You step back so as to throw your opponent off balance (boxing again).

There are occasions, of course, when you have your back to the wall . . . there is no room for retreat . . . all escape routes are cut off . . . Then remember the advice given to policemen, in similar but physical circumstances. 'Tuck yourself neatly into the corner and use your fists, your knees, your truncheon . . . At least if you are in that corner, they will not be able to get a knife in your back . . .' Unless, of course, they knock you unconscious and drag you out . . .

Try these gambits, when absolutely desperate:

If you see fit to make these allegations to third parties, we shall have no hesitation in putting the matter in the hands of our solicitors . . .

Your threats are as empty as the premise upon which your allegations are based is groundless. Nevertheless, if you wish to take the matter further, we must refer you to our solicitors . . .

We regard your allegations as both impertinent and groundless. If they are repeated, we shall take such steps as we are advised by our lawyers, to protect both our position and our good name . . .

If you are so ill-advised as to carry out your threats, then kindly direct all future correspondence to our solicitors . . .

In one, last, desperate attempt to remedy a situation which (we repeat) is not of our making, our Mr Jones will contact you and try to arrange some convenient time to visit your office . . .

Our chairman will be in touch with your's . . .

31 *The venue*

Very often, the speaker has no say as to where his speech must be made. The company meeting, organizational gathering or dinner-party is to be held in a place chosen by others. But even there, the experienced speaker may be able to make the best of his surroundings, if he knows what to look for. In many other cases, the speaker can influence (if not choose) the venue for his talk.

The first essential is to try and match the size of the room to the number of the audience. If the room is packed, the chances are that an atmosphere will be easy to create and the speaker's task made vastly simpler. If the room is half empty, his difficulties are enhanced. Take fifty people and squeeze them into a drawing-room and you are likely to have a lively, happy meeting. Lose those same fifty in a hall and the evening is a failure before it has even begun. So underestimate your audience. If a few get left outside, never mind. Next time they will come earlier. If some have to stand, or perch, on radiators, that cannot be helped. You must avoid at all costs the echoing emptiness of a half-filled hall.

If you do find yourself with a sparse audience, do not panic. Suggest to the organizers that they ask all those present to come right up to the front. People hate being at the front, preferring to tuck themselves away in a nook near the door, the better to make their exit if they get too bored. And it is not only speakers who are sometimes shy. But a capable chairman can wheedle most people into 'helping our distinguished speaker'. If your chairman is inexperienced, then (having obtained his permission) you ask your audience to 'gather round'.

Many times, it is better to abandon the platform, draw the curtains and come down to your audience. If the formal gathering has failed to draw in the crowds, then at least ensure that you have an informal chat, so that your audience go home satisfied with their evening. It is most unlikely that they would be if they were to be regaled from above with an oration more suitable to a packed and cheering hall than to an almost empty room. Someone overestimated the audience in the first place and created your unfortunate situation. It is now up to you to make the best of it.

Other suggestions? If the room is too hot, stop and ask for a window or a door to be opened. Your audience will bless you. If it is too cold, speak to the organizers and see whether they can do anything about it. The chances are that they cannot. But at least your audience will know that you are thinking of their comfort. If there are aeroplane noises overhead, stop until they pass. To speak on regardless is a sure sign of inexperience. If a carpenter is banging next door, then ask the chairman to use his influence to obtain silence for you. Then wait whilst the results of his efforts appear.

Of course, it is far preferable to have these distractions dealt with in advance. If you can get to a meeting sufficiently early, you can sometimes induce the organizers to rearrange the seating so as to suit your theme or your plans. You may want to avoid the use of a platform or to have the chairs arranged informally in a horseshoe, or conversely, to speak to your audience from a higher level. It helps everyone to have things arranged beforehand.

Again, it may pay dividends to have the sound equipment tested before the audience arrives or the lighting adjusted to suit your requirements (see Chapter 21). No theatre audience expects to have these changes arranged in their presence. No audience for a speech or lecture, a discussion or debate, likes to to see them done after their arrival. Punctuality pays. If you wish to make a triumphal entry at a later stage, you can always disappear from the scene until the appropriate moment. And if your chairman or hosts know their business, they will have organized some small room at the back for you to use for your coat and hat and for your refreshment.

But so much depends on the occasion. As we shall shortly see.

32 *Lessons*

The British businessman tends to be an amateur. We have no real equivalent of the Harvard Business School, and the average British speaker has seldom had any formal training. Even the barrister, who makes his living out of advocacy, is entitled to qualify without ever having opened his mouth in public. He learns on the job (or not, as the case may be)—all of which just does not make sense.

We all know that there is, in this country, a certain prejudice against taking lessons in public speaking. A book on the subject is not so bad. (Have *you* put this one into a plain, white cover?) 'But my dear fellow . . . fancy taking lessons in speaking . . .'

Yet there is no good, logical reason for this curious attitude of mind. Speaking in private may come naturally. Speaking in public does not. It requires experience. And without the appropriate flair, no amount of teaching can produce really outstanding results. But if you find that public speaking is a burden upon you . . . that you need to practice in private, but with an experienced audience . . . then do not despise the lesson. There is no need to advertise to your customers, clients, friends or family that you are indulging in that particular form of masochism. But whether you are simply an inexperienced speaker in need of practice or (and more especially) a sufferer from any form of speech defect or accent impediment, a good teacher is worth his weight in the compliments he will bring upon your head.

How do you find the right man? He may advertise in the local Press. Your local Education Authority or Citizens' Advice Bureau may put him in touch with you. In general, beware of the local school of drama—but an experienced speech therapist may either be your man or know of him. Do not, of course, lay out money for any long series of lessons until you are satisfied that the individual suits your purposes. Try a lesson—and do it on the basis that you will pay a single, once-off fee if you do not decide on a course, but that if you do opt for the longer and more expensive training, then the first lesson will form part of it.

The same principles apply to courses in public speaking which you may want for your staff or executives. Find an expert and call him in. Negotiate a fee and then watch out for results. Given even moderate material, the first-class teacher can be a very great help. The speaker in public may be an amateur, but there is no reason for him to be untrained. If more speakers had more training, listeners would have a much happier time.

My Lords, ladies & gentlemen—
Pray silence
for ...

Part III
Occasions

33 *After dinner*

A captive audience, well wined and amply dined, should be an orator's joy. But more often than not the speaker is too apprehensive to enjoy his food—and instead makes a meal of his speech. Which is quite unnecessary, if he would only follow a few basic rules.

First, wait for silence. When you have it, look around amiably and begin: 'Mr Chairman, ladies and gentlemen . . .' or as the case may be. Those few words are useful. You discover that you have not lost your voice after all. And your audience (at that stage at least) is ready to listen—and to be entertained.

However heavy the dinner or the company, however important the occasion or mighty the listeners, no one wants a dry lecture on top of a wet repast. So however important your message, do your audience the courtesy of exerting patience. Start with a joke . . . a witticism . . . a story.

The best jokes are usually impromptu. A friendly jibe at the chairman, the restaurant, the food . . . an oblique reference to the headline in the evening papers (those of the audience who have read it are delighted to be in on the joke). Otherwise, there are many good opening gambits such as:

'A few moments ago, the chairman turned to me and said: "Would you like to speak now—or shall we let them go on enjoying themselves?".'

Not long ago, an after-dinner speaker was greeted by a woman, at the evening's end, who said to him: 'Mr Jones . . . that was a terrible speech!' He composed himself as best he could—and was then greeted by another woman who said: 'I'm awfully sorry about Mrs Brown . . . she has such a long tongue . . . and she's such an idiot—she hasn't got a mind of her own . . . She only repeats what she hears other people saying!'

'I wish you could have seen the chairman, at the nineteenth hole . . .'

However weak the wit, dry the humour or wet the joke, provided that you put it across with verve, courage or at least a friendly smile, you are on your way to establishing *rapport* with your audience. They will settle back into their chairs, relaxed—and either be receptive to a continuation of merriment or, at worst, they will be the better braced for such message as you care to give.

Now you launch into the speech. Brevity should be its keynote. Have you ever heard anyone complain that a post-prandial offering was too short, too condensed? When addressed by the best after-dinner men, they may say: 'I could listen to him for ever . . .' But even if they think that they mean it, practice would prove them wrong.

The lower down you come in the toast list, the greater the premium to be put on brevity. So why is it that many of the most nervous speakers find it necessary to be the most long-winded? Do they think they can make up for their lack of wit, their terror or their dearth of wise words, by length? You may argue your bank manager into submission . . . stifle the opposition of your competitors by talking them into the ground . . . exhibit superb salesmanship by making it clear that you are not going to leave until you get what you want. But all this is in private. Enter into the public arena in general, or the dinner table in particular, and you must be brief.

As for the after-dinner speech itself, it requires the same careful construction as any other. It needs a flow of ideas as well as of words. And the more the words are laced with wit, the more likely that their wisdom will strike home.

So watch your audience. If they drop off to sleep, either tell them a joke or sit down. If they start jiggling the cutlery, wind up your sermon. If you want to be asked again, do not outlive your welcome.

As you approach your end, remember what it is you have been

called upon to do. If you are responding to a toast, you should start by thanking the man who made it and complimenting him on his wit and wisdom. And you should finish where you began —by repeating, once again, your delight at having been asked . . . your pleasure at the privilege of responding to the toast . . . and your good wishes to the organization which has asked you.

More important, if you are making the toast—then do so. Nothing is more discomforting than for the chairman to have to say: 'And now, kindly rise and drink with me . . .' That is your job. So do it.

The standard formula? 'Ladies and gentlemen, I invite you to rise and drink with me a toast to the continued success and prosperity of . . . the health and happiness of . . .' or as the case may be. By all means vary it. But by no means forget it.

One toast, incidentally, which should never be varied is that to: 'Her Majesty, the Queen'. If you are privileged to propose the loyal toast, then do so—in those words. No one wants a speech from you, extolling the beauty and majesty of the monarch—still less a defence of hereditary peerages, royal privileges and the like. The same applies to a toast at Jewish dinners: 'Mr Chairman, ladies and gentlemen—the President of the State of Israel'. This is no time for a Zionist outburst. The presence of an ambassador calls for a toast to the head of his state—but unless a toast to that state is one of the non-formal variety, reserve your eulogy to some proper occasion. Of course: no one should smoke until after the loyal toast and others of the formal, national variety. This explains why some kindly chairmen call on the proposer of these toasts when the waiters are collecting the soup. At least the proposers can thereafter relax and enjoy the rest of their meal, in an aroma of Havana cigar.

34 Feasts and funerals

The businessman may be called on to 'say a few words' on festive and funereal occasions, involving family, friends or colleagues. In general, similar rules apply to those outlined for the after-dinner orator—and elsewhere in the book. But here are some special suggestions for particular occasions.

THE FUNERAL

Naturally, no ill must be spoken of the departed. But, as usual, praise should be sincere and, where possible, deserved. Tact is essential. You are really expected to sum up all the pleasant and happy thoughts and memories which your audience would like to recall about the departed . . . to encourage and support those who remain behind, with the knowledge of the affection in which they are held . . . to indicate the immortality of the deceased—through those of his works which will live after him.

The obituary will range in length from a full-blown oration to (more likely) an introduction to a request for the audience to stand in memory of a departed friend. The following might serve as a model:

'Ladies and gentlemen, colleagues and friends. Before we start our meeting, I know that you would want me to express our deep regret at the loss of our well-loved fellow director, James Smith. He was a man of enormous enthusiasm, energy and initiative. He was loyal both to his friends and to the company for which he worked so well for so long. The organization which he created—in particular in our branch factories—will remain as a permanent tribute to his commercial acumen. We—his friends and colleagues—will miss him. So will the company. I ask you all to stand for a moment in memory of . . . James Smith.'

*　　*　　*

FEASTS

Happily, whilst every lifetime contains the seeds of its own sorrow, there are far more gay occasions than sad ones. Births and baptisms, christenings, confirmations and first communions . . . The Brit Milah and the Bar Mitzvah (Jewish ritual circumcisions and confirmation of 13-year-old boys) . . . engagements, weddings (including silver and gold) . . . each is the occasion for a word of congratulation at the start of a meeting or of a speech —or for a celebration at which a speech is required.

Of the full-blown variety, the after-dinner speech may form the mode (see Chapter 33). Perhaps the best advice of all is contained in the saying: the secret of talking to the public is the same as that of speaking to your wife—keep your tongue in time with your thoughts; if either gets ahead, you are done for!

35 Overseas speeches - and foreign customers

The isolationist businessman is (or should be) as extinct as the proverbial dodo. If you can export, then you should, says every government the world over. If you must import, then do so—but at the most competitive prices. You must bargain with the foreigner, eat with him, drink with him and even expense-account with him—and, in the ultimate, you may well be thrust into making speeches to or at him.

Naturally, if you are blessed with equal facility in the foreign language as you have in your own, your problems are minimal.

Then you only have to follow the rules laid down in the rest of this book and all should be well. Subject, of course, to cutting your forensic cloth to the style of your overseas audience, there is no essential difference between rousing, holding, interesting, convincing—or boring—an audience of Englishmen, Frenchmen, Russians or Greeks.

The proviso is a considerable one. Examples? Melodrama goes over a good deal better in the United States than in Britain. The florid oratory that went out in Britain many years ago still thrives in some parts—and with some audiences—abroad. But not all. And, in general, if you play up to the image expected of you—if you give your audience a touch of urbane wit, rather than roistering slapstick—you are likely to come across best.

In fact, stick to your style when in America and you have every chance of a friendly welcome. The writer once toured the United States, talking about Britain . . . the Welfare State . . . even what they choose to call 'socialized medicine'. He met a certain surprise that the Englishman was not cold, reserved, humourless, upper crust and frosty. The image of the icy Anglo-Saxon who will only speak when introduced—and, preferably, warmed with alcohol—dies hard. So the friendly, humorous opening acquired an extra significance and importance. Establish *rapport* and you are well away.

Once the overseas audience knows that you really do intend to entertain as well as to instruct—to talk across and not down—they are even more ready than your fellow countrymen to give you a warm hearing. The best tip for heating the atmosphere? To use the language of the country.

English and American is the same? In general, yes. But the idiom differs—and so do the allusions. The American speaker in Britain who takes the trouble to look at his daily newspaper and to joke about the current crime wave, strike outbreak, political disaster or other local misery does well. When you are talking to overseas listeners, return that sort of compliment.

A sample, well-tried opening in the U.S.A.: 'You will be relieved to know that I am not about to launch into discussion of whether or not that which is good for General Motors is good also for the country as a whole . . . as to the merits or otherwise of the political efforts of the Cabots, the Kennedys or' (here insert names of local politicians, currently in the news). 'If I am asked whether I support the Yankees, the Dodgers or' (here insert the name of the local baseball team), 'I shall refuse firmly to enter into your local politics. We British have enough trouble trying to run our own affairs, without risking another Boston tea-party. No. I shall confine myself, you will be pleased to know, to a discussion of . . .'

Another invaluable story. 'I have been asked to comment upon your current commercial crisis. I must respectfully decline. You may know the tale of the dying man who was visited by his priest. "My son," said the priest, "do you renounce the Devil, now and for ever more?" "Oh Father," said the dying man, "this is no time to be making enemies—anywhere!" Ladies and gentlemen, as the solitary Englishman in your ranks, I wish to make enemies, nowhere—so I shall tell you about our troubles—rather than venturing to discuss yours.'

Once you have established friendly relations with the overseas buyers, suppliers or fellow traders, if you stick to subjects which interest them, all should be well. They are as anxious to pick up profitable tips from you, as you are from them. Provided that you assume a cloak of modesty, they will wish to hear of your achievements. After all, that is why you have been invited to speak. So do not be shy. Talk freely of your doings—and you never know—the effort may prove more profitable than you had expected.

Now suppose that you are forced to launch into your speech, to people for whom English is not the mother tongue. There are two main possibilities. Either you address them in English and hope that they understand—following the Englishman's ancient theme: 'It's not for me to learn their language—the foreigner should educate himself'—or you may speak in the foreign language. The second possibility is infinitely preferable, provided that you have a command of the tongue concerned.

If you are really talking business—putting across facts, figures, theories or ideas in respect of which words must be given their

precise meanings . . . if what you say may create misunderstandings if the words are not used with their correct nuances . . . if
shades of meaning matter—then you should stick to English
and work through an interpreter, if necessary. It is no tribute to
your bravery if you venture into foreign seas without wearing a
lifebelt.

On the other hand, it may be that this is the occasion where
it would be worth while preparing your speech beforehand and
having it translated—and then reading it. Make a friendly,
impromptu opening (or one which is apparently not read) and
the audience will just have to put up with what may not be an
oratorical masterpiece but will at least be strictly accurate. That
will teach them to invite an overseas expert to speak to them!

In this case, you should do everything possible to mitigate the
misery by looking up from your speech as much as you can . . .
talking to your audience, whenever you can manage it . . . paus-
ing from time to time, to throw in a joke in English—or an
apology for having to read your script . . . and make sure that
you do try to put it across in the accent of the native.

We have all heard the Englishman who speaks the foreign
tongue as if it were his own. French words read in broad Scots,
Yorkshire, Welsh or upper-crust Bath or Tunbridge Wells have a
distinctly humorous flavour on the music-hall stage. But to the
foreign listeners, it is just plain silly.

There is an exception. If you are going to make your speech
in English, then you should always prepare a few words, right
at the start, in your host's language—or, if you are the host, then
in that of your guests. It matters not how badly you mispronounce the words—that adds to the fun. Nobody cares if you
make a hash of the grammar—that will be taken in good part.
Even if you manage to make a ghastly boob, which gives words
their opposite meaning, all will be well. What matters is that
you make the genuine effort to speak to folk in their own tongue.
You pay them the compliment of making what is obviously a
genuine attempt to be friendly—and in the most genuine possible
way.

The best formula? Start with your usual opening, in English.

'Mr Chairman, ladies and gentlemen, fellow workers in the—industry . . .' If you then break into the foreign tongue, you will produce just that element of surprise which should give rise to a very friendly reception. 'You did not know that I was learning Greek/Spanish/Hebrew/Chinese . . . did you?' (This, of course, in the language concerned.) 'After I'd met Mr. . . . in . . . who speaks such marvellous English, I was shamed into trying. I am only sorry that my efforts have been, as you hear, so very unsuccessful. To avoid any future misunderstandings of what I have to say, I hope that you will forgive me if I return—very gratefully—to English!' All that in the foreign language. Memorize it if you can. Otherwise read it. The fact that you will have got the information and the translation from one of the nationals of the country concerned is irrelevant. The compliment you have paid your audience will undoubtedly be appreciated.

There is an alternative. You can launch right into the 'Mr Chairman, ladies and gentlemen . . .' in the foreign tongue, following it up with: 'Welcome to Britain—we are very happy to have you and hope that you will have a very good time.' Do that in the foreign language—and then add: 'I know that you will forgive me if I return to English—I have a feeling that the way I pronounce French/Hungarian/Japanese/Italian, you are more likely to understand me in English than in your own tongue.'

If you cannot manage all that in the foreign language, then at least start with: 'Welcome to England' and end with 'Farewell—and come back soon', in the language of your guests. As usual, if you get the start and the finish of your speech 100 per cent right, the rest will fall into shape.

Naturally, if your audience happen to be a mixed bag, then the above rules will have to be modified. I have heard a very successful opening: 'Ladies and Gentlemen, Messieurs et Mesdames, Señores y Señoras, Meine lieben Herren und Damen . . . welcome to you all—and if I have managed to mispronounce even the few words in your language which I have ventured to speak, I know that you will appreciate why I am going to make the rest of my speech in English—I think it will be easier for us all'. Pause whilst the audience nod, smile, and

chatter. 'Misunderstandings that are created by speakers—
especially by politicians—who stick to their own tongue are only
exceeded by those who have the temerity to create vast international misunderstandings by murdering the languages of
others—and murder is a crime in every country in the world!'

Finally, an anecdote with a message. There is a famous prison
in Massachusetts, U.S.A., called the Norfolk Penal Colony.
Although a maximum-security unit, it takes pride in its debating
team, which plays no away games but welcomes guests from all
over the world, who make speeches in the prison hall before the
assembled inmates. Together with another ex-officer of the Cambridge Union, then studying with me at Harvard Law School
(and now, incidentally, a distinguished Q.C.) the writer once
debated at Norfolk : 'That this house deplores the advance of the
Welfare State'. Our opponents were a forger and a convicted
killer. Both were absolutely charming Boston Irish. Their opening gambits were classic and brilliant, tailored for any audience
—and especially for the one they had.

'The arguments you have heard from the gentlemen from
England,' the manslaughter man began, 'are as phoney as my
partner's cheques!' That brought the house down.

'We live in a welfare state,' began the forger. 'Does anyone
want to stay?' Roars of 'No, no' were the obvious result.

We did our best. 'My partner is Britain's favourite export . . .
Britain asks that you do not send him back . . .' We lost the
debate, but at least we did better than the previous English
guests, one of whom had ruined the atmosphere by making the
most elementary of mistakes—offending and talking down to his
listeners at the same time. 'This is the first occasion that I have
spoken to a captive audience,' he had begun. His speech collapsed
into immediate and well-deserved embarrassment.

36 Appeals and fund raising

The art of extracting money from the listener requires careful thought and ready adaptation to the circumstances. The Chancellor of the Exchequer may have political problems, but at least he can enforce his financial requirements. The businessman seeking to raise funds for his trade charity . . . an industrial benevolent fund . . . or even for some less apparently altruistic outlet . . . he must win the cash, pound by pound. How? That depends on the audience and the cause. But here are a few suggestions.

*   *   *

There are those who give out of pure kindness of heart. But guilt and self-interest are usually more powerful motives.

There are those who work very hard for a charity—and others who do not. But the latter may play their part by contributing the money they have earned whilst not striving for the good cause. In their own way, they can do as much for the needy as their more apparently energetic colleagues. Tell them so—by implication.

'There are those of us who are in the happy position of being able to spare time to work for this important charity. There are others who find it impossible to do so. May I make a special appeal to them? Give us the means and we will do the job. It is a job that desperately needs every penny that you can afford to spare—and more . . .'

What, then, of enlightened self-interest? Maybe it is a question of insurance. The charity deals with the aged, infirm, ill or needy? And you are young, middle-aged or at least fit? That is now. What happens when you get dumped on the scrap heap . . . sacked . . . struck down by (Heaven forfend) some fell disease? You have a pension? Well, maybe the company will not be in a position to pay it . . . it will not suffice for the needs of your widow. So now, when you are in a position to assure your future, do so.

Naturally, this is never said. The approach is more like this: 'I ask you to give as an expression of gratitude for the fact that you do not need to make use of this great trade charity for yourself. I hope that none of us will need at any time to occupy a bed in this convalescent home . . . to receive a payment from this fund . . . to rely upon the benevolence of others in the industry . . . But who knows?' Pause, significantly. 'And even if, as we all hope, we escape the necessity for help of this sort, we can be very proud indeed that those who do require it can look to us. They have given good service . . . they have earned every penny that comes to them . . . they have been smitten by the ill-fortune that we have managed to avoid . . .' And so on. We all spend money on insurance, do we not? Well, this is a healthy and helpful form of outlet for the same, intelligent response to potential misfortune.

Consider always the best way to confer a bargain. This is generally done with the kind aid of the tax man. If a businessman feels that he can give more by paying less, you are far more likely to get your money . . . to have a bed endowed in the trade home . . . to acquire your 'Smith House' or 'Jones Hall'. So check on covenant schemes, charitable trusts and the like.

'Think of it, ladies and gentlemen. Any person paying income tax at the current standard rate can confer a benefit on this charity, out of all proportion to the amount which he has to give up from his own spending. Here are some examples . . .' Then say how much a gift of £X per year or £Y per year will mean gross, to the charity. Remember, of course, that when a charity receives covenants, these can provide good security for loans, if it needs the money at once. And it is sometimes possible to get people to give a lump sum right away on the basis that it will be grossed up for tax purposes over the years. But this is a matter for the charity's accountants to work out.

Then, remember that lawful blackmail is the charitable fund raiser's most potent weapon. You phone your supplier. 'Jimmy,' you say. 'We've had such a tremendous call on our benevolent fund that we simply have to raise an extra £50,000. Can I count on you for a thousand?'

Jimmy groans inwardly. 'Certainly, Bill,' he smiles. 'Shall I send an advertisement for the Ball Brochure?'

Use the same tactic in public speech. Look at Jimmy when you ask for funds. He may turn away his gaze, but he may not dare to keep his cheque book closed. After all, when he came to the function or the meeting, he realized that the skinning knives were likely to be out. Or, even better, corner him in advance. Find out how much he is willing to give. Announce it—as a bait for others, or to shame them into raising their donations to an appropriately announceable level. If you have goodwill, then use it for the benefit of the less privileged. No one will ever tell you of the resentment they feel. It's all in a good cause, is it not?

Of course, whether you can use this sort of direct attack or whether you have to be more subtle . . . whether you can announce donations at the meeting or have to let the word go round from mouth to mouth . . . whether you conduct a mock auction at inflated prices, a raffle, a tombola . . . all depends on all the factors in the unhappy case. But one rule applies to nearly all: you cannot afford to be bashful, or to worry about rebuffs, if you are looking for money from the pockets of others.

The best time to attack those pockets is when the mind is weak through the stomach being overloaded or the heart touched by your words. If you have people in a happy, receptive and giving mood, then (literally) cash in on the situation. Either ask them for their donation at the time—and pass round the appropriate banker's order or covenant forms—or at least write to them the very next day saying: 'It was very good to see you last night . . . I enclose herewith banker's order . . . I am sure that I can count on your further support . . .'

Have I strayed from the straight and narrow of the public speechmaker? Not really. The speech can never be regarded as a separate entity, divorced from the project it encompasses. If you want funds, then you may have to appeal for them. But the appeal must be tied in with the campaign before and after. The very nature of the speech will depend upon that of the appeal, its preparation, its follow up, its needs. The production of goods depends upon the market . . . the resources at your disposal . . . the economic situation . . . and all the facts of the case. A speech must be matched to the audience and the circumstances—and no speech more so than that which incorporates an appeal for money.

*   *   *

POSTSCRIPT

Jews are great givers. Any professional appeals organizer will tell you that if you can interest the Jewish community, you are well away. And whilst Jewish people are willing givers to their own communal and Israeli causes, they take pride in taking part in the appeals of others. Perhaps even more important, they are excellent fund-raisers for charities of all sorts. So I reproduce with gratitude—and with due acknowledgment to *The Jewish Observer and Middle East Review*—an interview in which a successful Jewish appeal-maker gave away some of his secrets:

'I know plenty of people who can make an excellent speech,' he said, 'but not an appeal. The technique is quite different. The man who makes a speech can create the right atmosphere for someone to follow on. The appeal-maker must not waste time making speeches. He needs a couple of minutes to say what it is all about. And, of course, an appeal-maker must never be satisfied with his audience. Whatever he says, he must have the people in a frame of mind where they want to give. He should know when to stop.'

An audience, then, should be like a 'juicy orange—you squeeze, but not until the pips fall out. When you stop is a matter of psychology or intuition.'

When you have finished your appeal, can you tell whether the audience is still with you?

'If they applaud you as loudly when you sit down as when you got up, you can be happy with the job done.

'An appeal-maker must never read a speech. What he has to say must be spontaneous. It must come from the heart. He must never embarrass people but make them feel happy about their giving and leave them in a good frame of mind, thanking him for a successful job. People recognize the sincerity of the appeal-maker. An appeal-maker must be somebody who sincerely believes in the cause he puts forward . . .

'Finally, the appeal-maker must set an example in giving.'

Give, and the world gives with you . . . the mean man is not an appealing figure, in any sense of the word.

37 *Out in the open*

The open-air speech is a comparative rarity. But you must be prepared to make one. Maybe it will be at the factory gates, at the dockside, or at some open-air trade show. Perhaps it is only a vote of thanks at your local sports day . . . a talk or a lecture on site . . . or maybe you have to speak at a rally in Hyde Park, Trafalgar Square or at your local war memorial? Whatever the place and whatever the circumstances, there are certain basic rules on open-air oratory which should help you succeed in any such appearance you may be called upon to make.

* * *

Human voices carry poorly in the open air. So the prime essential for the outdoor speaker is to be heard.

If you have a microphone, use it. The same sort of rules apply as set out in Chapter 21. But more so. The chances of outdoor amplifying equipment going wrong are far greater than with their indoor brethren. The variety that hooks on to a motor-car battery is particularly vulnerable. Listen to the men of politics, next election time. Pity their attempts to be heard—especially when a crowd is all around them and the amplifying equipment points only to the front.

If you have a microphone, remember its outdoor limitations. For instance, if ever you have to speak in a moving vehicle— from the front of a car or the back of a truck, for instance—talk very slowly and distinctly and get the driver to proceed as slowly as possible. People do like to hear what is being thrown out at them from a moving object. But they get extraordinarily aggravated when it flies by without giving them the chance to pick up the words—however banal or trite those words may be. Usually, there's time for a slogan only. 'Today's the day . . . come to the carnival . . . 12.15 p.m. at the Rectory . . .' Then you are gone.

Still, most outdoor speaking is stationary. And—mike or no mike—many of the indoor rules go out the window. For instance:

The outdoor speaker can be far freer with movement and gesture.

Old-fashioned oratory—of the rabble-rousing variety—is much more effective and appears far less insincere when out of doors.

Instead of having an audience ready made, you may have to collect it. Whereas indoors there is no point in speaking to yourself, outdoors you may have no alternative—so the louder and more provocatively you rant, the greater your chances of an eventual audience.

But some rules of indoor speaking require special emphasis out of doors. For instance:

Do not be afraid to pause . . . to wait . . . to give every possible indication of complete calm and confidence.

Never panic, no matter what may be thrown at you—even if this is more than mere words. Remember always that the man on the platform has a vast advantage over his hearers. If he is firm and refuses to be ruffled, in the long run he should be bound to win (but see Chapter 26 on 'Interruptions').

Make certain that your voice carries. If you use a battery-operated, hand megaphone, pull the trigger tight. As one famous Harvard professor used to put it: 'Take your voice and throw it against the man at the back of your audience and make it bounce off'. If you get hoarse as a result, do not worry. You have joined the ranks of the outdoor speakers. You have hit one of the hazards of the trade. Lose your voice and it will come back. But lose your audience and it is gone for ever.

38 Presentations and awards—as giver and receiver

THE GIVER

You can come at presentation or award speeches from two angles —that of the giver and that of the receiver. In either event, 'a few words' will be expected of you. But in either case, the key-note of the speech is sincerity.

Everyone likes to be honoured. The art of the well-turned compliment is appreciated more than almost any other. Flattery given freely and wholeheartedly is always welcome—but it must be given in moderation.

'Mr X is the most brilliant businessman, straightforward and sweet-tempered, a paragon of commercial virtue . . .' Rubbish. No one will believe it—not even Mr X. Compare this: 'On the one hand, Mr Smith has been the head of a large and successful commercial concern. He has had to see that business became and remained thoroughly competitive. His has been the unpleasant duty of striking the hard bargain, ensuring that the business was tough and competitive, enabling the enterprise to survive and flourish in spite of all the economic circumstances, the bitter and fierce rivalries within the trade, the battle for manpower.

'On the other hand, Mr Smith has sought to preserve the good name of the company and its good relations both with its suppliers, customers and competitors and with its own staff.

'That he has succeeded in building up the business without destroying the foundations of goodwill . . . that he has promoted the economic welfare of the business without demoting or undervaluing the honour and integrity or the goodwill of the Board . . . that he has earned such a warm regard not only for the company but for himself—those are the reasons why we are delighted to honour him this evening—and why we are so sad at his impending retirement.'

Or take the manager, foreman or operative, leaving after long service, or receiving an award for distinguished, long-term conduct.

'We were thinking of presenting Mr Jones with a watch. But we do not believe our staff really want to know the time just when it has became least important to them. And so we felt that this electric tea-maker would be more appropriate and much more useful. It comes with the thanks and admiration of the company—and its gratitude. But it is also given with the affection and goodwill of his fellow members of staff. They have contributed towards it and I know they hope, as much as I do, that it will remind him—and his wife and family—of the affection and esteem in which we all hold him, and of our thanks to him for his loyal service. We wish Mr Jones, together with his charming wife, a long and happy retirement, blessed with the very best of health. And we hope that he will visit us whenever he comes this way. He will always have the warmest of welcomes from all of us, his colleagues and friends.'

No flowery insincerities. No 'schmaltz' as the overdone compliment is sometimes called in the United States, but straightforward, sincere and sensible words which are bound to be appreciated by the person concerned.

Sometimes, of course, the presentation of an award is really an excuse to encourage people to come to a dinner or other function, knowing that they would not wish to offend the recipient by being absent. With this sort of award or presentation, it is expected that the toast to the recipient will be coupled with a eulogy of the organization which he represents—and/or of the virtues represented by the organization which is conferring the award. This sort of excuse for an oratorical jamboree is becoming increasingly common, and is a not altogether welcome transatlantic importation. The public relations man has created a new vehicle. But if it comes your way, you must be prepared to steer it.

'In the new and expanding sauna bath industry, we are proud of our pioneers. This dinner is in honour of Mr Finn, whom we are all delighted to welcome to England.' Hear, hear!

'Mr Finn has helped to put our industry on to the English map. Close on the heels of the central-heating boom has come the realization that sauna-bath treatments bring health and true family relaxation. Whilst no public authority should be without one, there is an immense, untapped demand for them in the larger private homes throughout the country.' (The Press start scribbling.) 'What better occasion could there be than this to launch the great new drive for British-built sauna baths—we shall create a home demand so as to build up an economic, export potential . . .' And so on. 'And we wish to express our admiration and thanks to our honoured guest, Mr Finn, to whom I am delighted to present this gold pin, in the shape of a sauna bath, as a token of our respect and gratitude.' Loud cheers. The audience rises. Flash bulbs pop.

This is only a slight exaggeration of the sort of award occasion which occurs somewhere, every day of the week. If you are the presenter, the more fatuous the occasion . . . the less deserving the recipient . . . the bigger the publicity hoped for—the more

your sincerity becomes vital, if the occasion is not to deteriorate
into sickening slush.

How, then, do you appear sincere, even when you are not? By
playing down. By avoiding exaggeration. By excluding melodrama, theatricals, tears in the eyes or choking in the throat.
'I am so moved that I can scarcely speak . . .' Then don't. 'Mr
Jones is fabulous, fantastic, magnificent . . .' Superlatives are
seldom either sincere or accurate. A few, quiet words of praise
are worth paeans of exultation.

THE RECEIVER

With a bit of luck, you, too, may be at the receiving end of an
honour, an award, a presentation or a toast. Praise may be heaped
on your receptive shoulders. How do you cope with it?

'I am very grateful to Mr Smith for his most generous obituary.'—Adlai Stevenson.

'There is one difference between a speech of this kind heaping
praise on the living, and a funeral oration, extolling the dead.
In the former case, but not the latter, there is one listener who
is ready to believe in the truth of all that was said.'—Chaim
Weizmann.

More common: 'I would first like to thank Mr Jones for his
very kind references to my wife and myself. We are very grateful—and only wish that half of it were true.' Or: 'I am deeply
grateful to you, Mr Chairman, for the very generous way in
which you have referred to my organization and to myself. We
shall do our best to live up to your high regard.'

What it comes to is this: just as it is vital for the maker of the
speech of praise to be patently sincere, so the recipient must be
clothed in decent modesty.* It would be ungracious to say: 'It's
all untrue . . . you shouldn't have said those things . . .' And
anyway, no one would regard that sort of attitude as bearing the
true mark of sincerity. On the other hand, one can hardly say:

* See also **Chapter 11.**

'Every word is an understatement . . .' You may be immodest about your wife: 'All that has been said about my wife is true. I am very proud of her—she's a gem!' But then you must go on to say: 'I only wish that I could believe the same of the words about myself. Nevertheless, I am most obliged to Mr Smith for having spoken them. Maybe he convinced my wife of their truth, even though he left me in a good deal of doubt.'

The next stage is to return the compliment by speaking well of the individual or organization that has had the good sense to honour you. 'I have been very lucky to have had the opportunity of serving this company over the years . . . It has been a privilege to work with you all . . . I shall miss you . . . I hope that we shall meet again, very often . . .' Or: 'Whilst this fraternal organization has been good enough to make an award to me, I should in fact have been making a presentation to the organization. The honours are flowing in the wrong direction. I shall try to redress the balance a little by saying why it is that I regard the work of this organization to be of such enormous significance, especially in the present state of the industry . . .'

Or: 'It was very good of Mr Smith to speak so well of me. As everyone here knows so well, most of the virtues that he was kind enough to attribute to me were in fact his own. This company is very fortunate to be led by a man of his calibre . . .'

Sincerity and the nicely-turned compliment, then, should not be the prerogative of the giver.

Finally, the conclusion. 'And so, Mr Chairman, my speech— like my time with the company—has drawn to its close. Thank you, Mr Smith, once again for your very kind words. Thank you, my colleagues, for your goodness to me, over the years— and for your most generous gift. My wife and I will treasure it always—as we shall the memories of our association with you. Good luck to you all.'

Or: 'And so, in accepting this award, I thank you all for the compliment you have paid to me—and through me to my organization. My colleagues and I are all happy to have been able to carry out our work—and we undertake to attempt in the future to exceed the achievements in the past which have caused you to honour us in the present. Our gratitude to you all.'

The sentimental anecdotes you have slipped into the body of your speech . . . the reminiscences, memories, tales with a moral —all of which go down so well in this sort of situation . . . these are all rounded off with a final word of thanks. To end, where you began, with your gratitude. It has been a fine occasion— and an excellent speech.

39 Credits

Few men object to being thanked or resent receiving credit, even where it is not strictly due—and in this instance at least, 'Man' (as Churchill once put it) 'embraces Woman'. But most people get upset from time to time if their merit is not recognized or thanks are withheld—especially if credit due to one goes to another. So the good advocate is as liberal with his praise of others as he is parsimonious with his praise of himself (see Chapter 38). The listener who feels that you recognize—and are prepared publicly to laud—his worth is far more likely to be receptive to your arguments.

Here, then, is a good opening attack upon an audience, even if it happens to be friendly towards you:

'First, I would like to express my appreciation to various people here. Were it not for Mr Brown, this gathering would never have been organized at all. Were it not for Mr Black, the company would be in grave difficulty. Were it not for Mr White, the scheme we are about to discuss would never have been born. In paying tribute to them, I express my gratitude to all of you for giving them the support and backing without which they could not have put forward this essentially constructive project.

'Now, let us look at the project.' Your audience is softened up. They are ready to listen to some constructive criticism from you.

Alternatively: 'Under the chairmanship of Mr Green, this project has made great headway. With Mr Brown as treasurer and Mr Blue as honorary secretary, it is hardly surprising that it has gathered momentum. And now it is up to us to help them by applying constructive minds to the scheme they have created. I know they welcome criticism designed to forward their work. We all appreciate that their enthusiasm is only increased by suggestions, coming from people like ourselves who only want the scheme to succeed. They know that there is no element of destructive intent in the views that some of us hold. Mr Chairman, we are with you all the way—and if we take the liberty of suggesting that the way may not be quite as simple as some think, I am sure that you will give careful consideration to our submissions.' Flattery? Certainly—but legitimate. Praise? Yes, indeed, and with every appearance of sincerity. Credit, thanks, tact—and all designed to prepare the ground for your forthcoming attack. It is not only armies that do best when they advance from the side, and there is no shame in a swift strike from the rear.

To see the importance of these rules, all you have to do is to listen to someone who ignores them. Beware the benefactor scorned . . . the doer of good deeds which go unrecognized . . . the creator whose idea, invention or brainchild is fathered on to another.

There exists, of course, the occasional *eminence grise*—the spectral backroom boy who takes as much pride in praise going to others whom he has built up as does the father who basks in the reflected glory of the exploits of his child. But even he appreciates the oblique reference to the power that made the throne secure, the modest mind that 'wishes to remain anonymous but must not go without being thanked . . . Those of us who are fortunate enough to realize just how and by whom the work has been done salute our silent and modest friends—we are indeed grateful to them.'

Just as the editorial mention and the praise of a product which appears in the general pages of a newspaper are the public relations man's delight—and worth a good deal more to him than the advertisement which he has to pay for—so the 'plug' given in the course of a speech and as part of it is often a good deal more valuable to the maker and appreciated by the person referred to than the formal and expected vote of thanks. But even that is a weapon not to be despised in the campaign to get your own way—as we shall now see.

40 Votes of thanks

The formal vote of thanks to the speaker is a mark of courtesy and just as necessary as the word of gratitude to the hostess at the end of the evening. You may not have enjoyed your meal. The company may have been excruciatingly dull. Unlike the fabled hostess who was said to have made her guests feel at home even when she fervently wished that they were, Mrs Black may have caused you to be thoroughly ill at ease. Nevertheless, as you leave you thank her—and no doubt compliment her as warmly as you can on the excellence of her cooking and the pleasure you have had in the company of her other, well-chosen guests. Because the compliments are apparently unrehearsed, they may well be believed. Anyway, they must be given.

So it is with the guest speaker. He must be thanked. In America, it is customary to make handsome payment to those who lecture, even to rotary clubs, friendly societies or business or charitable organizations. They are given tangible thanks, in financial form. In this country, the speaker is thought to have been the recipient of a compliment. When he says: 'It was very kind of you to invite me to this splendid, peaceful Highland resort,' he probably means, 'I wish I could have thought of some way to refuse your invitation to trek up to your God-forsaken development area slum.' So at least bathe him in the warmth of your thanks.

Incidentally, have you remembered to offer to pay the man's expenses? He would probably be too embarrassed to ask for them and he may even refuse your offer. But to beg for and receive the benefit of the time of a busy speaker and then to expect him to pay for his fare or accommodation is a typically British stupidity. All speakers know the wretchedness of being dragged many miles for a few minutes of speech to a minute audience. That is one of the hazards of the trade. But when he does so entirely at his own expense, in money as well as in time, it is hardly surprising if he feels bitter.

What, then, of the vote of thanks itself? How do you best put it across?

Sincerity is the keynote. This rests upon a genuine (if possible) and topical (certainly) assessment of the positive and helpful aspects of the visitor's speech. Refer, perhaps, to the speaker's wit and wisdom, the full and frank way in which he has dealt with the subject, the particular interest which you have had in that portion of his talk which dealt with . . . By all means elaborate on a point or two, to show that you have really taken it in— or to indicate that you have been taken in, as the case may be. But do not use the occasion to launch into a tirade of your own. Your job is to thank. Do it.

A vote of thanks is a mini-speech. So the general rules apply, in abbreviated form.

By all means write out your first sentence and the skeleton of the speech (see Chapter 1). But to have the whole speech written in advance is a travesty. 'We have all been extremely impressed with the wise words of Mr Stout,' the speaker reads from his typed card. 'He gave us a very clear exposition of the subject. We have much to think about as a result.' Terrible. Obviously written before the speech was heard and not worth the paper it was written on. In fact, of all the speeches which should never be written out, votes of thanks head the list.

'We are very honoured to have had Mr Slim with us this evening. We realize and appreciate how far he has come. We know and understand the effort that it has cost him. And I know that I am expressing the feelings of everyone here when I tell him how deeply grateful we are to him.' At this stage, you must pause for applause. If you rush on, your audience will not know what is expected of them. There will be a few embarrassed hand-claps and the speaker will not be complimented.

'We listened with great interest to Mr Slim's views on . . . Personally, I was especially impressed with the concept of . . . If my own company does not take steps to put this system into effect, it will not be through any lack of enthusiasm on my part, nor any failing on the part of our distinguished speaker. He has paid us the compliment of laying out before us in the clearest terms the essence of the organizational method which he has distilled through years of trial, error and experience. The greatest tribute which can be paid to him will be through our adoption of his ideas.' Every speaker likes to feel that he has sown good seed on fertile soil. Treat his words as pearls and he will not think of you as the proverbial swine.

'But perhaps our greatest delight, Mr Chairman, has been in the way in which Mr Slim has succeeded in bringing his some-what recondite subject to life. He has proved that to tell a tale of . . . need not be dull. He has enlivened our evening with wit and humour.

'And so, in thanking Mr Slim for his good words this evening, I can only hope that we shall have an early opportunity of hear-ing him again. We wish him every success in his ventures—and a speedy return to our midst. Thank you, Mr Slim, very much indeed.'

And thank you for a terse, appropriate, sincere, friendly and well-constructed vote of thanks. Just to think that the audience inwardly groaned when you were called upon to speak, worry-ing in case you were about to make the late hour even later . . .

to cause them to lose the last bus or train or the services of their aggravated chauffeurs . . . or, possibly, to embarrass them by saying what they really thought about their guests. So they were pleasantly surprised—and are likely to invite you to perform the same service again. Or maybe they knew all the time that you would perform this under-rated chore with aplomb, which is why they asked you to do it. In that case, their trust was not misplaced. Thank you indeed.

41 *Brains trusts*

Curiously, even very prominent people are prepared to sit on so-called 'brains trusts'. The audience gets at least two views for the price of one evening. The speaker—who might otherwise resent the competition and the feeling that his audience really should be satisfied with an evening of him—accepts, perhaps because he is delighted not to have to prepare any set speech. Each or all of the speakers are often fooled into accepting because they think that the others on the panel have already done so—or they turn up because they have been asked by someone whom they cannot refuse. Whatever the circumstances, most speakers have to perform at brains trusts some time or another. So here are some suggestions.

*   *   *

The organizers ought to provide each speaker with a pencil and pad. But they often fail to do so. You should never turn up at any meeting without pen and paper, but both are absolutely vital for a brains trust.

When a question is asked, jot it down. Alongside it, put any random ideas which leap to mind. If you have none, then indicate to the chairman that one of your colleagues should open the batting. Something will come to your mind whilst the answer is given. If it does not, then do not be afraid to say: 'I agree', or 'I'd rather not comment on this one, thank you'. And there are questions which may provoke all sorts of possible answers, none of which you think it politic to give. Do not be browbeaten into words you may later regret.

Each answer you do give should be a small, neat speech. It should have a beginning, a body and an end. But it must be concise. And precisely because it must be extempore, you may find it considerably more difficult than the ordinary, set effort. There is a definite art to brains trusting.

You may have to cope with interruptions from your colleagues or from the chairman. You must take them in your stride. React to the informality of the occasion. Do not be afraid to break your train of thought—or, if you cannot return to it, say: 'Now, where was I, before Mr Brown's witty intervention?' Someone will remind you.

Conversational informality—that is the key to a successful brains trust performance. You are performing at a dinner party, with an audience to play up to. Make use of your powers of showmanship. React to your audience. By all means fish for applause and laughter. Relax and enjoy yourself—and the odds are that your audience will do the same.

Well-chosen brains trust panels include people with different backgrounds, viewpoints and ideas. With any luck, there will be a friendly clash. Speakers can engage in gentlemanly teasing. Jokes against yourself will be appreciated. And smart retorts to points made by other speakers seldom go astray. But the tradition is still that of the dinner party and not of the political tub-thump. Aggressive and unfriendly rejoinders . . . rude or unkind rebuttals . . . personal remarks to or about other speakers, which hurt (whether or not they are calculated to do so)—these are all to be avoided. The object is to demonstrate your brains, not to tear out those of the other panelists.

On the other hand, if things get too dull, some provocative remarks are appreciated. Well-prepared brains trusts have some questions provided in writing at the start, so as to get things moving or to fill in dull moments. But if the dread moment arrives when the audience is silent and the questions do not arise, say: 'I wonder whether I could take this opportunity to ask Mr Large something I have wanted to get out of him for some time? I appreciate, Mr Chairman, that he might prefer to answer this question in private. But if you would allow me to put it to him, at least we shall see whether or not he is prepared to allow his views on this subject to appear on the platform.' The chairman will doubtless be delighted. And Mr Large will probably be pleased and flattered to know that his opinions are sought. Speakers, on the whole, are a pretty vain lot, who like expressing their views for all to hear. Those on brains trusts are no exception.

42 *Interview techniques—from both sides*

The difference between speaking in public and in private depends largely upon the formality of the former, the informality of the latter. Some private occasions are sufficiently formal to require the speaker to give careful thought to his statements. Into this category come most interviews. Some public occasions are so informal that the speaker can conveniently 'chat' to his audience. Here we have some private gatherings, perhaps around the hearth—or, on occasion, when what was expected to be a large public meeting turns into a small gathering. The speaker can save the day by turning to complete informality, asking his audience to sit around him, himself remaining seated—and throwing his notes out the window.

There are nearly as many techniques for interviewing as there are interviewers and situations. The head of an organization which specializes in supplying sales teams for industry and who spends the bulk of his days interviewing prospective representatives reckons on a five-minute maximum. Take any longer, he claims, and you start overlooking the defects of the interviewee because you find common ground with him. The chief personnel officer of a giant retail organization reckons on each interview taking at least fifteen minutes and preferably thirty. 'It takes you a quarter of an hour,' he says, 'to put the interviewee thoroughly at ease and to be able to start finding out what he is really like.'

Each of us, then, acquires a technique to probe the talents and character of the interviewee. The only vital rule is to allow the other man to do the talking—and to prod him into speech.

What guidance, then, have we for the interviewee?

First, he must be as natural as the situation allows. Ideally, of course, he should have a shrewd idea of what the interviewer wants to find—and then hint as broadly as possible (but with the maximum appearance of subtlety) that he is everything that is required. But one can be a good deal too clever. So relax as much as you can. Be yourself. And if that is not good enough—well, even if the interview had proved more successful perhaps you would not have fitted the assignment anyway. One door closes. Another will doubtless open before long.

Do not prepare a speech in advance—unless, of course, you are being interviewed for a Parliamentary candidature and are expected to deliver a ten-minute set piece. In that case, the ordinary rules of speeches would apply. But in the more common circumstances—where you are facing, perhaps, a Board of interviewers—the interview will take the form of question and answer. The less you are tied to a memorized script, the more natural you are likely to be, and the less inhibited.

The only question you are almost certainly to be asked is why you want (or think that you are suited for) the particular job, scholarship, assignment or position for which you have applied Be as frank in your answer as you can. If you think it will give you the opportunity to serve, in a way that you have always desired, then say so. If you are at present in a rut and feel that the new situation will provide an exciting outlet for your enthusiasm, then speak up. Tell them. But be careful not to overplay your hand. An interviewee was applying for a senior executive post in a particular European country. 'Why do you want to go to that country?' he was asked. 'Because I have always found it fascinating,' came the ready answer. He then discovered that one of his interviewers was an expert on that country's affairs—about which, despite his alleged fascination, the interviewee (as soon became pathetically apparent) knew practically nothing. He had failed at the first hurdle.

How much better he would have done had he answered: 'I have the terrible feeling that I am in a rut. I have always wanted to work abroad and have never had the opportunity. I must admit that I do not know a great deal about conditions and circumstances in the country in question. But I am anxious and willing to find out. I have had to adapt myself to all sorts of work in England, and I am sure I could take to the situation which you have to offer abroad.'

Regard an interview as an examination, and prepare for it. If, to return to the same example, you wish to obtain an appointment abroad, at least take the trouble to read a book or two concerning the country in question, its political, commercial and economic situation and the state of the particular trade or industry with which you are concerned, in that foreign land. Make sure that you are able to discuss the prospects . . . the work . . . the difficulties. By all means play down your knowledge—but put yourself in a position to surprise the interviewing panel with what you do know.

You are selling yourself. So apply the ordinary rules of good salesmanship. In most cases, the 'soft sell' is infinitely preferable to a show of immodesty, pomposity or omniscience. You may be better than your interviewers, but it is tactful not to make this too obvious. Of course, if your interview concerns a product, then the fact that you are dealing with an interviewing panel rather than with one potential customer only means that you must spread your usual wiles more widely.

Before you come up for the interview, sit down and think about its purpose. Be prepared to answer questions clearly and comprehensively. Consider the sort of background information which you would require if you were doing the interviewing. Make sure that you have it available at the front of your mind.

Answer the questions you are asked, in an informal, conversational style. Avoid oratory, rhetoric or platform fineries. By all means show a sense of humour, but do not be 'too clever'. Do not be afraid to show enthusiasm, ideas, imagination. The chances of your failing the interview through over-enthusiasm are as nothing compared to the fair certainty of failure for those who appear indifferent, unenthusiastic, uninspired.

Of course, what you really need at an interview is good luck. But good speech certainly helps.

43 *Lectures and visual aids*

A lecture has been defined as 'a discourse before an audience or class upon a given subject, usually for the purpose of instruction' (*The Shorter Oxford English Dictionary*). The lecturer, then, is expected to instruct or, at least, to describe. He is likely to have to speak for at least twenty minutes and possibly up to an hour. He will probably be forgiven if his notes are more extensive and his reading and quotations more lengthy and apparent than would otherwise be expected. But the word 'lecture' is not synonymous with the word 'bore'. All the rules as to preparation, notes, humour, the structure of the speech and the like apply. But the lecturer will normally be expected to be expert in his subject—and to demonstrate his expertise.

If you do have to 'read a paper' and prepare a speech, word by word, you can generally reckon that, at the ordinary rate of delivery, you will need somewhere about 110 words a minute. But by all means check your own delivery time by reading out the first few paragraphs and using a stop-watch. Remember that you will probably speak faster when the time comes. But remember also that a good speaker varies his pace (see Chapter 25) as well as his volume and tone. Like a first-class record player, his output is variable.

One great advantage of the properly briefed lecturer is that he may make use of visual aids and these are well worth preparing, especially as a lecture (unlike most speeches) can often be repeated.

Slides and films are useful. But do make sure that you would have a projector or, if you bring your own, that the appropriate electrical supply, plugs and the like will be available. If you have to 'get set up', then come early.

You may also be able to obtain film strips. Or your hosts may have one of those ingenious projectors that enable the speaker to put charts, graphs or maps on to a platform and have them projected on to a screen. Discuss your visual aids with your hosts and make sure you obtain and use the best that the equipment available will justify.

Remember, too, that if you do not have your own slides or photographs or film strips, there are various firms that hire projection equipment and machinery. Maybe your hosts will be able to help. Alternatively, some Government departments and local authorities are extremely co-operative. If you can get hold of visual aids, then you should certainly do so. An uninterrupted lecture of considerable length may hold an audience if the speaker is sufficiently experienced, witty and wise and if his material is really of absorbing interest to his audience. But—as any recipient of lectures, university or other, knows to his cost— the chances of a lengthy lecture proving pleasurable as well as instructive are not great, in the absence of visual aids.

44 *On radio—and TV*

To the performer who makes his living on radio or TV, a 'fluff' may mean disaster. In a television studio, in particular, the moment before the cameras are turned on is fraught with tension. If the show is 'canned'—that is, pre-recorded—then a disaster may be cut out. Or if the radio programme is on tape, mistakes can be erased or re-recorded. But the 'live' show never loses its expectancy. 'Good luck, darling,' say the experts, and then compliment the visiting celebrity, the amateur speaker, the non-professional guest, on his calm. He is probably thoroughly enjoying the experience. He should be. At worst, he will not be asked back. At best, he talks to the camera, the microphone, the technicians behind the glass screen— and forgets about the thousands (or even millions) who will see his performance when it eventually 'goes out'. But his path will be smoother and his calm as real as it is apparent if he knows a few of the basic techniques.

*   *   *

As a speaker, you will appear in one of two ways. Either you will be interviewed or you will deliver a set talk.

The interview lives on its informality. The interviewer may take you through in advance some of the questions he will ask. But seldom all of them. When the show is on, they will in any event take a different form, if only in their wording.

The interviewer's job is to encourage you to talk. The chances are that the questions he will ask will be pointed but either non-committal or friendly. But they may be hostile. Forget about the microphones, the cameras with their green eyes glinting when they are 'live', the studio audience. Chat with the interviewer as if the two of you were on your own. Choose your words with care, especially if you are criticizing others. A defamatory statement made on television is a libel and not a slander (see Chapter 14). Do not be rushed or bullied. Relax and be yourself.

If yours is a set speech, then the chances are that you will have to provide a copy in advance. This will then probably be put on to an ingenious machine which sets your words on to a large, paper tape and runs them across your vision, just above the camera. The operator ensures that the words match the speed at which you speak. You will be reading—but your audience will be admiring your fluency and powers of memory. All you must remember is to read as if you were talking. Once again, be natural and conversational and you have nothing to fear.

For a sound broadcast, the chances are that you will have a script. This will probably have been retyped for you on to special paper that does not 'rattle'. If the pages are stapled together, remove the clip. Underline in black, red or green, so as to help to remember what to emphasize. Above all, do as the producer tells you.

He will run through your script with you, and you may well have had to attend the studio for a rehearsal or two beforehand. Your voice will be tested, if you have not broadcast before. The object is not to remove any regional accent or spoken peculiarities but to ensure that your words will come through clearly and understandably.

The producer will give you your directions. Normally, he will operate a green cue-light, to tell you when to start. If you slow down too much, then you may receive a flashing signal to speed up. But if you have included a penultimate paragraph which can be cut out without adversely affecting the sense, he may not trouble. If you go too fast, you will probably receive the equivalent of a slow handclap on the green light. But, as in bridge, you and your partner (in this case, the producer) will arrange your signals in advance.

You may also have to co-operate with an announcer. He will give you your cue, and its nature will be agreed at rehearsal.

Common troubles? Dry throat. Stop and sip your glass of water. The urge to cough. Give way to it, if necessary—but turn your head away from the microphone. Loose dentures. Make sure that they are firmly in place before your talk begins or you may produce whistling sibilance, reminiscent of 'interference' from nearby stations.

When preparing your script, you can probably reckon on about 125 words a minute. As in the case of a lecture (Chapter 42), count your words and then declaim them to a stop-watch. If in doubt, add a few words to the minute. You can cut them out later, if the producer so directs. But remember that the chances of your being allowed to overrun are remote. Every second of radio time is allotted in advance.

You will probably speak a little slower on television. Once again, the producer will help you. Your talk will probably be directed straight at the lens of the 'live' camera and you may never have to look away. But you may be told to move around ... to pick up some exhibit or to point to a visual aid ... to speak to your announcer or to a fellow guest or to an interviewer. Do as you are told. When you do move, do not rush. And use as few gestures as possible. The camera tends to exaggerate the false and the unnatural. So be yourself. Talk as if you were at home, and you will not be returned there uncomplimented.

POSTSCRIPT

The smallest mistake or the most apparently innocuous remark made in the most obscure radio or TV programme may let loose shoals of protests. Mistakes in print may sometimes be ignored and forgotten. But heaven help the man who broadcasts without due care. He may not lose his licence, but it may be a long time before he gets back on the air. So be extra careful to get your facts right if you do not want to regret your words for long afterwards.

45 *Titles*

If in doubt as to how to address a particular person, check with a reference book, telephone an information service (in London, *The Daily Telegraph* service is excellent), or get your secretary to check with the guest's office to find out. If there is a toast-master, he will soon put you right. If you have an experienced chairman, follow his lead. Here, in any event, are some common examples. The lower you go down their scale, the more likely you are to meet them. Still, you may be privileged to start a speech with: 'Your Majesty' (for a king or queen); 'Your Royal Highness' for a royal prince, princess or duke; 'Your Grace' for an archbishop, a duke or a duchess; or 'My Lord' or 'My Lady' for members of the peerage below the rank of duke or duchess, children of peers who bear courtesy titles, the Lord Chancellor, Lord Chief Justice and Lords of Appeal and all bishops.

If there is only one bishop present, you may say 'My Lord Bishop'. The Lord Mayor (any lord mayor) is usually referred to as 'My Lord Mayor'. Reference to a particular honoured guest by name is generally appreciated, provided you get the name right (see Chapter 80). The word 'honourable' should be left together with 'right honourable' to those addressing their Parliamentary colleagues. 'Brothers' and 'comrades' have their place. But 'Ladies and Gentlemen' will usually do, even when you consider that your audience are nothing of the sort.

46 *A postscript—pastimes whilst others speak*

Part of the price of the pleasure of hearing your own voice is the necessity to endure the speeches of others. You may, of course,

be lucky. The sole guest speaker of an evening only has the introduction and vote of thanks to sit through. During the former, he
will be thinking of his speech—and, if he takes the advice given
in this book to heart, trying to find something in the words of his
introducer to quote, adapt or answer, and so establish a *rapport*
with his audience. During the vote of thanks, he must simply
try to believe that the words spoken of him are true. And no one
need exhibit false modesty to himself.

But inevitably unlucky is the after-dinner speaker, no matter
what his place in the toast list. The chairman of a committee may
be able to regulate the speeches of others, but the rest must put
up with them. If you happen to be a Member of Parliament, you
may be able to escape from the function after you have spoken,
perhaps alleging a three-line whip. ('Mr Jones must now return to
his Parliamentary duties, I'm afraid. But we appreciate all the
more that he has spared us some of his most valuable time to be
with us.') But heaven help anyone else who leaves before the
other speeches are complete.

So the art of listening is worth some cultivation.

In private, the good listener is generally credited with great
powers of perception, intelligence and even eloquence. In public,
to fall asleep whilst others speak is the height of bad manners.
But how can you avoid it?

Every practised speaker is, of course, a skilled doodler. So
much so that there is one handwriting expert who is alleged to
make his living largely by interpreting the doodles of famous
men. But much more constructive is the writing of those neglec-
ted letters.

The dinner is dull? Too bad. You must try to get your neighbour to talk about his speciality and, with a little luck, you may
find that he is more interesting than you had realized. The after-
dinner speeches are a misery? Then use the back of the menu or
toast list or guest list or brochure. Take out your pen and write
your correspondence. Look up every now and again at the
speaker. And no one—least of all the speaker himself—will suspect that you are doing anything other than paying him the
compliment of noting his words. My relatives in Australia always

know when I have been cursed with dull speeches to hear. They receive missives on agendas, minutes, jotting-pads . . . anything that happens to be handy.

Of course, you could instead be jotting down notes for the current work which you have on hand. In the unlikely event of the speaker sparking off a constructive chain of thought, make a note of the idea before it flees for ever. If he happens to tell a good story, write it down. It may come in handy one day. If all else fails, and you can fight off slumber no longer, then you must do your best to organize your forty winks so as to attract the least possible suspicion. An acquaintance has, through long years of experience, learned how to sleep whilst sitting bolt upright and with his eyes open. Most of us must be content with the head rested on the hand, the elbow on the table. Alternatively, the head droops forward and the notes or brochure or agenda are in front of you so that it may (with luck) appear that you are reading—or at least engaged in deep thought.

It has been said that women knit to give themselves something to think about whilst they are talking. Every speaker should learn to amuse himself during the unamusing speeches of others. What matters is to do so without any appearance of flagging attention or concentration. Spare a thought for the diplomats who must do it all the time.

Part IV
In Courts and Tribunals

47 Introduction

Courts and Tribunals provide a highly refined and specialized area for speech-making. You may be lucky and only forced into the witness box or (woe is you) into the dock, on rare and isolated occasions. However, those occasions are likely to be of supreme importance—if not to you then to those on whose behalf you testify.

Today, though, businessmen are stepping into the legal arena with increasing frequency, not only to give evidence but also as advocates.

Industrial Tribunals now have vast powers. They may award up to £11,760 to the employee who is unfairly dismissed—and you may need their help either in your capacity as employer or as employee (however mighty). They rule over redundancy disputes and battles over equal pay, sex discrimination, race discrimination, notification to trade unions of intended redundancies and most areas of employment protection. In addition, they are the proper forum for appeals against improvement or prohibition notices, served under the Health and Safety at Work Act.

Now, you will employ a lawyer (through necessity or wisdom) to represent your interests or those of your business, in civil courts (County Courts—with jurisdiction, in general, up to £1000; the High Court—above that sum); or Criminal Courts (Magistrates' Courts or Crown Courts). But you may prefer to represent yourself or your business in an Industrial Tribunal. There is no legal aid and (for all practical purposes) no provision for the recovery of costs from the loser, in any Industrial Tribunal.

So this Part of the book is designed to help you and those at your command, if and (as is likely) when you are faced with the miseries of court or tribunal proceedings. I offer: A guide to Courts and Tribunals and checklists for those who must appear as witnesses, as advocates—or both. I hope that these guides will be needed as little as possible. As the famous Rabbi in *Fiddler on the Roof* said of the man who controlled the temporal destinies of his flock: 'God bless the Tsar—and keep him as far away from us as possible'. The best view of the Courts is from a distance—but if you come close to the flames, these guides should help to keep you intact.

48 Courts and Tribunals—the legal framework

THE LAW—CIVIL AND CRIMINAL

The *civil law* is designed to provide remedies for citizens (or their companies, firms or other organizations)—one against the other. The *criminal law* sets minimum standards, demanded by the community.

Some wrongful acts have both civil and criminal consequences, e.g. negligence on the road or at work—the guilty party may be prosecuted; and/or sued by the injured party. But civil courts seldom apply criminal sanctions—nor do criminal courts often give remedies to sufferers.

POWERS OF THE COURTS

Civil courts generally award *damages*, as compensation. They may also make *declarations*, setting out the rights of the parties; grant *injunctions*—orders, restraining the continuation of wrongful acts, e.g. nuisances; and orders for the *specific performance* of contracts, where damages would not be an adequate remedy, e.g. contracts for the sale of land.

A *civil court* may imprison for contempt of court. It is a criminal offence to flout the orders of a civil court.

A *criminal* court may fine, imprison, bind over, grant discharges (conditional or absolute)—and occasionally, e.g. to compensate sufferers with up to £400, under the Trade Descriptions Act, order those convicted to pay compensation.

THE COURTS

The High Court—with unlimited civil jurisdiction—is divided into the *Queen's Bench Division* (general, common law jurisdiction)—as opposed to the *Chancery Division*, which has a so-called 'equitable' jurisdiction (deriving from the authority of the Lord Chancellor to supplement the ordinary powers of the common law courts, and now dealing with disputes regarding companies, overlaps that of the Queen's Bench Division). *The Family Division* deals with matrimonial disputes and their ramifications.

The County Courts have jurisdiction up to £1000—although sometimes smaller claims go to the High Court, e.g. under special procedures seeking swift, summary judgments.

Appeals from both County Courts and High Court go to the *Court of Appeal* and thence (with leave from the Court of Appeal or from the House of Lords) to the House of Lords (judicial committee).

Criminal Courts—All criminal cases commence in the Magistrates' Court—although the more serious ones (from theft to murder) may (and in some cases, must) be tried by the *Crown Court*. The accused may have a right to elect for trial (and will have in the most serious cases). Advantage of trial by jury : much greater prospect of acquittal; disadvantages—extra delay and cost. Where cases are committed by Magistrates to a higher court, the 'committal proceedings' are usually formal—but may be detailed and lengthy. Magistrates must find that there is *prima facie* case to proceed.

Appeals from Magistrates' Courts on points of law go to a special criminal division of the High Court (three Judges); but for rehearing on facts before jury, to Crown Court.

INDUSTRIAL TRIBUNALS

Industrial tribunals exercise primarily a civil jurisdiction, including disputes about: redundancy pay; unfair dismissals; equal pay and sex discrimination; and under Employment Protection Act. But they also (and rarely) consider appeals against improvement and prohibition orders under Health and Safety at Work Act (essentially a criminal statute, providing penalties for unsafe practices at work, etc.). Appeals from industrial tribunals go to Employment Appeals Tribunal.

WHO JUDGES?

High Court Judges (all) and Circuit Judges (most) are ex-barristers—ex-solicitors may sit in some Crown Courts. Magistrates' Courts are staffed either by lay Justices (usually—but not always—legally unqualified—and assisted by clerk)—or by 'stipendiaries', who are paid a stipend and are qualified lawyers.

Industrial tribunals have legally qualified chairmen, accompanied by two lay members, usually one nominated by the CBI (with management experience) and one by the TUC (with shop-floor background).

Appointments of Judges are by the Lord Chancellor and of industrial tribunal members by the Secretary for Employment.

PROCEDURES

These range from the highly formal, jargon-ridden (House of Lords, High Court, County Court, Crown Court), through the comparative discipline of Magistrates' Courts to the informality of tribunals (no robes; everyone sits; members hunt for truth with varying regard for rules of evidence). In general, laymen may cope with procedures of tribunals but anywhere else they should recall the old adage: 'The man who is his own lawyer has a fool for a client'.

SCOTLAND: CIVIL COURTS

The equivalent of the English and Welsh County Court is the Sheriff's Court, with wide jurisdiction. The Court deals with actions of debt or damages with no upper limit—so while some 95 per cent of claims are for less than £1000, some are frequently higher.

Where a claim is for damages in excess of £250 these may (with certain exceptions) be remitted to the equivalent of the High Court—the Court of Session in Edinburgh, for a jury trial.

The Sheriff's Court also deals with landlord and tenant and rent restriction cases; with separation actions; with petitions for the adoption of children; with bankruptcy cases and with ordinary cases of contract and tort.

Where the value of the case does not exceed £250, the sheriff's decision is final. And in the civil sphere, the Sheriff's Court also incorporates a Court of Appeal—cases first heard by a sheriff may be appealed to the sheriff-principal. So this curious appeal from one single judge to another may be anomalous but it does enable people to appeal locally and without undue pressure.

The equivalent of the High Court is the Court of Session—the superior civil court. This is also both of first instance and a Court of Appeal. It sits in Parliament House, in Edinburgh.

The Court of Session deals with all actions concerning status (marriage, nullity, divorce, legitimacy); and with petitions for the winding-up of companies whose paid-up capital exceeds £10,000. And its shares jurisdiction with the Sheriff's Court in actions for damages, debt, etc., normally dealing with those involving the largest sums.

SCOTLAND: CRIME

The equivalent of the English Magistrates' Courts is the Sheriff's Court (criminal). Minor prosecutions may also be brought in District Courts before a stipendiary magistrate (in Glasgow) or justices of the peace—but the bulk of cases come before the sheriff. There is no appeal to the sheriff-principal.

About 90 per cent of prosecutions on indictment and more than 50 per cent of prosecutions on complaint, i.e. a summary prosecution, are dealt with in the Sheriff's Court. The prosecutor decides which mode of trial is appropriate and the accused has no right to elect for trial by jury.

Appeal in criminal matters goes to the High Court of Justiciary —made up of judges of the Court of Session. Apart from hearing appeals, it tries all serious crimes—including murder and rape and goes on circuit for the purpose.

49 Witness-boxing

One of the potentially most uncomfortable audiences for any businessman is the court of law. With a bit of luck, you will avoid appearing in the dock. But the day is almost bound to come when you find yourself in the witness-box. With reasonable good fortune, you will be there as a witness for or against some-one else. But you may be a defendant. Still worse, you might be an accused. Or you could be a plaintiff. In any event—whatever the capacity in which you appear—you must know the basic rules of successful witness-boxing. It is said that a judge must ensure not only that justice is done but that it is manifestly seen to be done. It is equally true that a witness must not only tell the truth but make it manifestly apparent that he is doing so. After all, it is no use being accurate and precise, is it, if no-body believes your story?

Your ordeal generally begins by the taking of the oath. Assuming that you have religious beliefs, you will be able to swear on the Holy Book of your choice. Every witness-box has an Old Testament as well as a New—and a Jewish witness would be well advised to bring a hat with him and make sure that his head is covered. Judges, who have no conception of the different

rituals of the various Jewish sects, look askance at a Jewish witness whose head is not covered when he takes the oath. He may
be relieved if a Chinese witness dispenses with the traditional
ceremony of smashing a saucer to seal his promise to tell 'the
truth, the whole truth and nothing but the truth'. But he tends
to be baffled by a Jew who swears hatless or covering his head
with hand or handkerchief.

If you have no religious beliefs or your religion forbids the
taking of oaths, you will be allowed to affirm. This simply
amounts to a declaration that you will tell the truth to the
court—a declaration that is intended to be binding upon your
conscience.

When you take the oath, do not rely on your memory. The
usher will hand you a card. Read from it. It is extraordinary
how many intelligent people misread the oath. This may be due
either to nervousness or overconfidence—or perhaps a state of
partial shock induced by the usher's loud roar of 'Silence' just
as you are about to intone the formula. But you need not have
worried—no one is allowed to talk other than the oath-taker, and
you were therefore the only person to whom the usher's injunction was not addressed.

'And now, Mr Jones,' your counsel will say, 'will you kindly
address your remarks to the learned judge and do please remember to keep your voice up.' Better advice you could not be given.
Do not talk to counsel. One of them is already sufficiently or at
least apparently convinced (even if only temporarily) that you
are right and the other that you are wrong. It is the judge—or
magistrate or magistrates or jury, as the case may be—who will
need the convincing. So speak to them. This applies whether
you are being examined by your own counsel or cross-examined
by counsel on the other side. And in the latter case, it will save
you from being put off by a favourite trick of some barristers—
attempting to unnerve witnesses by asking them questions while
looking in a completely different direction. Talk to the judge and
you won't notice it.

'But how does one address a judge?' you ask. If it is a justice
in a Magistrates' Court, he is called 'Sir' (or, on occasion,

'Madam'). If it is a judge in a County Court, he is 'Your Honour'. And if it is a judge of the High Court, you address him as 'My Lord'. If you call a magistrate, 'Your Honour' or 'My Lord', he will be flattered. But don't call a County Court judge 'Sir' or a High Court judge, 'Your Honour'—that is almost insulting.

You are now speaking to the judge and calling him by his correct name. Now is the time to remember to 'speak up'. Nothing irritates a judge more than not being able to hear what a witness is saying—and this is particularly important if the judge is elderly and possibly a little deaf. If you have a case, tell the world. If you have something to say, say it so that the world—including counsel, the jury (if any), the shorthand-writers, in fact, everyone in the court—can hear without straining.

'What is your full name?' your counsel goes on. 'And where do you live?' So starts the 'examination in chief'. Your barrister will do his best to prompt you and to help you along, but he cannot ask you 'leading questions'. A leading question is simply one which suggests the answer. For example, take an ordinary car accident. You are describing how it occurred. Your counsel cannot say to you, 'The van crossed against a red light, didn't it?' That is leading you to say yes. What he will ask is, 'What happened?' Then it's up to you to explain, in your own words, the facts about the case. (Incidentally, 'That's a leading question,' is one of the legal phrases most misused by laymen. 'And with whom did you spend last night?' is not a leading question, so don't try to hedge by telling your interrogator that it is!)

When your 'examination in chief' is finished, opposing counsel will weigh in with his questions. And he can ask as many leading ones as he wishes. He will try to needle you, to irritate you, to provoke you. Be not provoked, irritated or needled. Remember that he is only doing his job and he is not being nasty because he has any personal feeling against you.

Equally, if he treats you to a charming smile and asks you his questions in a respectful or a kindly tone of voice, do not be fooled. He is not doing it because he likes or respects you, but because he thinks it the best way to get you to drop into his little trap or to give your evidence in the way most favourable to his client.

So listen to counsel's questions. If you do not understand them, ask that they be repeated. And then reply, calmly and carefully. Don't lose your temper. That's what the other side wants you to do. And don't be afraid that counsel will take an unfair advantage of you—if he tries to do that, your own counsel will leap to his feet, objecting vigorously. But by then, if counsel really has been unfair, the chances are that the judge will already have choked him off.

When you are asked a question, answer it—do not reply by asking another one. You are not there to ask questions. 'What is your full name?' begins the classic examination in chief. 'What's my name?' replies the witness. 'Yes. What's your name'. 'Dai Jones,' says the witness, 'and what might your name be, pray?' It may get a giggle from the back of the court—but it won't please the judge.

Of course, there are exceptions to every rule. We remember with affection a Dutch gentleman who was claiming commission as agent for a chocolate firm. He told Judge Block, of the Mayor's and City of London Court, of the excellence of the firm and its prospects—but continued with a sad tale of woe, ending with his leaving the employment. 'But if the job was such a good one,' queried the counsel on the other side, 'why did you leave?' The witness turned round to the judge, spreading his arms out wide. 'My Lord,' he cried appealingly, 'if you were treated like that, would you stay on as judge?' His question was never answered—but he won his case.

Another good rule is—don't make jokes. Leave that to counsel and to the judge. If you try to be facetious or funny, you are asking for trouble. And if the court or counsel do laugh about matters which you consider terribly serious, forgive them—if they were to become emotionally involved in the troubles that surround their lives, they would be sad folk indeed. So don't let their jokes upset you.

Not long ago, a small boy appeared before Mr Justice Stable in the High Court, claiming damages from a shop-keeper who he claimed had sold him a firework with which he had seriously injured one eye. When his mother came to give evidence, counsel cross-examined her, suggesting that she had put words into her little boy's mouth.

'Have you discussed this case with your son?' he inquired.

'Naturally,' she replied.

'Often?'

'Not too often—I didn't want to remind him about his bad eye.'

'But I suppose you did discuss it with him when you knew that he was coming to court?'

'I did.'

'And I suppose you discussed his evidence with him?'

'Yes.'

'So you told him . . .'

'I told him to tell the truth, and that if he didn't there'd be one man who'd know—and that would be God.'

The judge turned round to her, wagging his finger, and beaming from ear to ear. 'And what about me, Madam?' he asked, amidst roars of laughter.

The lady was greatly discomfited. She need not have been. The judge had already made up his mind that her son was telling the truth—and in due course, he gave judgment to that effect.

Which brings us to one of the most common questions put to a witness—and one which upsets them the most. 'Have you discussed this case with anyone recently?' counsel asks. 'If I say yes,' the witness say to himself, 'then he'll suggest that I'm party to a cooking of the evidence. But if I say no, then he'll say I'm lying.' Quite right. But the answer is still, yes. First, you will undoubtedly have discussed the case with your solicitor. It is extremely doubtful whether you will have kept it back from your wife, your secretary . . . in fact, you'll probably have been dining out on it for months. So reply, 'Certainly I've discussed it —but what I've told the court is what I saw—and it's true.' Do that, and you will have edged around yet another trap laid for the unwary and the liar.

Always remember, too, to treat the judge with tact. The

witness who says, 'The man I'm talking about was really very old and decrepit,' when the man referred to was sixty and the judge is over sixty-five, is hardly out to make friends and influence the court in his favour. Equally, it is rude and discourteous to talk to the court with your hands in your pockets, still less rattling coins in them.

But it is not impolite to take your time before replying to a question. A very self-confident businessman came a cropper recently simply because he took no time to think. He was asked to mark on a map the place where a collision happened—and counsel passed him the document. With a slash of his red pencil, the witness marked the spot. But he only made one little mistake —counsel had handed him the map upside-down—he failed to check that it was the right way up—and as a result he marked the spot exactly—on what everyone agreed was the wrong side of the crossroads. After that, it will hardly surprise you to hear that his evidence was completely disregarded by the court. So bear witness with care—and remember that it's up to you to say what's on your mind. Do not take anything for granted. Your counsel will do his best to prompt you—but he cannot lead you. So do make sure that you tell your own story—and do not be one of those who says to himself, when the case is over and he's lost it, 'If only I'd said . . .'

And now a last word about your relationship with solicitors and counsel. If you are yourself instructing solicitors, they will instruct a barrister on your behalf. You can pick your own counsel if you want to, but a solicitor prefers to do the choosing for you. If you make your own choice, then you will have to bear the responsibility. The normal rule is, you instruct a solicitor, and he briefs counsel.

The story is told by a distinguished colleague of an occasion when he was called upon at the last minute to rush off to do a police-court case. It seems that the counsel whom the accused businessman had asked for was not available and, as a personal favour to the solicitor concerned, our friend filled the gap.

He arrived at the court and won the case. Then, for the first time, he met his client outside. 'Thank you so much, Mr Jones,' the man effused.

'Oh, you're quite welcome,' counsel replied. 'But I'm afraid Mr Jones was in another court, I'm Mr Brown.'

'Mr Brown?' snorted the client. 'Who asked for you? What are you doing here? How dare you conduct my case when I didn't ask for you?'

The question was obviously rhetorical—but it does make it clear why counsel is happy that professional etiquette will not permit him to interview his lay client when a solicitor is not present. So you mustn't phone up your barrister for a private chat. Nor must you try to see him without its being in a proper conference, arranged by the solicitor. Just as you cannot go direct to a specialist in medicine—you have to arrange it through your G.P.—so counsel must be approached through the proper channels.

Mind you, if you are only a witness, counsel will not talk to you at all before the case—unless, that is, you are an expert. Once again, etiquette permits him to discuss the evidence only with experts and clients. The interviewing of other witnesses is done entirely by solicitors.

And now, knowing the ropes and the rules, advised by solicitor and counsel, you sally forth to the witness-box. May the best man win. May you be the best man!

50 *A witness's checklist*

Before giving evidence in any court or tribunal, check the following:

1 Do you know your case? Work out in advance what questions you are likely to be asked and ensure that you either know the answers or are prepared to say that you do not know. Therefore

2 Have you prepared (and preferably had typed out) a proper 'proof of evidence'—that is, a statement concerning all relevant facts? Read it through carefully before you give your evidence. You may not take it into the witness box with you (unless it is 'a contemporaneous document'—see below). But you are fully entitled to absorb and re-absorb its contents.

3 Can you get a colleague or friend to cross-examine you—to test and to probe your evidence, so as to prepare you for the cross-examination you will probably face? The better prepared the witness, the greater his prospect of being believed.

4 Are you satisfied that your evidence is correct? Check it out with any documents (those in the possession of your own side or those revealed by your opponents)—with special reference to dates, names, time, places, etc., which can be ascertained with certainty.

5 Have you prepared all contemporaneous documents (notes, letters, etc.) which you will need with you—not only at the hearing but also in the witness box? Remember that (like the policeman's note book) these documents may be referred to while you are giving evidence—although they will have to be shown in that case to the other side.

6 Are you dressed for the occasion? Respect for the court or tribunal—together with recognition that those who sit in judgment are likely to have to rely on first impressions—should encourage you to dress smartly and conservatively. (A young accused who declined to have his hair cut was warned by his lawyer that the result might be an even shorter crop, in one of Her Majesty's institutions. Unfortunately, appearance counts here—as elsewhere in business).

7 Are you afraid of the witness box? If so, spare time to visit the scene of your future ordeal. Courts and tribunals are nearly always open to the public and you may sit in on someone else's troubles and imbibe the atmosphere and observe the procedures. Watch in particular:

a Usually, the witness may say what he has himself seen or heard—but not what someone else said that he (the other person) heard or said. This is known as 'the hearsay rule'.

b Watch how advocates 'cross-examine' witnesses on the other side, asking 'leading questions' (that is, questions which suggest the answer) to their heart's content—but how they avoid 'leading' their own witnesses. Your advocate will not be able to put the words into your mouth, nor suggest the answers to the questions which he asks you.

c Note with care the idiosyncracies of the court or tribunal—or, if you happen to know the individual Judge, Magistrate or Tribunal before whom you will appear, then those of the individual or individuals concerned. Judges decide cases—and each has his own ways. Also: The lower down the scale (especially at tribunal level) procedures are less rigid, more varied and are frequently decided by the presiding chairman.

8 Have you watched other witnesses and their mistakes—so as to avoid them: Examples: Unpleasant mannerisms of speech ('To tell the truth . . .') or of manners (picking noses, rattling coins); rudeness to court or counsel; speaking too fast, so that court cannot write down replies (most Judges etc. have to keep long-hand notes); speaking so that they cannot be heard; and above all, failing (or refusing) to answer the questions asked.

9 Are you aware that you will be watched when you are not giving evidence? The demeanour of witnesses when sitting in court or tribunal and not realizing that they are being observed is highly revealing to any experienced Judge, etc.

10 Have you checked on the time when you will probably be needed at the court or tribunal? Although there are occasions when witnesses (like litigants) have to hang around and wait their turn, courts and tribunals do try to oblige by hearing witnesses when they are available (some-

times even slotting in at convenient hours—perhaps at the start or end of a day or after the luncheon break). If in doubt or difficulty, ask your lawyer. He may, if necessary, make application to the court.

11 Recognizing that (unless you are an expert witness—and hopefully, well paid) you will waste a good deal of time and cash through the proceedings, are you satisfied that your evidence is really necessary? If not, can you convince whoever is trying to call you that you are dispensable?

12 Have you received a *subpoena* or witness summons—which requires you to attend? Or a *subpoena duces decum*—one requiring you to bring with you the documents named? If so, then you must turn up. But if you do not want to come, do not hesitate to tell those who have seen fit to require your presence that they may regret putting you into the witness box. Every witness is a hostage to the other side—which (unlike the side which called him) may submit him to cross-examination.

13 If you are prepared to give evidence but do not wish to testify voluntarily against the other side, why not ask for a *subpoena* or witness summons? Then you can say to any objector, 'I couldn't help myself ... I was subpoenaed ...'

14 If lawyers are involved, have you discussed your evidence with them? Unless you are an expert, you will not be able to talk to your barrister—but it is part of the solicitor's job to 'take proofs of evidence' from witnesses and to discuss cases with them.

*   *   *

Remember that in a criminal case, no witness is allowed into the court after the trial has begun, until he gives his own evidence—after which, he may remain. In civil actions, unless the court otherwise orders, witnesses may (and should) listen to all the evidence which precedes theirs.

The more important the case; the longer it is since the incidents you will describe; the more time you will have to invest in the hearing—the more important it is to check this list and to follow the rules. Witnesses may discredit themselves as well as the side on whose behalf they are called.

51 An advocate's checklist

In the High Court, the County Court or the Crown Court, the company will inevitably be represented by solicitor or counsel (that is, by a barrister). The solicitor (roughly, the general prac- titioner of the legal world) has limited right of audience, mainly in lower courts and in tribunals; counsel (barrister) may appear in any court, up to the House of Lords. There are two ranks of bar- rister: 'Junior' (who may, in experience, knowledge and tech- nique be very senior—but who has not 'taken silk')—and 'Queen's Counsel' (sometimes called 'Leading Counsel' or 'Silks', because they wear silk gowns). You will choose your solicitor (preferably, by recommendation) and he will select counsel, when he needs a consultant or an advocate or an expert with time to look up the law.

Lawyers are, of course, trained and experienced advocates (although most solicitors do little advocacy and not all barristers are at the top of their profession).

In the past, executives and managers seldom appeared as advo- cates—either for themselves or, still less, for their business organi- zations. With the advent of the Industrial Tribunal, though, managers have taken to advocacy, for various reasons:

1 When the sum at stake is small and legal costs are high, tribunal advocacy becomes worthwhile.
2 You are usually better off in a Tribunal to represent your- self or your company than to employ anything other than an experienced (and hence, expensive) lawyer. And
3 Many top people bring their own claims—with potentially £11,760 (at least £5000 thereof tax-free) as the top prize for

an unfair dismissal, claims are not solely for lesser business mortals. But as such claims are brought by people who are (by definition) 'dismissed'—and frequently, still out of work—and as legal aid is not available for representation in Industrial Tribunals and executives and managers are seldom members of trade unions (which supply representation) —they represent themselves.

Happily for the advocate, Industrial Tribunal chairmen invariably attempt to help those who are not good at helping themselves (or their companies or firms). But there are certain basic rules to follow. Here is a list of some of the most important:

1 Do your homework. Know your case. Be prepared to answer questions about it.
2 Know what is contained in your own documents. Put them into proper (which usually means, date) order.
3 Find out what documents the other side intends to produce. Ask for them and if they are either not produced or you think that there are others which are being hidden from you, go to the Tribunal in advance and seek an order for the production of these documents. An order for 'discovery' and 'inspection' is almost invariable in civil actions—too few industrial tribunal litigants realize that the same order can be obtained there. Do not be taken by surprise by documents produced in court by the other side.
4 Prepare your documents in proper (which usually means date) order. Make them into a bundle and number the pages. Then make copies—three for the tribunal; one for your witness; at least one for the other side.
5 Obtain statements (technically called 'proofs' of evidence) from potential witnesses. Remembering that each witness is a hostage to the other side—and likely to contradict himself under cross-examination—keep the list as short as possible. Call those who are essential; bring second liners to the tribunal, prepared to give evidence if necessary. You do not have to decide in advance.

6 Ensure that all witnesses who can produce 'contemporaneous documents'—that is, file notes, records or letters, made
at the time of the occurrence—have the originals available
in order to refer to them in the witness box.

7 Take all witnesses through their 'proofs'; discuss their evidence—and ensure that they know their case and are prepared to answer questions about it. Naturally, you must not
tell them what to say—but you are entitled to ensure that
they know what they are about.

8 Decide whether you wish yourself to testify. In tribunals,
you may both present the case and give evidence.

9 If possible, attend the tribunal in advance so as to study the
procedures and the atmosphere. If in doubt, ask the clerk
or the usher—enquire, especially, about any idiosyncracies
of the individual chairman. (You will probably not know
the composition of your own tribunal until a few minutes
before the hearing.)

The normal routine in a case is :

i The party on whom the burden of proof falls 'opens'
the case, explaining the facts and calling evidence. In
dismissal cases, if the employer admits that he 'dismissed', then the burden falls on him to show the reason
for the dismissal and that he acted 'reasonably' in treating that reason as sufficient to warrant depriving the
employee of his livelihood. Therefore he will usually
kick off. But in 'constructive dismissal' cases, where the
employee must prove that he was 'dismissed', he will
start.

ii The other party will then call his evidence—and address
the tribunal. The claimant will then make his submissions.

iii The person who calls the witness may not 'lead' him—
but only ask questions which do not suggest the answers.
The other advocate then 'cross-examines'—asking any
questions that are relevant. Then the witness's advocate

may 're-examine'—that is, ask further questions arising out of the cross-examination.

10 In their presentation and manner, advocates should follow the same rules as those for witnesses (see witness's checklist). In particular, they should speak clearly; be concise; answer directly any questions asked of them by the tribunal; and always remain calm and courteous. He who panics or gives way to anger loses his temper and his case at the same time.

11 Finally: Arrive early; prepare yourself, your evidence, your witnesses with time on your side; do not be afraid to ask for a few minutes' grace, if your preparations are not completed—or (especially) if you are trying to negotiate a settlement with the other side. Just as litigation is an expensive luxury, to be avoided by potential litigants whenever reasonably possible, so members of tribunals are happy to have cases disposed of by agreement, rather than by argument.

The good advocate is frequently the man who can win the best settlement—which requires that skill in negotiation for which the businessman ought in any event to be prepared.

52 *Winning cases—in Courts and Tribunals*

The businessman who can avoid ever appearing before a court or (today, more likely) an industrial tribunal is indeed fortunate. This checklist should help ensure that your trials (in both senses of that word) are as few as possible—and their outcome as favourable as you would wish.

PREPARE FOR BATTLE

Documents

1   Documents win cases. Is your system of documentation pro-fessionally prepared and properly used? Check especially: con-tracts of employment or written particulars of terms of service; written statements under the Health and Safety at Work Act; written warnings of intended dismissal—and letters of dismissal; safety systems—including reproofs and warnings to employees who do not follow your systems; and requests to mothers that they give notice in *writing* of their intention to return.

2   All the above documents—and almost any other relevant document which is not specifically prepared for the purpose of litigation (and which is 'privileged' from disclosure) will have to be produced if trouble arises. Beware of carelessly phrased inter-office memos and notes scrawled on files. Conversely:

3   If you have a whiff of legal trouble, remember: documents avoid litigation—the other side can see your strength; they win cases—because they are more reliable than memory; and—if made at the time—they may be referred to while in the witness box.

OTHER PREPARATIONS FOR TRIAL

Other preparations for trial include:

1   Take careful statements from all potential witnesses, before you see your solicitors. You will save their time and (hence) your money.

2   If you make statements to anyone else (including the police or other people's lawyers) say as little as possible. Most liti-gants lose cases out of their own mouths.

3   Instruct your lawyers early—when they still have time to guide and to help you. Even if you decide to 'go it alone'

before a tribunal, your lawyers should help you prepare your case—including your documents.

4 Put all documents into date order and make them into a bundle. Make at least five copies of the bundle for a court and seven for a tribunal, (one for each judge or tribunal member; two for your side; two for your opponents—witnesses may need copies while giving evidence).

5 If you are not satisfied that the other side is producing its documents in advance of the hearing, you may apply for 'discovery'—even industrial tribunals have the power to order disclosure.

Finally: ask your solicitors to give an estimate as best they can of the likely costs involved; weigh up your chances of success or failure; never despise a sensible compromise; and settle the case if you can because you will, in any event:

1 Spend your time and that of your staff in the preparation of the case and at the hearing.

2 Never recover all your costs, even if you win (from a tribunal, you will get none). And

3 You are likely to suffer anxiety and adverse publicity.

TRIAL TACTICS

If the case must be heard, then check the following:

1 Do you need solicitors or counsel to represent you? In court, the answer is almost always: Yes (a company, in any event, cannot represent itself). Before a tribunal, the answer is probably: No—unless the sum involved is great and/or there are complicated questions of fact and/or of law to be sorted out.

2 Choose the right lawyers when you need them: horses for courses and lawyers for cases. Recommendation is your best guide.

3   At the trial, dress conventionally—reckon that those who judge your case are likely to be middle class and middle aged.

4   When giving your evidence:

   a Speak up—reckon that those who listen to you are deaf— they probably are.

   b Answer the questions you are asked—as briefly as possible; if you wish to add a rider or some additional comment, say so.

   c Tell the truth—however unlikely it may sound.

   d Look at the judge, magistrate or chairman—and not at the person who is asking you the questions. And if the chairman or judge is writing down your answers, give him time to do so. Watch his pen.

   e Avoid unpleasant mannerisms of conduct (rattling of coins; picking of teeth, etc.) and of speech ('To tell the truth . . .', 'To be frank with you . . .').

   f Laugh at the jokes of others; make none yourself.

   g Finally: Watch your behaviour when you are not in the witness box. Wise observers (including experienced judges, etc.) watch the demeanour of witnesses when they (the witnesses) do not realize that they are being watched.

*   *   *

If you have to appear in a Tribunal or Court—in any capacity —familiarize yourself as best you can with its style, procedures and atmosphere. Take time to sit in on someone else's troubles before your own are reached. And if in doubt about the ways and customs of the court or the idiosyncrasies of the Bench—ask the usher or the clerk. The more humble the official and the more distinguished the questioner, the more flattered he is likely to be.

*   *   *

The basic rule remains, of course: Let someone else be the test

case. Only the lawyers are bound to win legal battles. Keep away
from them if you can. But if you can't—then at least follow the
above rules and you stand a good chance of winning—particularly if you happen to have truth and justice on your side.

53 *Guide to legal costs*

The costs of the law are mighty—but knowing their outline may
save you much money. So here is your guide to legal costs—and
how to avoid or to reduce them.

INDUSTRIAL TRIBUNALS

Tribunals only have power to award costs to the successful party
if the loser behaved in a way that is 'frivolous and vexatious'. The
Employment Appeal Tribunal has ruled that 'reasonableness' is
taken into account.

If you are taken to a tribunal by an ex-employee reckon on
paying your own costs in any event—but none of those of the
employee, if he chooses to engage lawyers. (Note—legal aid is not
available for tribunals, although help with preparation may be
given under the Legal Aid and Advice Act.)

When considering settlement of Industrial Tribunal claims,
then, take into account your own time and that of colleagues
or employees; potential bad publicity; and inevitable legal cost
if you employ lawyers.

If the sum demanded by the claimant is too high—or you feel
that you must set an example to others by fighting, then consider whether you should not keep the legal costs down by representing your own firm or company or getting a manager or
executive to do so for you. If you do decide to employ a lawyer

(perhaps because the sum claimed is high or the legal points involved are intricate) spend enough to get one experienced in tribunal battles.

COSTS WITHOUT LITIGATION

If you use lawyers to negotiate the settlement of a dispute (perhaps over alleged defects in machinery or in your repair service), you will probably have to pay the costs yourself unless: (*a*) payment of your costs by the other party is made part of the settlement; or (*b*) you start proceedings and win them.

THE COSTS OF A LAW SUIT

The costs of litigation in the County Court (usually, claims of up to £1000) or in the High Court (usually, above £1000) depend upon all the circumstances of the case, including: (*a*) the number of documents to be examined, copied and produced; (*b*) the complication and length of any pre-trial ('interlocutary') summonses or appeals; (*c*) the length of the hearing; and (*d*) the stature and fees of the lawyers employed by the parties.

Ask your lawyer how much he thinks the costs of an anticipated law suit are likely to be. Then put a limit on your expenditure (actual—on your own costs; potential—on those of the other side) —and tell him to report back when that figure is reached—if the case is not settled in the meantime.

THE WINNER'S COSTS

In a civil action, normally 'costs go with the event'—in other words, the winner is entitled to an order that the loser pay his costs. But these will normally be payable only on a so-called 'party and party' basis—that is, the loser will only have to pay those costs which are assessed (or 'taxed') by a court official or agreed as having been necessarily incurred in order to achieve the victory. Other (less important but still properly incurred) costs will be payable by the client to his solicitor (hence called 'solicitor and client' costs).

Because of 'solicitor and client' costs—or, if you prefer, because costs are seldom awarded on an 'indemnity basis'—even if you win a case, you are unlikely to emerge scot free.

LEGALLY AIDED OPPONENTS

In general, a litigant who receives legal aid will only be ordered to pay costs equal to the amount of his legal aid contribution— and by the same instalments—even if he loses. So if you are sued by a legally aided plaintiff, enquire what is his contribution to the legal aid fund—and you will then know what amount of your costs he will pay if you win. Result: It may be cheaper to pay the whole of the claim than to fight the case and to win it.

CRIMINAL COSTS

Legal aid apart, if you are prosecuted, e.g. under the Health and Safety at Work Act, you must expect to pay your own costs— although criminal courts do have power to award costs to innocent defendants (power normally only exercised when the prosecution should not have been brought).

However: If you bring a private prosecution with the co-operation of the police, you are likely to get your costs awarded out of public funds. A similar award (paid by the public) is available to those (rare) civil cases in which hardship is caused to the opponent of the legally aided litigant who cannot pay his costs.

INSURANCE

Where insurers step into the litigious shoes of their assured, e.g.

in personal injury claims by employees, cover includes legal costs. So it also does under many road traffic policies. Insurance against the legal costs of industrial safety prosecutions is also available.

PAYMENTS INTO COURT

In civil cases, it is usually possible for the defendant to pay money into court with a denial of liability. The plaintiff may then take out the money paid in—and recover his costs up to that date. But if he decides not to accept the sum paid in, he takes a chance— because even if he wins his case and is awarded no more than the sum paid in, he will have to pay his costs and those of the other side, from the date of the payment in.

CONVEYANCING AND OTHER NON-LITIGIOUS COSTS

To find out how much your solicitor will charge to execute the conveyance of your property; to make your will; to draw up standard terms and conditions; to prepare contracts of employment for your staff—ask him. Sometimes there are fixed scales based on the sum involved. Usually, you are back in the market place, finding the best lawyer at the most reasonable price— in the same way as your customers must search for the best bargains in your line of trade.

RELIEF AGAINST FORFEITURE

Where a tenant fails to pay his rent and is sued for possession, he can normally apply for 'relief against forfeiture'. At any time before he is actually put out of the property, he may pay the rent properly due—and escape from having to forfeit his tenancy. But it will almost always be a term of the Court's grant of relief that he pays all of the landlord's cost on an indemnity basis.

SCALES

In both the County Court and the High Court, scales of costs are frequently laid down, setting out the maximum payable to solicitor and/or to Counsel (barrister—'junior' or Q.C.)—in return for the work stated. Details from your lawyer.

BEWARE

So take care over costs—they often amount to more than the sum in dispute between the parties to a legal battle. If you are going to settle your case, try to do so early—the longer you wait, the higher the costs . . . the higher the costs, the more difficult it becomes to reach a compromise . . . the harder the compromise, the longer the battle and the greater the costs . . . which can only (and properly) benefit the men and women of the law.

54 Settling legal cases—a checklist

Any legal dispute that is settled on reasonable terms should be regarded as a victory. Rare indeed is the winner of any legal battle because:

1 In any court case, the winner is normally entitled to his costs. But normally the loser will only be ordered to pay those costs which were regarded as essential for the winning of the case—the winner is likely to find a balance which was properly incurred and which he must pay to his solicitor out of his own pocket (or out of the winnings).
2 If faced with a legally aided plaintiff (e.g. in an industrial injuries case), even if you win, the plaintiff will only be ordered to pay a sum towards your costs equal to his contribution to the Legal Aid Fund (and by the same instalments).

This means that you will probably have to pay the bulk of your costs out of your own pocket.

3 Industrial tribunals only order the loser to pay costs in very exceptional cases, e.g. where there has been an 'abuse of the process of the court'. In practice, regard money spent on industrial tribunal proceedings as an investment in success. Do not expect its return.

4 Proceedings take time—hours and days and sometimes weeks, spent in preparing for trial; waiting for cases to be called or heard; enduring the trial.

5 Law suits—civil and especially criminal—are 'trials', in all senses of that word. Anxiety . . . the possible bad publicity . . . possible bad effects on industrial relations . . .

The lawyer who advises you to accept a sensible compromise is not a coward—nor is he saving money for himself, because most lawyers who take on litigation make far more from the trial than from the preliminaries. A lawyer's advice to 'settle' should be as welcome as that of a surgeon to avoid the knife, treating an ailment with drugs.

So here is a checklist of some of the essential rules for settling.

*   *   *

1   Regard the settlement of a legal claim in the same way as any other business transaction. Exclude emotion and 'principles'—you are engaged in a commercial battle. Balance the probable cost of proceeding (estimates from your lawyers) against the probable loss involved in a settlement. Remember to include allowance for time, anxiety, etc. (see above). If the balance is in favour of settlement, then write off the loss and cut clear.

2   Everything has its price—even a law suit. So even if you did originally intend to fight (perhaps to show others that you are not prepared to be beaten down or ill treated), then prepare yourself for battle—but do remember that litigation is a most chancey affair and even the best cases are sometimes lost and the most

unlikely ones are won. Fight by all means—but recognize that you are involved in a gamble.

3   If you are a defendant in a civil action, you can normally reduce the odds by making a payment into court. If the plaintiff takes the money paid in (with denial of liability), then that is the end of the case. He gets the payment in plus his costs to that date. If he does not accept the money paid in, then if he wins his case and recovers no more than that sum, he will have to pay most of your costs from the date of payment in—even though he got judgment. So if you have nicely judged that payment, you put him on the spot. You should pay in as much as you are willing to lose, to get rid of the case—although you may pay in a smaller amount first, then add to it later if necessary. If the sum paid in is not taken out, the judge will not know of its existence—still less of its amount. So remind your lawyer of the possibility of a payment in, at an early date.

4   Efforts to settle a case may begin with the threat of litigation and end at the door of the court—or even when the case is under way. Some 95 per cent of all cases are settled before judgment.

5   About 50 per cent of all unfair dismissal claims are either withdrawn or settled before they reach the tribunals. Remember that claimants cannot normally contract out of their right to take a case to the tribunal. Exception: Where an agreement is approved by the conciliation officer. The Advisory, Conciliation and Arbitration Service (ACAS) provides conciliators who can frequently bring parties to terms. Use them—their advice is free and often as well informed as that of any lawyer except those specializing in employment work.

6   Use 'without prejudice' conversations and correspondence whenever you are negotiating and do not wish to risk any offer being treated by a court as a sign of weakness. Once a letter is marked 'without prejudice' it cannot be produced in any legal proceedings without your consent—unless it leads to a settlement,

in which case it may provide evidence of that 'accord and satisfaction'.

7   The art of negotiating a settlement is (again, like all business transactions) one requiring experienced and delicate handling. If you negotiate on your own behalf, good luck—but once you have placed the negotiations in your lawyers' hands, let them get on with it. Do not 'keep a dog and do your own barking', otherwise you will inevitably get the worst of all worlds.

8   If you do reach a settlement, make sure that the terms are clear. Even if you have done your own bargaining, have those terms checked by your lawyer, if you have any doubt as to their precision or enforceability. Once you have reached an agreement to settle, it (like any contract) is enforceable through the courts. The original dispute has then been overtaken by the agreement and a dispute over that agreement becomes a new battle, on revised territory.

9   Once you have settled a case, have no regrets. Do not complain: 'If only we had fought, then . . .' After all, you might have lost—far more than the compromise cost you. And the earlier you settle, the less you will have to pay in legal costs. Conversely, once you reach the door of the court (where so many cases are compromised because the parties become reasonable when in sight and fear of the witness box), the costs may (and in many cases do) equal or even exceed the amount in dispute between the parties.

Book II

The Businessman's Guide to the
Laws and Conduct of Meetings

Part I
Meetings

55 Company meetings

What meetings must a company call? What meetings may it call? And when may members of a company themselves requisition a meeting—either directly or with the help of the court?

*　　*　　*

Within a period of not less than one month nor more than three months from the date at which a public company is entitled to commence business, a general meeting of members must be called. This is known as 'the statutory meeting'.

Thereafter, a company is bound to hold an Annual General Meeting every year, and notices calling the meeting must specify it as such. Not more than 15 months may elapse between the date of one Annual General Meeting and the next—subject only to the proviso that a new company has 18 months from the date of its incorporation within which to hold its first A.G.M.

If a company in which you are interested has not held its A.G.M., and you can get satisfaction no other way, you should (either directly or through your solicitor) contact the Board of Trade. The Board may then itself call or direct the calling of a general meeting 'and give such ancillary or consequential directions as the Board think expedient . . .'

Suppose, now, that a member wishes to call a special meeting of the company to discuss some particular matter. To get results, he must either himself hold at least one-tenth of the paid-up capital of the company or be able to get the backing of enough shareholders to make up that proportion. Under Section 132 of *The Companies Act, 1948* (which we will call 'the 1948

Act', for convenience) 'the directors of a company, notwithstanding anything in its Articles, shall, on the requisition of
members of the company holding at the date of the deposit of
the requisition not less than one-tenth of such of the paid-up
capital of the company as at the date of the deposit carries the
right of voting at general meetings of the company ... forthwith
duly proceed to convene an extraordinary general meeting of the
company.'

The requisition must state the objects of the meeting and must
be signed and deposited at the registered office of the company.
The requisition itself may be in a single document or it may
'consist of several documents in like form each signed by one
or more requisitionists.' The directors then have 21 days from
the date of the deposit of the requisition in which to convene the
meeting. If they fail to do so, the requisitionists or any of them
who represent more than one-half of the total voting rights of
all of them, may themselves convene a meeting. But this may
not be held after the expiration of three months from the date
of the deposit of the requisition.

The Act lays down the length of notice which must be given
before meetings are called. Twenty-one days' written notice is
required for the A.G.M. Meetings other than the A.G.M., or
those called for the passing of a special resolution, require 14
days' written notice.

If insufficient notice is given, the meeting may still be valid.
If, in the case of a meeting called as the A.G.M., all the members
entitled to attend and vote agree that the meeting shall be
treated as validly convened, all will be well. And in the case of
any other meeting, if there is a majority who together hold not
less than 95 per cent in nominal value of the shares giving a
right to attend and vote at the meeting and if they resolve that
the meeting was properly convened, then once again the irregu-
larity is waived.

So if ever a shareholder wishes to call a meeting, he should
check the Articles of the company to see what provision they
make as regards procedure and voting. In the absence of anything to the contrary in the Articles, he should look at the

'Table A' clauses, which are usually made to apply where there
are no special, contradictory Articles. For instance, 'two or more
members holding not less than one-tenth of the issued share
capital . . . may call a meeting . . . In the case of a private company two members, and in the case of any other company three
members, personally present shall be a quorum . . . Any member
elected by the members present at a meeting may be chairman
thereof . . . In the case of a company originally having a share
capital, every member shall have one vote in respect of each
share or each £10 of stock held by him, and in any other case,
every member shall have one vote.'

Suppose, now, that the company will not call a meeting which
a member believes is necessary, though he cannot himself muster
sufficient share power to requisition it. All is not necessarily lost.
Under Section 135 of the 1948 Act, 'If for any reason it is impracticable to call a meeting of the company in any manner in
which meetings of that company may be called, or to conduct
the meeting of the company in the manner prescribed by the
Articles or this Act, the court may, either on its motion or on
the application of any director of the company, or of any member of the company who would be entitled to vote at the meeting,
order a meeting of the company to be called, held and conducted
in such a manner as the court thinks fit. Where any such order is
made, the court may give such ancillary or consequential
directions as it thinks expedient . . . Any meeting called, held
and conducted in accordance with an order under the foregoing
subsection shall for all purposes be deemed to be a meeting of
the company duly called, held and conducted.'

It is not often that the court can be convinced or cajoled into
calling a meeting. But here is a powerful, residuary right given
to investors who feel that otherwise they are not going to have
the opportunity to ventilate their grievances.

Finally, a word about voting at meetings. If a member believes
that a proper poll ought to be taken, then he is entitled to demand one. 'Any provision contained in a company's Articles
shall be void,' says the 1948 Act, 'in so far as it would have the
effect either of excluding the right to demand a poll at a general

meeting on any question other than the election of the chairman of the meeting or the adjournment of the meeting; or of making an effective demand for a poll on any such question which is made either by not less than five members having the right to vote at the meeting or by a member or members representing not less than one-tenth of the total voting rights of all the members having the right to vote at the meeting, or by a member or members holding shares in the company conferring a right to vote at the meeting, being shares on which an aggregate sum has been paid up equal to not less than one-tenth of the total sum paid up on all the shares conferring that right.'

Five members with the right to vote at the meeting may demand a poll. So may those holding one-tenth of the total voting rights or one-tenth of the paid-up share capital.

Parliament, then, has done its best to see that company meetings are properly conducted and members' grievances properly aired. But that is hardly surprising. Who does not wish to encourage self-imitation?

56 *The secretary*

The company secretary, director-general, general secretary—whatever you may call him—is probably the kingpin of the organization. As such, he must be prepared to speak in public, from time to time. And most of the suggestions in this book apply to him, quite as much as to the chairman or managing director, the treasurer or honorary secretary. But there are some additional responsibilities and liabilities which attach to his professional capacity.

The secretary is the chairman's right-hand man, even when

the presence of a guest of honour obliges him to sit to the chairman's left. As such, he must know the procedure . . . the rules . . . the constitution. Hence the parts of this book which detail those rules should be his special preserve.

When he himself is called upon to speak, he will need to exercise a special form of diplomacy. He is a civil servant, in all senses of both words, neither of which imply servility.

Tact is the secretary's greatest weapon. He needs to be on good terms with all. He cannot afford to attack those who employ him, or to sow seeds of discord between them. If he speaks evil in private, that is bad enough. In public, his words must not only be impartial, but manifestly so when it comes to personalities.

On the other hand, he may have to speak out on behalf of his Board, his organization, or his employers. He may even have to speak his own mind, at the behest of the company, the partnership, or the charity, and though he will be expected to have a mind of his own, he will be in trouble if he speaks it too loudly.

There is only one, short, general rule, then, for those who are employed to guide and direct. If you cannot be non-controversial —or at least pleasant about your controversial views—be silent. Public disputation is not for you, if you can possibly avoid it. But knowledge of the rules in this book is doubly vital for you.

57 The agenda

The chairman should decide upon the agenda for his meeting. Naturally, he will be guided by the company secretary, the firm's accountant or solicitor, his own secretary, the general secretary of the organization—in fact, by the individual who shares his secrets with him. Where the meeting is a large one, the agenda may have to be fixed, discussed and, where necessary, altered by a smaller group. An organization's executive may be its parliament, whilst its honorary officers are the cabinet. The Board of a large company may appoint a small agenda sub-committee. There are no laws about it.

But the agenda must be ready before the meeting starts. The good chairman will have sorted out the likely sticky patches and done his best to prepare the ground for constructive discussion rather than bitterness or personal animosity. It is so much easier, in so many cases, to exercise diplomacy in private. Not for nothing do so many professional diplomats do so much of their work behind closed doors. Anyway, the smaller the group, the more potent its power. 'If Moses had been a committee,' goes the old saying, 'the Israelites would still be in Egypt.'

However, committees there must be and it is up to chairmen to keep them on the rails. And the rails are laid down by the agenda.

First, apologies for absence. 'I have apologies from Messrs Black, White, Grey . . . I know you will be sorry to hear that Mrs Brown is in hospital. I have written to her on your behalf wishing her a speedy recovery . . . Mr Black is, in fact, celebrating the arrival of a small boy. I have written to him to express our congratulations.' If there are too many apologies, then say: 'Our secretary has a list of those who have sent in their apologies.' It is very depressing to have more people expressing their regrets than attending, so get off that subject as fast as you can. Or perhaps add: 'Considering the weather, it's remarkable how many of you have been good enough to attend. I'm very grateful to you.' Forgotten words of thanks cause frequent offence, and few chairmen have ever been criticized for being thankful too often.

Next, welcome any new members and publicly greet any distinguished arrivals or guests.

Then, the minutes of the last meeting should either be read

or, if they have been circulated, taken as read. If there are in-accuracies, these should be expunged. Then: 'May I now sign these minutes as a correct record?' Silence or nods of approval. 'Thank you, gentlemen.' The minutes are then signed. If any question arises as to past decisions, the answer will be found in the minute-book.

'Next, matters arising. Are there any matters arising out of the last minutes which are not covered by items lower down the agenda?' If there are, then deal with them. If there are none, then the meeting continues.

Sometimes it is sensible to take first those items which can be dealt with swiftly. Uncontroversial material should (unless you are up to some plot) be cleared out of the way whilst latecomers are still arriving. If you know that members have particular interests, try to make sure that these are dealt with in their presence. If someone intimates that he must leave early, ask him whether there is any particular item upon which he wishes to speak. If there is, then push it up the agenda. If you are warned that someone will be arriving late, ask him in advance if he has any particular views to express on anything on the agenda. If so, then hold it down until he arrives.

An agenda, then, is nothing more than a series of convenient headings under which the business of the meeting can be dis-cussed. It is a guide, not a strait-jacket, and essential if the meeting is not to deteriorate into a waffling session. It allows the business to be done in a coherent order and enables you to judge the length of the session. Just as your notes should in-dicate the skeleton of your speech (see Chapter 3), so the agenda provides the skeleton of the meeting. It is for the chairman to see that the body of the business is fleshed out in a sensible and helpful way.

When the listed business is done, two items remain. 'Is there any other business?' You deal with points not on the agenda and which did not arise out of the minutes of the last meeting. And then: 'Date of next meeting. Is the same time and place on the same day next month convenient. . .?'

If no one looks at his diary, you can fix the next meeting entirely to suit your own convenience, and you may even find yourself the only one present at it. But if everyone looks at his diary, the meeting has obviously been a success and the members are looking forward to the next of your gatherings. In that case you may congratulate yourself on your chairmanship.

58 Quorums

There is a story told—and it is a true one—of a shareholder who (apart from the company secretary) was the only person present at a company meeting. He took the chair; produced the proxies of other members; proposed and passed a resolution to make a call on the shares—and concluded by passing (unanimously, of course) a vote of thanks to the chairman! Eventually, other members took him to court and obtained a declaration that, despite the proxies, he could not constitute a valid meeting. In general, it takes two to make a quarrel or a meeting. The call on the shares was improper and a nullity. Before any business can properly and validly be transacted, there must be a quorum— that is, the minimum number. And that number can rarely be only one.

But there are exceptions. For instance, if one member holds all the shares of a class, he on his own may constitute a class meeting. And the Board of Trade or the court may, in certain circumstances, direct that one member shall be deemed to constitute a meeting.

In normal circumstances, however, you should look at the Articles of a company, or the rules of any other sort of organization, to find what quorum must be present when the meeting starts its business.

Section 134 of *The Companies Act, 1948,* provides that 'in the case of a private company two members, and in the case of any other company three members, personally present shall be a quorum.' Note the 'personally present'. Article 53 of Table A (commonly incorporated into a company's Articles) says that three members present in person will constitute a quorum in the case of a public company. Again, proxies cannot be included for this purpose. But Table A also fixes two members present in person 'or by proxy' to be enough in the case of a private company. No quorum, then no resolution can validly be passed. So if you intend to propose a resolution, make sure that a quorum is present.

In one case, directors had to repay fees received by them on the authority of a resolution passed by a general meeting at which there was no quorum. But third parties are entitled to presume that the internal proceedings of the company have been carried out in a proper manner. So, unless they have been 'put upon inquiry' by some unusual circumstances, a resolution passed in the absence of a quorum may still bind the company, in so far as third parties are concerned.

Article 54 of Table A says that if a quorum is not present within half an hour of the time appointed for the meeting, then —if convened upon the requisition of members—it shall be dissolved. In any other case, it shall be adjourned to the same day, time and place on the following week or to such other day, time and place as the directors may determine. If there is no quorum within half an hour of the start of the adjourned meeting? Then the members present will form the quorum. One single member can then probably be a quorum on his own.

Once the meeting has started, the quorum may depart. Business dealt with after the number of members remaining has been reduced below that required for the initial quorum is valid. So rally the troops for the start of the battle, even though they are later allowed to depart in peace.

Most organizations do require the presence of a certain

number of members if business is validly to be conducted. To find out the situation in any particular case, look at the organization's constitution or rules.

59 Proxies

There are so many meetings to attend, that often a choice must be made. Then there are absences through illness . . . other business engagements . . . family responsibilities. So the law recognizes that arrangements must often be made for people to attend and to vote 'by proxy'—that is, through appointing someone else to take their place.

Section 136 of the 1948 Act, says: 'Any member of a company entitled to attend and vote at a meeting of a company shall be entitled to appoint another person (whether a member or not) as his proxy to attend and vote instead of him and a proxy appointed to attend and vote instead of a member of a private company shall also have the same right as the member to speak at the meeting:

'Provided that, unless the Articles otherwise provide:

'(*a*) This sub-section shall not apply in the case of a company not having a share capital; and

'(*b*) A member of a private company shall not be entitled to appoint more than one proxy to attend on the same occasion;

'(*c*) A proxy shall not be entitled to vote except on a poll.'

In every notice calling a meeting of a company with a share capital, there must appear 'with reasonable prominence' the statement that a member entitled to attend and vote is entitled to appoint a proxy or, where that is allowed, one or more proxies to attend and vote instead of him, and that a proxy need not also be a member.'

The Articles generally deal with votes—and with proxies. Articles 68 to 72 of Table A (often incorporated into the Articles) are very much in point, and provide the appropriate form for the appointment of a proxy.

60 *Admitting the Press**

You may welcome the Press to your meetings, or you may prefer to meet in private. The Press are not entitled to attend a private meeting without the consent of the organizers. Where the meeting is held either on private premises or on public premises hired for the occasion, their position is the same as that of any other member of the public (see Chapter 78 on 'Trespass'). If you admit them, they are there as your guests. If you ask them to leave, they must go.

Local authorities may, in general, resolve to exclude the public (including the Press) from all or part of the proceedings of a meeting whenever it is considered that publicity would be prejudicial to the public interest. Neither the public nor the Press can, in practice, force their way into a council meeting, contrary to the wishes of its members. (For details, see *The Public Bodies (Admission to Meetings) Act, 1960.*) The same rule applies to newspaper men as to the public at large.

* See also Chapter 13.

61 Bugging—and the age of the tape-recorder

In the old days a company office was filled with people—half of them at least with pencils at the ready. Today, it is filled with machines, and ladies with pencils are rare, highly-paid super-women. Much of the rest of the staff are machine attendants . . . words pour into their ears and out on the typewriter. But have you ever wondered just how far the law would protect you if those machines were to turn against you? What, for instance, are your rights if your conversations, conferences or meetings are 'bugged'?

Some of the more refined models which doubtless decorate your desk can be used—by you or anyone else—for eaves-dropping . . . for invading the privacy of others. But could the police use the recording in court?

There is no law against recording the conversations of others and no reason, therefore, why you should discontinue your practice of installing a secretary on the extension when you speak on the telephone. And if you decide to enter the machine age by sticking some contraption to the receiver and using a tape instead of a human recorder, that is a matter for you.

Equally, you are entitled to record a conference. The fact that you do so without the knowledge of the other conferees does not mean you are committing any sort of offence, criminal or civil. There is no law which guarantees the citizen his privacy, though many citizens fervently believe that there should be.

There is in fact, a very lively argument going on at present, expressed by one man as being about 'the necessity to strike a balance between personal freedom and police efficiency'. As far as the law is concerned, provided the police do not assault prisoners, that is about all that is required of them. Evidence may be excluded by the trial judge if it has been unfairly obtained or if the accused has not been given the proper warnings. But although it is said that the police are 'sensitive to criticism from the Bench' and tape-recorded evidence is unlikely to be offered if a particular judge is known to be averse to it, it can and will be given in other circumstances.

In a recent case, two prisoners who were thought to have been involved together in a brutal murder, were left alone in a room. Not only convinced that they were in private but satisfied that their foreign dialect (they were Pakistanis) would protect them from prying ears, they spoke freely. They did not realize that a microphone was hidden behind the waste-paper basket and that the tape-recorder in the adjoining room was taking down all that they said. They made some very incriminating statements which were later used in evidence, and helped towards their conviction. The Court of Criminal Appeal said that the recording was properly used. 'The criminal does not act according to Queensberry rules. The method of the informer and of the eavesdropper is commonly used in the detection of crime. The only difference here is that a mechanical device was the eavesdropper. If in such circumstances the appellants by incautious talk provided evidence against themselves, then in the view of this court it would not be unfair to use it against them.'

It follows then that there is nothing improper in the use of tape-recorded evidence. So when you know that a tape-recording is in the hands of your opponents, watch out. True that, just like a photograph, a tape-recording can be faked, and will not, therefore, automatically be accepted by the court. Its contents will have to be proved. But this can be done.

A more common case for the ordinary company is a good deal more prosaic, and far more important. Your tapes are important records of your doings and of your sayings, and they should not always be blithely rubbed out by re-use or erasure as soon as they are finished. Your records are vital for your protection, and if a dispute arises as to what was said, you may be in difficulties without them.

Letters survive with a top copy and a carbon which remains impaled for ever on your files. But conferences, meetings, telephone conversations with clients or customers are another matter and though these may subsequently be confirmed in writing, no evidence can be as satisfactory as that made at the time. If, for instance, you reach some agreement or another speaker commits himself—or you are accused of doing so— all you would need to do in the event of some later dispute would be to produce the tape-recording.

Some companies keep marked tapes until a transaction is concluded, or the decisions taken at a conference have been fully implemented. They have specially-built drawers for these tape-recorded messages, and protect themselves by keeping recordings of conversations, knowing them to be more accurate evidence than letters of confirmation. Gone are the arguments about what was actually said. If you hold the tape, you can prove your case up to the hilt, and the more important the spoken occasion, the more helpful a tape-recording may be.

62 Insolvency—the end of the road

All good things, it is said, must come to an end. Fortunately, this will not apply to the successful business, but even the business-man who successfully manages to avoid a winding up of his own company, the dissolution of his partnership or his personal bankruptcy, may sometimes have to attend the sorry funerals of his competitors' business hopes. After all, he may be in the market for a take-over. One way or another, then, he needs to know the basic rules on meetings in insolvency, corporate and incorporate, personal and impersonal. Here they are.

*   *   *

Many a businessman with creditors howling hungrily around his door has considered Carey Street as a possible solution. And many have rejected it because of the effects of the Bankruptcy Acts, carefully designed to make it unpleasant for the man who too readily attempts to rid himself of his liabilities. Quite apart from the stigma attaching to a bankruptcy, an undischarged bankrupt is forbidden to obtain credit for £10 or more without revealing that he is an undischarged bankrupt—so there goes any hope he may have had of casting off one hungry heap of creditors and starting right away on accumulating another. It isn't so easy to get rid of your bankruptcy, either. You will have to apply to the court for an order of discharge, but even if you do manage to get one it may be made conditional. The court has an absolute discretion.

Again, you may not be given the opportunity voluntarily to throw in the bankruptcy towel; others may count you out whether you like it or not. If you fraudulently convey your property, conceal yourself or abscond to avoid paying your debts, fail to satisfy the judgment of the court—in fact, commit any 'act of bankruptcy'—then you may have a bankruptcy notice served on you. A receiving order will be made and an official receiver placed in control of your property—all of it. You may treasure secrets from your wife, your mistress or your private secretary, but the Official Receiver will know all. His job is to get in as much as possible for your creditors, and your debts will be paid according to strict and settled priorities.

Top of the list come funeral and testamentary expenses. This may prove troublesome to your widow, but is unlikely to make you turn over in your grave any faster than your stock managed to during your lifetime.

Next come a series of so-called 'preferred debts', which 'rank equally'. If there is money enough to pay them all, then well and good; if there is not then they share in the proceeds in the same proportion. These include rates and taxes (or, in any event, most of them); some wages and salaries and most National Insurance contributions; accrued holiday pay; guarantee payments; remuneration during medical suspension; payments for time off work (under the Employment Protection Act), and under a protective award (where a trade union has not been given proper notification of proposed redundancies).

Better still for the employed victim of a business downfall: If there is not enough money in the kitty to pay off the preferential debts, he is likely to have a substantial right to claim from the redundancy fund. Items include: Up to 8 weeks arrears of pay and six weeks holiday money (maximum: £80 per week); basic award for unfair dismissal; and even 'reasonable reimbursement' of any premium paid by an apprentice (those were the days). Anyway, if and when all the preferential creditors are paid off, the rest of the world's lenders can then queue up for the crumbs.

'Aha!' you exclaim. 'But how naïve can one get? The law may choose the preferred creditors—but I will get there first. And then it's woe betide the mean and nasty people who have trodden me down—and the best of luck to the kindly folk who've picked me up. The latter will get paid before I go down the drain—and the others can gurgle for their money.'

'Aha to you!' replies the law. 'We've thought of all that. If you attempt to favour one creditor at the expense of the others and go bankrupt within six months of any such preferential payment, the payment will be void as being "a fraudulent preference" and your effort will have been entirely in vain.'

'But suppose that one creditor threatens to sue me if I don't pay up, while the others don't bother me. Will it be a fraudulent preference if I pay the one applying pressure?'

'No, it won't. You are not then voluntarily preferring anyone —you are submitting to pressure which you cannot be expected to resist.'

All of which goes to show that kindness to prospective bankrupts just doesn't pay.

So much, then, for the downfall of individual business brilliance. What now of two penniless genii in concert? How can one terminate an unhappy or an unsuccessful partnership?

The answer all depends on the type of partnership in question. If it is for a fixed period, when that period expires that is the end of the combination. You can revive it if you wish; if you don't, it will slip silently into oblivion without further ado. Again, if it is a partnership of which the duration is not fixed, then it is a 'partnership at will' and can be dissolved at any time by any partner. If the partnership has been made by deed, then the partner breaking it up must given written notice to his colleagues. In any other case, no particular form of notice is required.

A partnership will also come to an end if any one of the partners dies or goes bankrupt. The old firm will never be the same again. True, the sad survivors can dispose of the body, pay off the widow and close ranks. But they are not obliged to. They —or any of them—can make it the occasion for the final bust-up. But if something happens which would make the partnership illegal, then it will dissolve automatically—and irrevocably.

Finally, the court can dissolve the partnership, if any of the partners applies, in any one of six circumstances. Here they are:

1 If the Court is satisfied that any partner is of permanently unsound mind, or a lunatic.
2 When any partner, for any other reason, becomes permanently incapable of performing the duties required of him under the partnership agreement.
3 When any partner has behaved in a way 'calculated prejudicially to affect the carrying on of the partnership business.'
4 When any partner persistently or intentionally breaks any term of the partnership agreement or in other ways behaves so that it is not reasonably practicable for the others to carry on in partnership with him.
5 When the partnership business can only be continued at a loss.
6 When the Court, in its discretion, decides that it is 'just and equitable' that the partnership should be wound up.

One warning: except in the case of the Official Solicitor applying on behalf of a lunatic partner, a partner who is guilty of an offence which is causing the breakup cannot apply to the court for the partnership to be dissolved. It is an old rule of equity that you must come to the Court 'with clean hands'—and in this case, the rule has been effectively enshrined in the Partnership Act.

When the firm is dissolved, its assets are used first for the paying of partnership debts, on similar lines to those governing payment of creditors in a bankruptcy. If the assets exceed the liabilities, well and good—the debts are paid off and the partners share the balance. But if the liabilities exceed the assets, then it's heaven help the partners—they have to share the losses in the same proporion as they shared the profits and each is liable for the partnership debts to the full extent of his worldly possessions. If any.

Which leaves companies. Assuming they are not extinguished by being struck off the register, they can be wound up in any one of three ways. First, there may be a voluntary winding-up, secondly there may be a winding-up under the supervision of the Court, and third, the Court may order a compulsory winding-up.

If the shareholders decide by special resolution (see Chapter 63) to dissolve the corporation, then they voluntarily put an end to their own misery. If the directors deliver to the Registrar of Companies, not more than five weeks before the passing of the resolution, a statutory declaration confirming that the company will pay all its debtors in full within twelve months of the start of the winding up, this is then known as 'a members' voluntary winding-up'. Its advantage is that the liquidator will be appointed and controlled by the shareholders who will, in effect, control the passing of their own, corporate legal entity.

If the directors cannot make the statutory declaration, the winding-up is described as 'a creditors' winding-up'. The day following the resolution, a creditors' meeting is called and a liquidator is appointed. And if the shareholders and creditors disagree, it is the creditors' man who will do the job.

Even where there is a voluntary winding-up, the Court is still entitled to step in if it thinks fit. It may order that the winding-up proceed under its supervision, and it will then appoint an additional liquidator to keep his eye on the proceedings.

A compulsory winding-up is much more unpleasant, and a Court can wind up the company for any of seven reasons. They are these:

1 If the company has by special resolution resolved that it be wound up by the Court.
2 If default is made in delivering the statutory report to the Registrar or in holding the statutory meeting.
3 If the company does not commence its business within a year from its incorporation, or suspends its business for a whole year.
4 If the number of members is reduced, in the case of a private company below two, or in the case of any other company below seven.
5 If the company is unable to pay its debts.
6 If the Court is of the opinion that it is just and equitable that the company should be wound up. Or
7 If on a petition by the Official Receiver or by any other person authorized to present a winding-up petition, the Court is satisfied that an existing voluntary winding-up, or a winding-up subject to supervision, cannot be continued with due regard to the interests of creditors or contributories.

The most interesting of these grounds is 'inability to pay debts.' This again is divided by the Companies Act, and comes under four heads:

1 If a creditor who is owed more than £50 has demanded payment—but has gone three weeks without being satisfied.
2 If, in England or Northern Ireland, execution is levied in an attempt to realize money owing under a judgment—and that execution is returned unsatisfied, in whole or in part.
3 If, in Scotland, certain specified debts (such as 'the induciae of a charge for payment of an extract decree' . . . or certain other matters, equally mysterious to a Sassenach) have gone

unpaid.
Or
4 If it is proved to the satisfaction of the Court that the company is unable to pay its debts; and, 'in determining whether a company is unable to pay its debts, the Court is to take into account the contingent and prospective liabilities of the company'.

It's not really quite as complicated as it sounds. If the Court considers there is a good chance of the company getting back on its feet, it will not be wound up. But if it seems that extra time would only lead to further and deeper wallowing in the mire, the company will have to go.

A company's creditors are paid off on much the same basis as those of a bankrupt, but the shareholders will only be liable for debts to the extent of any unpaid portion of their share capital. And—unless they are shareholders, or have committed some fraud or other—the directors will not be liable at all. The reason? An individual is a legal entity. The partners in a firm are separate legal entities—though the firm is not. But a company, while it has life, exists in law and has an existence entirely separate from those of its shareholders. And that is why limited liability is the greatest boon to business ever invented by fertile, legal minds.

63 Meetings in insolvency

No one just 'goes up the spout'. There are always meetings, speeches, obituaries, obloquies.

The initial decisions concerning the winding up of an insolvent company are taken by contributories and creditors. Section 213 of *The Companies Act, 1948,* defines 'contributory' as meaning 'every person liable to contribute to the assets of a company in the event of its being wound up.' Every holder of fully paid-up shares is a contributory 'since every member of the company is primarily liable to contribute, subject to the limit of the amount which he may be called upon to pay'. But only those who still owe money on their shares are liable to make contribution to the assets. So a holder of fully-paid shares will only be placed on the list of contributories at his own wish.

As for creditors, they may, of course, be members or non-members, friends or foes. You borrow your money where you find it.

In the case of a creditors' voluntary winding up, Section 293 of the 1948 Act provides that 'the company shall cause a meeting of the creditors of the company to be summoned for the day, or the day next following the day, on which there is to be held a meeting at which the resolution for voluntary winding-up is to be proposed, and shall cause the notices of the said meeting of creditors to be sent by post to the creditors simultaneously with the sending of the notices of the said meeting of the company.'

The company must cause notice of the creditors' meeting to be advertised once in the *London Gazette* and once in at least two local newspapers circulating in the district where the registered office or principal place of the business is situated. Creditors must know of their gathering.

The directors of the company must then 'cause a full statement of the position of the company's affairs together with a list of the creditors of the company and the estimated amount of their claims to be laid before the meeting of the creditors . . . and appoint one of their number to preside at the said meeting.' The director appointed to preside at the creditors' meeting must attend and preside in accordance with his appointment.

Failure to call a creditors' meeting or failure by a director to do his duty in accordance therewith may lead to a fine of up to £100 on the company and/or each of the directors in default.

The creditors and the company at their respective meetings may nominate a liquidator 'for the purpose of winding up the affairs and distributing the assets of the company'. If they nominate different people, the creditors' wish predominates. If no one is nominated by the creditors, then any person nominated by the company is liquidator. In the case of different people being nominated, any director, member or creditor of the company may, within seven days after the date on which the nomination was made by the creditors, apply to the court for an order either directing that the person nominated as liquidator by the company shall be liquidator instead of or jointly with the person nominated by the creditors, or appointing some other person to be liquidator instead of the person nominated by the creditors (Section 294).

The creditors, at their meeting, may (if they think fit) appoint 'a committee of inspection consisting of not more than five persons. If such a committee is appointed, the company may, either at the meeting at which the resolution for voluntary winding-up is passed or at any time subsequently in general meeting, appoint such number of persons as they see fit to act as members of the committee, not exceeding five in number.' But the creditors may resolve that any or all of the people appointed by the company ought not to be members of the committee of inspection— in which case, such people shall only be qualified to act as members of the committee if the Court so directs. Application may be made to the Court to appoint other persons to act as such members in place of the people mentioned in the resolution.

If the winding-up of a company continues for more than a year, the liquidator must summon a General Meeting of the company and a meeting of the creditors at the end of the first year from the commencement of the winding-up—and another at the end of each succeeding year, 'or at the first convenient date within three months from the end of the year or such longer period as the Board of Trade may allow'. He must lay before the meetings an account of his acts and dealings 'and of the conduct of the winding-up during the preceding year'. Failure to do so may result in his being fined up to £10. (Section 299.)

'As soon as the affairs of the company are fully wound up, the liquidator shall make up an account of the winding-up, showing how the winding-up has been conducted, and the profit in the company has been disposed of, and thereupon shall call a General Meeting of the company and a meeting of the creditors for the purpose of laying the account before the meetings and giving any explanation thereof. Each such meeting shall be called by advertisement in the *Gazette* specifying the time, place and object thereof and published a month at least before the meeting.'

Within one week after the date of the meetings (or, if the meetings are not held on the same day, after the date of the later meeting) the liquidator must send to the Registrar of Companies a copy of the account, and must make a return to him of the holding of the meetings and of their dates. Once again, he may be fined for default. If a quorum is not present at either of these meetings, the liquidator must make a return that the meeting was duly summoned, that no quorum was present and that he shall be deemed to have complied with the rules. (Section 300.)

64 *Members' voluntary winding-up*

Where the members wish to wind up the company, a General Meeting must appoint one or more liquidators 'for the purpose of winding up the affairs and distributing the assets of the company'. The meeting may fix the remuneration to be paid to the liquidator or liquidators. Once a liquidator is appointed, 'all the powers of the directors shall cease, except so far as the company in General Meeting or the liquidator sanctions the continuance thereof.' The Board hands over its powers to the liquidator.

A liquidator may be appointed at the same General Meeting

at which the winding-up resolution is passed. No special notice need be given that a resolution will be proposed for the appointment of a liquidator. But, in practice, the notice usually does state the name of the person who will be proposed as liquidator. But if the resolution in question is not passed, then someone may be appointed in his place, without any further notice. (Section 285.)

Note that the liquidator's remuneration should be fixed by the General Meeting. If it is not, then the Court may fix it.

If the liquidator appointed dies or resigns, the company may hold another meeting and 'subject to an arrangement with the creditors', fill the vacancy. Any contributory may convene such a meeting.

The essence of a voluntary winding-up lies in the directors (or a majority of them) making a statutory declaration at a Board meeting 'to the effect that they have made a full inquiry into the affairs of the company and that, having so done, they have formed the opinion that the company will be able to pay its debts in full within such period not exceeding 12 months from the commencement of the winding-up as may be specified in the declaration.' (Section 283.)

But the liquidator may take a different view. If he considers that the company will not be able to pay its debts in full within the period stated in the declaration under Section 283, he 'shall forthwith summon a meeting of the creditors, and shall lay before the meeting a statement of the assets and liabilities of the company.'

If the winding-up continues for more than one year, then the liquidator must summon a General Meeting of the company at the end of the first year from the commencement of the winding-up, and of each succeeding year—or, once again, at the first convenient date within three months from the end of the year concerned.

As soon as the affairs of the company are fully wound up, the liquidator must make an account of the winding-up, showing how it has been conducted and how the property of the company has been disposed of. He 'shall thereupon call a General Meeting of the company for the purpose of laying before it the account, and giving any explanation thereof'. The meeting is called by advertisement in the *Gazette*, specifying the place, time and object thereof and published at least one month before the meeting. Within a week after the meeting, the liquidator must send to the Registrar of Companies a copy of the account, and must make a return to him of the holding of the meeting and of its date. If a quorum does not turn up, the liquidator must make a return that the meeting was duly summoned, that no quorum was present, and he shall be deemed to have complied with his duties. (Section 290.)

65 *Provisions applicable to every voluntary winding-up*

In the case of a members' voluntary winding-up, the liquidator may, with the sanction of an Extraordinary Resolution of the company—and in the case of a creditors' voluntary winding-up, with the sanction of the Court or the committee of inspection or (if there is no such committee) a meeting of the creditors—exercise most of the powers given to a liquidator in a winding-up by the Court. And he may in any event summon General Meetings of the company for the purpose of obtaining the sanction of the company 'by special or extraordinary resolution', or 'for any other purpose he may think fit'. (Section 303.)

66 Arrangements with creditors

Naturally, where a company is able to make some sensible arrangements or compromise with its creditors, it should do so. But the power to compromise is hedged about with precautions.

'Where a compromise or arrangement is proposed between a company and its creditors or any class of them, or between the company and its members or any class of them,' says Section 206, 'the Court may, on the application in the summary way of the company or of any creditor or member of the company, or, in the case of a company being wound up, of the liquidator, order a meeting of the creditors or class of creditors, or of the members of the company or class of members, as the case may be, to be summoned in such manner as the court directs.'

A creditor includes everyone 'having a pecuniary claim against a company, whether actual or contingent'. And even if some of the creditors are also members, the different classes of those affected must have separate meetings. If application is to be made to the Court under Section 206, it is done by Originating Summons (but you can leave that to your solicitor). Someone will have to swear an affidavit setting out the relevant facts showing the need for the proposed scheme of arrangements and sufficient details to enable the Court to decide who should be appointed chairman, where the meetings ought to be held, how they should be advertised and so on.

At the meeting itself, 'if a majority in number representing three-fourths in value of the creditors or class of creditors or members or class of members, as the case may be, present and voting either by person or by proxy at the meeting, agree to any compromise or arrangement, the compromise or arrangement shall, if sanctioned by the Court, be binding on all the creditors or the class of creditors, or on the members or class of members, as the case may be, and also on the company or, in the case of a company, in the course of being wound up, on the liquidator and contributories of the company.'

So a minority of 25 per cent or fewer may be forced to accept a compromise, even though they may think that the arrangement is unreasonable. But before the Court will approve such a compromise, it will have to be satisfied that 'the class of creditors or members have been fairly represented' by those who attended and that the statutory majority who approved the scheme were acting '*bona fide* in the interest of the class it professed to represent'. But if everyone was acting *bona fide* and a reasonable man of business would approve the arrangement as fair and reasonable, then the Court's sanction should be obtained.

'Where a meeting of creditors or any class of creditors or of members or any class of members is summoned under Section 206,' says Section 207, 'there shall:

'(a) with every notice summoning the meeting which is sent to a creditor or member, be sent also a statement explaining the effect of the compromise or arrangement, in particular stating any material interests of the directors of the company, whether as directors or as members or as creditors of the company or otherwise, and the effect thereof of the compromise or arrangement, in so far as it is different from the effect of like interests of other persons; and

'(b) in every notice summoning the meeting which is given by advertisement, be included such a statement as aforesaid or a notification of the place at which and the manner in which creditors or members entitled to attend the meeting may obtain copies of such a statement as aforesaid.'

You do not simply call together the creditors and members—they must know why they are coming and have the chance to consider in advance whether the arrangement or compromise is one which should meet with their approval.

'Where the compromise or arrangement affects the rights of debenture holders of the company, the said statement shall give the like explanation as respects the trustees of any deed for securing the issue of the debentures as it is required to give as respects the company's directors . . .

'Where a notice given by advertisement includes a notification that copies of a statement explaining the effect of the compromise or arrangement proposed can be obtained by creditors or members entitled to attend the meeting, every such creditor shall, upon making application in the manner indicated in the notice, be furnished by the company free of charge.' (Section 207.)

67 Committees of inspection

When a winding-up order has been made by the Court, 'it shall be the business of the separate meetings of the creditors and contributories summoned for the purpose of determining whether or not an application should be made to the Court for appointing a liquidator in place of the official receiver, to determine further whether or not an application is to be made to the Court for the appointment of a committee of inspection to act with the liquidator and who are to be members of the committee if appointed.' (Section 252).

If a committee of inspection is appointed, it 'shall consist of creditors and contributories of the company or persons holding general powers of attorney from creditors or contributories in such proportions as may be agreed on by the meetings of creditors and contributories or as, in the case of difference, may be determined by the Court.'

The committee of inspection 'shall meet at such times as they from time to time appoint, and, failing such appointment, at least once a month.' The liquidator or any member of the committee may also call a meeting of the committee 'as and when he thinks necessary.'

The meeting may act 'by a majority of their members present at the meeting which shall not act unless a majority of their members are present.' A member may resign 'by notice in writing signed by him and delivered to the liquidator'. A member may be removed 'by an ordinary resolution at a meeting of creditors, if he represents creditors, or of contributories, if he represents contributories, of which seven days' notice has been given, stating the object of the meeting'.

If a vacancy occurs in the committee, the liquidator must at once summon a meeting of creditors or contributories, as the case may be, to fill the vacancy. The meeting may, by resolution, 'reappoint the same or appoint another creditor or contributory to fill the vacancy'.

68 *The Court—and the meeting*

'The Court may, as to all matters relating to the winding up of a company, have regard to the wishes of the creditors or contributories of the company, as proved to it by any sufficient evidence, and may, if it thinks fit, for the purpose of ascertaining those wishes, direct meetings of the creditors or contributories to be called, held and conducted in such manner as the Court directs, and may appoint a person to act as chairman of any such meeting and report the result thereof to the Court ...

'In the case of creditors, regard should be had to the value of each creditor's debt ...

'In the case of contributories, regard shall be had to the

number of votes concerned on each contributory by this Act or the Articles ...' (Section 346).

So if no one else wants to call a meeting, the Court is entitled to do so.

69 *The liquidator—and meetings*

In a winding-up by the Court, the liquidator has very considerable powers. These include the making of compromises or arrangements with creditors, the bringing or defending of actions, the carrying on of the business of the company 'so far as may be necessary for the beneficial winding up thereof' ... and so on. But Section 246 lays down some controls over those powers. In general, 'in the administration of the assets of the company and in the distribution thereof among its creditors,' he must 'have regard to any directions that may be given by resolution of the creditors or contributories at any General Meeting or by the committee of inspection, that any directions given by the creditors or contributories at any General Meeting shall, in the case of conflict, be deemed to override any directions given by the committee of inspection.'

The liquidator 'may summon General Meetings of the creditors or contributories for the purpose of ascertaining their wishes'. But it 'shall be his duty' to do so 'at such times as the creditors or contributories, by resolution, either at the meeting appointing the liquidator or otherwise, may direct—or whenever requested in writing to do so by one-tenth in value of the creditors or contributories as the case may be.'

The liquidator may also apply to the Court for directions in relation to any particular matter arising out of the winding-up.

And so may any person 'aggrieved by any act or decision of the liquidator'.

70 Bankruptcies

Similar rules apply to the individual bankrupt as to the insolvent company. The trustee in bankruptcy, for instance, 'may from time to time summon General Meetings of the creditors for the purpose of ascertaining their wishes, and it shall be his duty to summon meetings at such times as the creditors, by resolution, either at the meeting appointing the trustee or otherwise may direct, and it shall be lawful for any creditor, with the concurrence of one-sixth in value of the creditors (including himself), at any time to request the trustee or Official Receiver to call a meeting of the creditors, and the trustee or Official Receiver shall call such a meeting accordingly within 14 days:

'Provided that the person at whose instance the meeting is summoned shall deposit with the trustee or Official Receiver, as the case may be, a sum sufficient to pay the costs of summoning the meeting, such sum to be repaid to him out of the estate of the creditors or the Court so direct.' (Section 79 of the Bankruptcy Act, 1914.)

Section 13 of the Act says: 'As soon as may be after the making of the Receiving Order against a debtor, a General Meeting of his creditors . . . (the first meeting of creditors) . . . shall be held for the purpose of considering whether a proposal for a composition or scheme of arrangement shall be accepted, or whether it is expedient that the debtor shall be adjudged bankrupt, and generally as to the mode of dealing with the debtor's property.'

Details as to the summoning of and proceedings at the first

and other meetings of creditors are laid down in the First Schedule of the Act (the Schedule is reproduced as Appendix 5).

A minute of proceedings at a creditors' meeting 'signed at the same or next ensuing meeting by a person describing himself as, or appearing to be, chairman of the meeting in which the minute is signed, shall be received in evidence without further proof'. In other words, a minute will be enough to show what happened at the meeting. And unless the contrary is proved, every meeting of creditors in respect of which there is a duly signed minute is deemed to have been 'duly convened and held, and all resolutions passed or proceedings had thereat to be duly passed or had'. So mind your minutes.

PARTNERSHIPS—DISSOLVED

As we have seen (in Chapter 62), the partners in a firm are jointly and severally liable for the partnership debts. If these are unpaid, then any one of the individual partners may be made bankrupt. One result will then be—meetings, as in the case of a bankruptcy.

71 *In conclusion*

In the world of insolvency, meetings play a major part. They seldom bring joy to anyone. But if you have to attend, the suggestions made in this book may at least, help you in the handling of yourself and of others. And let us hope that you will always be a creditor and that all your speeches may bring credit to you—in every sense of that word.

I think we are all agreed...

Part II

The chairman— and chairmanship

72 The company chairman

There are certain duties of a chairman which are prescribed by law.

Section 134 of the 1948 Act provides: 'Any member elected by the members present at a meeting may be chairman thereof.' That is all the Act has to say about the chairman, whose duties are usually set out in the company's Articles. Table A, which most companies adopt, provides (in Article 55) as follows: 'The chairman, if any, of the Board of Directors shall preside as chairman at every general meeting of the company, or if there is no such chairman, or if he shall not be present within 15 minutes after the time appointed for the holding of the meeting or is unwilling to act, the directors present shall elect one of their number to be chairman of the meeting. If at any meeting no director is willing to act as chairman' (Article 56 adds) 'or if no director is present within 15 minutes after the time appointed for holding the meeting, the members present shall choose one of their own number to be chairman of the meeting.'

So the company need not have a chairman at all. If the Board of Directors appoints a chairman, he presides over general meetings of the company, as well as over those of the Board itself.

At a directors' meeting, democracy prevails—'questions arising . . . shall be decided by a majority of votes'. But if the scales are evenly balanced, 'the chairman shall have a second or casting vote'. But note: A chairman is not entitled to a casting vote unless the Articles say so. And as the principle of 'one man, one vote' is intended to rule supreme . . . and as in any event a casting vote must not be used unless there is 'an equality of valid votes'—it is obvious that (the law apart) this chairman's bludgeon should be used as rarely as possible. The chairman, after all, is (in theory at least) an impartial creature.

Once ensconced in the chair, it is the chairman's job to keep order, to conduct the meeting in a proper and regular manner, and (as was decided in an 1894 case) to be careful to see that 'the sense of the meeting is properly ascertained' in connection with any matter under discussion.

Articles may give a chairman the right to order a poll. Such power must be used with discretion. Accusations of prejudice or bias are to be avoided.

Both sides are entitled to be heard—but not indefinitely. When opposing views have been given a fair airing, the chairman is entitled to accept a motion for the closure. A small minority need not be allowed 'to tyrannize over the majority' (said Lord Justice Chitty), by being able to prevent the meeting from coming to a decision.

On the other hand, a chairman must not only allow resolutions to be put and to be argued. If an amendment is moved and seconded but the chairman refuses to put it to the meeting, the unamended resolution, if passed, will be a nullity. He must allow amendments to be put.

'At any meeting at which an extraordinary resolution or a special resolution is submitted to be passed,' says Section 141 of the Companies Act, 'a declaration of the chairman that the resolution is carried, shall, unless a poll is demanded, be con-clusive evidence of the fact without proof of the number or the proportion of the votes recorded in favour of or against the resolution'. So when it comes to special or extraordinary resolu-tions, in the absence of a poll, the chairman's arithmetic is taken as final. And the same rule is usually put into Articles of Association, with regard to ordinary resolutions.

So the chairman has a casting vote in a deadlock—the right to conduct meetings and to declare conclusively the results of votes. Apart from deciding 'incidental questions' which come up during the meeting, that is normally the quota of required power. Unless there is some disorder, he cannot adjourn a meeting at his own behest. And if he purports to do so, the meeting may elect someone to act as chairman in his place, so that the business can go on. On the other hand, he is not bound to adjourn a meeting. 'The chairman may, with the consent of any meeting at which a quorum is present (and shall if so directed by the meeting), adjourn the meeting from time to time and from place to place, but no business shall be transacted at any adjourned meeting other than the business left over from the meeting from which the adjournment took place. When a meeting is adjourned for 30 days or more, notice of the adjourned meeting shall be given as in the case of an original meeting. Save as aforesaid, it shall not be necessary to give any notice of an adjournment or of the business to be transacted at an adjourned meeting.' So says Article 57 of Table A—which, once again, is commonly incorporated in a company's Articles.

As to the actual conduct of the meeting, to some extent this is laid down by the 1948 Act and by the Articles of Association. But otherwise, consider the words of Lord Russell (pronounced in 1937):

'There are many matters relating to the conduct of a meeting which lie entirely in the hands of those people who are present and constitute the meeting . . . It rests with the meeting to decide whether accounts, resolutions, minutes or notices and such like shall be read to the meeting or be taken as read; and when discussion shall be terminated and a vote taken; whether representatives of the Press, or any other persons not qualified to be summoned to the meeting, shall be permitted to be present, or if present, shall be permitted to remain; and whether the meeting shall be adjourned. In all these matters, and they are only instances, the meeting decides, and if necessary a vote must be taken to ascertain the wishes of the majority. If no objection is taken by any constituent of the meeting, the meeting must be taken to be assenting to the course adopted.'

So what does the law lay down about the conduct of a meeting?

First, resolutions (unless the Articles otherwise provide) are decided by a show of hands. One person, one hand. One hand, one vote. But then may come the poll. This is a formal vote.

Those present in person or by proxy (see Chapter 51) will probably be asked to sign a paper headed 'FOR' or 'AGAINST' the
motion. The poll is taken by counting these votes.

According to Article 58, a poll may be demanded in any
general meeting either by the chairman or by at least three
members present in person or by proxy or by any member or
members present in person or by proxy and representing not less
than one-tenth of the total voting rights of all the members
having the right to vote at the meeting. A member or members
holding shares in the company conferring a right to vote at the
meeting on which an aggregate sum has been paid up equal to
not less than one-tenth of the total sums paid on all the shares
conferring that right may also demand a poll. The demand for a
poll may 'be withdrawn'.

If a poll is demanded (and not withdrawn) on the election of a
chairman or on a question of adjournment, Article 61 says that
'it shall be taken forthwith'. Where a poll is demanded on any
other question, it shall be taken 'at such time as the chairman of
the meeting directs, and any business other than that upon
which a poll has been demanded may be proceeded with pending the taking of the poll'. Note: 'On a poll, votes may be given
either personally or by proxy' (Article 67).

What of the man who comes to break up your meeting? The
chairman has the right to order his immediate removal. Alternatively, he may adjourn the meeting for long enough to remove
'the disorderly element'.

Naturally, the chairman will generally have the company
secretary at his side—and he, one hopes, is a wise and experienced man who can advise on points of order and procedure.
Like the Clerk to the Justices, if he knows his job, he is in-
dispensable. Meanwhile, the above are the rules from the 1948
Act and Table A of the rules that the chairman needs to know.
If the situation gets out of hand so that the chairman needs
more detailed information, he should first consult the Articles
of the company—and then a solicitor.

73 The chairman as compère

The chairman of a meeting—any meeting—sets the tone. If he is a dull dog, the meeting will be a bore. If he is in gay mood, the meeting will be of good cheer. If he is long-winded, any members of his audience not bound to stay will disappear. If he is angry, aggravated, tactless or unkind, this will soon be reflected in the atmosphere. Not for one moment dare he be off his guard. He is the compère . . . the life and soul of the gathering—or its death and decay.

Consider the ordinary variety programme. The compère is the link man. He holds the show together. If he fails, then it falls apart. The same applies to the chairman.

To keep a meeting in good humour, here are some suggestions:

Do not allow yourself to get aggravated. The more difficult the gathering, the more important it is for you to keep your self-control and your pleasant manner.

Set the tone before the meeting begins. Try to do your colleagues or your audience the compliment of arriving on time. Spare a few minutes beforehand, if you can, to iron out difficulties and to prevent personal affronts (see Chapter 43).

If the meeting is a small one, try not to ignore people who come in late. 'Good evening. It's nice to see you.' Worthwhile words to make a guilty latecomer feel at ease—and obliged to you.

There is no need to take too literally the old, chairman's warning: 'Stand up, speak up and shut up'. But do try to let others do as much of the talking as you can. Time them beforehand, if possible. Introduce them . . . invite them to have their say . . . ask what they think. Link the speakers together and provide the channel through which they speak. But yourself—talk only when you must.

Let your audience feel that they have had their say. In the case of a large meeting, do your best to allow as adequate a question time as possible. Cajole your speakers into brevity and into agreeing to answer questions at the end. The audience that has its questions answered is almost always satisfied. Question Time in the House of Commons is easily the most interesting period of the day. And so it is with most meetings. But where the session is a small one—a committee or Board meeting, for instance—the same principle is even more vital. Let the others put their views before the gathering. Try not to choke off discussion before it comes to an end. Wait until you get the feeling of the meeting that time has come for the particular debate or argument to be wound up.

Let everyone feel that his presence is appreciated. One way is by saying so: 'We are delighted to have you all with us.' When the meeting is small enough, make sure that everyone has said something. 'What are your views about this?' The quiet man may have more valuable advice to give than the garrulous soul who monopolizes the discussion. The timid participant may be more expert than the exhibitionist. If talent is available, make sure it gets used.

Do not be afraid to season the proceedings with laughter. A few moments spent on a friendly joke may be more worth while than ten times as long devoted to argument. (But try to avoid the unkind cut—see Chapter 5). Round the meeting off with appropriate words of thanks—and set the atmosphere right for the next time.

*   *   *

Most of these suggestions could be brought under one word: tact. You are running the meeting. But (except in case of disorder) you should try not to let it be too obvious. The horse knows when it is mounted by a skilled rider. He does not have to keep tugging at the reins or hurting the animal's mouth. The best leaders give their followers the maximum feeling that they (the followers) are running their own show. The top compères keep the programme going and ensure that everyone stays contented and awake. The finest chairmen are those who rule through good humour, quiet tact and gentle persuasion.

74 Chairing a safety committee

From 1 October 1978 employers will not only have to recognize and consult with safety representatives appointed by recognized, independent trade unions. If two or more such representatives require the setting up of a safety committee, the employers will be bound to comply.

Naturally, a safety committee (like any other) will need a chairman. He may be a manager—the managing director, perhaps, or the personnel chief or the company doctor. Or one of the safety representatives may himself be a capable chairman—perhaps with experience drawn from work for the local authority. The law prescribes neither the identity of the chairman of a safety committee nor how he should do his job. But the success of the committee's work will depend on how he carries out his function. So here are some hints to help him (or you) to do this vital job.

*　　*　　*

1 Do your homework. This means:

- a Read and understand the new Regulations, Code and Guidance Notes. They are all neatly set out in a small pamphlet available from the Health and Safety Commission (Baynards House, 1 Chepstow Place, London, W2 4DF. Telephone: 01-229 3456).
- b Read the Minutes of previous meetings, so that you know what has been discussed and decided in the past—otherwise you are bound to forget to check on implementation of decisions and/or to waste time re-covering old territory.
- c Study the safety set-up, organization and problems within the unit concerned—if necessary, taking guidance from representatives or other committee members—so that you can guide the discussion in an informed and helpful way.

2   Prepare your agenda in advance. As in the case of all other meetings, you must know what is to be discussed. A typical agenda might read:

    a   Apologies for non-attendance.
    b   Minutes of last meeting.
    c   Matters arising from Minutes, not included elsewhere.
    d   Correspondence.
    e   Reports of safety representatives on incidents—including accidents or hazards occurring on inspections carried out since last meeting.
    f   Report of safety officer.
    g   Report of medical officer/nurse.
    h   Recommendations for action.
    i   Any other business.

3   Ensure that someone on the committee is capable of taking careful Minutes; that he in fact does so; and that the Minutes are circularized to all members before the meeting—so that at the start you can say: 'Minutes have been circularized. May I sign these as a correct record of what occurred at the last meeting?' If there are any alleged inaccuracies, these should be sorted out. Remember: The Minutes are neither more nor less than a record. They set out what happened—not what you or anyone else would have preferred to have happened.

4   Prepare the rest of the meeting in advance, insofar as you reasonably can. Help the safety representatives to have their reports ready and encourage them to discuss with you beforehand any queries on presentation. You may also find items which it would be better for the safety representative (at least initially) to deal with behind the scenes rather than in public. The job of the chairman is to get results and to encourage discussion—not disputes. Conversely: the more harmony he can achieve, the better.

5   Take special care to bring into the full discussion those whose

views may be valuable but who may be reticent or inarticulate. Particularly when dealing with people who have practical safety experience or interest but who are not used to committee work, it is the chairman who can make them feel valuable—and so encouraged in their efforts.

6 Guide the discussion so that it stays within the intended limits —of health, safety and welfare. Do not allow the meeting to turn into a battleground, with discussion or argument ranging over other areas. If a safety committee trespasses into the arena of (for instance) collective bargaining, union and management are likely to move back to their own sides of the table—whereas in a safety committee they should be brought and kept together.

7 The safety committee chairman's job is to focus attention all the time on the united purpose of management and unions—to preserve life and limb. There should not be two sides. If you are successful in bringing and keeping people happily together for this purpose, then you may indeed improve the atmosphere for all other purposes. But if management and unions cannot combine successfully for safety purposes, what hope can there be for industrial peace?

8 If disputes arise over the composition of the committee, check back to the Commission's Guidance Notes. Remember that management should certainly not constitute more than 50 per cent of the membership—and there is no reason why it should not be less. Yours is a practical committee with one, sole, crucial job—to reduce the risks of accidents. Keep your mind concentrated on that task—and ensure that the discussion does not drift away from it.

9 As in the case of all chairmen, keep cool; retain your good humour; and use tact, courtesy—and flattery—rather than sarcasm or the stick. A firm appraisal (especially when dealing with deviations from the health and safety area) should be fully acceptable.

10   Always try to achieve a consensus of opinion. But do not be afraid to call for a vote. Votes are rare on boards of directors but frequent at trade union meetings. Directors who chair safety committees are often too chary of calling for a vote where clarification of views becomes necessary. You will sometimes find that the vote brings results which are quite different from those that you would have expected from the discussion.

11   Always fix the date of the next meeting—and make sure it is one that is suitable for yourself. The Commission stresses that meetings should only be cancelled or postponed in the most rare emergencies. If you expect others to give priority to your committee and to its decisions and deliberations, you must do so yourself. A chairman's job is to lead. Chairmen of safety committees are leading the way into a safer industrial world.

75 Controlling the audience

Whether you are dealing with a committee of three or a crowd of three thousand, as chairman you must be in control. Except in the rare cases of people who have deliberately arrived with the intention of breaking up the proceedings, your audience have given up their time for a purpose. It may be the wish to advance the company's business and hence their own prospects. They may be seeking knowledge or entertainment. They may wish to extend the work of the trade charity. Whatever the reason, they wish the business to be done. And then they will want to get back to their offices or, at the end of the day and with even more fervour, to their homes. A chairman who controls his audience and hence the business of the meeting is appreciated.

So do not be afraid to put your foot down (metaphorically) or (literally) to tap with the gavel. You were elected or appointed chairman to keep order and if you do so, you will have the meeting behind you. This does not mean that you should shout. A firm: 'Order please, gentlemen'; 'Will you please give Mr Black a fair hearing'; or 'I must insist on quiet for our speaker, please' —these are the courteous and successful gambits. Occasionally you may need: 'I'm afraid that if those who are attempting to break up the meeting will not desist, I shall have to ask the stewards to have them evicted' (see Chapter 76). But much more common is the 'Thank you, gentlemen', addressed to those of your colleagues whom you hope to thank for their future silence.

Of course, it is essential for you to know precisely what you are doing. You must understand the basic rules of procedure (see, in particular, Chapter 77 on resolutions and amendments). But if you do make a mistake, then you have two alternatives, and one or other must be grasped as firmly as possible. Either you stand by your mistake or you smile and apologize.

In general, even when a chairman is wrong, the law will if necessary uphold his decisions. In one case, for instance, it was decided that a chairman who had incorrectly counted the votes on a show of hands could not be overruled because, in the absence of fraud or bad faith, the Court would not interfere with his decisions. So if you have chosen the wrong procedure or decided to rule that an intervention is out of order or have declined to allow a resolution to be put to the meeting, and you regret that decision, it may still be best to stand by it.

Alternative: 'It is clear that the meeting would, in fact, like to discuss this matter. So be it.' Or: 'You are quite right, Mr Jones. I should have allowed the discussion to go further. Please do carry on.' A graceful retreat. As the French put it: *'Se reculer pour mieux sauter'*—you recoil so as the better to jump forward. You are being decisive even about your indecision.

Still, it is 'the sense of the meeting' that usually matters. The chairman needs antennae. He must be able to judge what people want. He must employ his tact so as not to override the wishes of those who have seen fit to put him in charge of their proceedings. Whilst not pandering to the inevitable mischief-maker, abrasive irritant and aggravating nuisance whom nearly every organization or body or community seems to throw up, he must nevertheless give even such persons (who may be right on occasion and have a certain acid usefulness) the opportunity to let off steam. When the meeting has had enough of them, you will know. And so will the aggravators. Sense your meeting—and run it. That is your job as chairman.

76 Order—and disorder

To some extent, a speaker can and must control his own audience. He must command attention. He must know how to deal with his own hecklers (see Chapter 26). And, if necessary, he must be prepared to tongue-lash those who will not pay heed to his words. But if the speaker fails, the chairman must step in. Indeed, it is part of the chairman's task to ensure that the speaker gets a hearing (literally as well as metaphorically).

In most cases, a smart rap with the gavel and a command of 'Order' should suffice. (If you have no gavel, a smart rap on the table with a coin, pen-knife or lighter, will probably do the trick. It is also both more effective and more dignified than a pounding of the fist which may, in any event, prove painful.) But if disorder does break out, the chairman must know precisely how to handle it.

The main rule, of course, is to handle himself with restraint, calm and dignity. He must never lose his head, or he will have failed. With luck, he will have the secretary sitting beside him, to guide him on procedure. But to know the rules in advance breeds the confidence he needs. (And the secretary should know them, too). So here they are.

77 Debates and procedure

The chairman must know the rules of debate. His duty is to enforce them. Speakers must know the rules either to follow them or to attempt to evade them.

* * *

The chairman is in charge. He has been elected or appointed to his position and is expected to guide and control the meeting. He is in charge of proceedings.

When the chairman stands, everyone else is expected to sit and to be silent. If the chairman cannot obtain order by rapping his gavel and demanding silence, he may have to adjourn the meeting. Unless the meeting is closed, the chairman is entitled to speak whenever he wishes—and to prevent anyone else from doing so unless he wishes. He decides the order of speeches. He will have the agenda but may vary it (see Chapter 72). He is in charge.

But, of course, he should rule by consent. For instance, if he decides to change the order of business, he should explain his reasons. If the bulk of the meeting objects to the change, then he should normally revert to the original order. He is not a dictator.

Normally, each item of business should be discussed separately. If there are steps to be taken—or even if it is to be resolved that there be no action on the matter—a resolution or motion will be 'put'. This can be done quite informally, where there is either no opposition or a general consensus. But if after discussion has taken place there is no agreement, there should be a vote (see Chapter 72).

Where the formalities are being preserved, a motion will be proposed and seconded. It will then be thrown open to the meeting for discussion—and the chairman will attempt to call upon someone who will oppose the motion. After the matter has been sufficiently ventilated, the proposer will normally exercise his right of reply (see Chapter 24). Then a vote may have to be taken.

If the motion or resolution is not on the agenda, the proposer should be asked to phrase it as concisely and clearly as possible. The chairman who has to put a resolution which even the proposer has not put into sensible English (and into words which can be put into the minute book) is in a bad way. The motion should be clearly stated either by the proposer or by the chairman before it goes forward for debate.

The length and number of speeches will depend upon the chairman. But anyone may 'move the closure'. Or it may be resolved that 'the question be now put'. A show of hands will indicate whether those present have had enough of the subject or whether they wish to debate the matter further. If a chairman is in doubt as to whether or not the debate should be closed— or if he feels that it would appear partisan for him to terminate it—then he can easily test the feeling of the meeting, if necessary by asking whether anyone wishes 'to move the closure'.

If it is agreed that the question 'be now put'—then that is what happens. The motion is voted upon. If a motion is carried that the meeting move on to 'next business', then no vote is taken on the motion. It is often better not to reveal the split in the ranks. Or all sides may prefer to avoid a vote which no one is really confident of winning.

Some organizations allow the moving of 'the previous question'. The effect of this being passed is that the discussion on the current topic terminates and all reference to it is expunged from the minutes. No vote is, of course, taken on the matter in question. There are times when people feel that it would have been better for the organization or meeting had the discussion not taken place at all. 'The previous question' is a useful procedure.

Again, someone may move that the entire meeting be adjourned. It is not only the chairman who can terminate the proceedings. If those present at the meeting wish to put an end to it, they may normally do so. But, of course, there may be a lengthy debate 'on the adjournment'.

Whilst the debate goes on, there may be interruptions (see

Chapter 26). One common device is a 'point of order'. Anyone is entitled to raise any point he wishes concerning the order of the meeting, at any time. In theory, he is only free to query as to whether the procedure in hand . . . what the speaker is saying . . . the chairman's ruling . . . is 'in order'. He should not stray away to deal with side issues or to use the occasion to deal with the substantive issues. But skilled interrupters can often disguise their disruptive attacks in the form of 'points of order', and so insinuate extra speeches where none would otherwise be allowed.

In some meetings, the custom is for speakers to give way on 'points of information'—but generally, it is a matter for them (the speakers themselves) to decide. The chairman cannot force them to give way, or take any step if they decline to do so. But if the chairman himself addresses the speaker, the latter may remain standing but (like anyone else at the meeting) must accord the chairman the right to speak—and whilst he does so, must remain silent.

The speaker, then, must 'obey the chairman's ruling'. The fact that he 'has the floor' does not mean that he is entitled to occupy it in the teeth of objection from the chair.

If all motions were proposed, seconded, opposed and voted upon as they stood, a chairman's life would be moderately easy. But there are always amendments to be considered. In general, motions to amend a resolution must (if seconded) be allowed. They should be considered individually and voted upon if necessary. If accepted (whether or not after a vote) they become incorporated into the original motion, which must then be put, as amended. If rejected, they die. An amended motion, once put, can then be the subject of further amendment, with the procedure as before.

Often a skilled chairman can manage to induce the mover of a resolution to vary or extend its terms so as to incorporate the amendment. A peaceful meeting is a chairman's delight. But equally, if an amendment is really no more than an attempt to kill the resolution, he may rule it out of order and require the proposer of the amendment to put forward his views in opposition to the substantive motion. The chairman's job is to ensure that everyone is given a reasonable opportunity to express his views. But he is not bound to allow a minority to dominate. He is entitled not only to select the speakers (in the fairest possible way), but also to sort out the resolutions and the amendments, so that the feelings of the meeting may be tested in the fairest way.

Note, then, that once the meeting has a reasonable opportunity to express its view, the chairman himself may—with the consent of the meeting—close the debate and put the motion to the vote.

Some additional points:

Unless a company's Articles (or the constitution of the organization in question) require motions to be seconded and/or submitted in writing, neither will be strictly necessary.

No one has any right to speak more than once on any motion or amendment—although the proposer of an original motion (but not usually of an amendment) will generally be given the right to reply.

Once a motion has been defeated, it should not be allowed back into the meeting under some other guise.

No amendment can be proposed after the original motion has been passed or rejected.

Amendments cannot be proposed or seconded by those who performed that service for the original motion; but they can, of course, accept (or speak on) the amendments proposed by others.

If you wish to frame an amendment, the best way is usually to do so by moving that the words you have in mind be added to or omitted from or inserted into (as the case may be) the motion or resolution.

*   *   *

Meetings are usually governed by consent and common sense. The chairman must keep his head and never panic. Speakers should help the chair in every case except that in which the chairman has shown himself to be unwilling to act impartially. In that case, the battle is on.

78 Trespass—and who may be present

The occupier of premises has the sole right to decide who may —and hence, who may not—be upon them. Anyone who enters or remains upon premises without the occupier's consent (express or implied)—or, of course, against the occupier's wishes—is a trespasser. And proper steps may be taken to eject him.

The organizers of a meeting occupy the meeting-place. It may be your company, welcoming its members to a general meeting. It may be a trade organization, using a room in a local hotel. Or perhaps it is a political or charitable organization, which has hired a hall. Wherever the gathering, the organizers are (for the time being at least) the occupiers. They are entitled to decide who may or may not be present.

Now, if the meeting is advertised as open to the public, anyone is entitled to turn up and to take part. If special invitations are sent out (as to a company meeting) then the recipients are expressly invited. If people simply wander in to a gathering (perhaps one organized by a charity) they may well have an implied invitation to attend. They will be present as lawful members of the assembly.

But the fact that someone arrives lawfully does not mean that he is entitled to remain for ever. You are free to ask anyone to leave the premises over which you have control. He is then bound to go. If he fails to do so, he becomes a trespasser—just as effectively as if his initial arrival had been unlawful. You may start your visit as a welcome guest. The moment you become unwelcome and are asked to leave, the law requires you to comply. If you do not, you are a trespasser.

Take the ordinary case of the shopkeeper. He may specifically invite a particular customer to come to buy from him. That customer is no trespasser when he arrives. Nor is the potential buyer who comes in off the street. But then there is a dispute. The customer is asked to leave. He must do so.

Or a representative comes to your office. He probably had an implied invitation to display his wares. If you ask him to go and he stages a sit-down demonstration, he is a trespasser. He has no more right to be there than the man who gate-crashes a private meeting, breaks into a factory or home or trespasses upon someone else's land.

Trespassers cannot normally be prosecuted. Only military establishments, certain Government departments and others with special statutory powers can bring criminal proceedings against those who set unlawful foot on their property. But—the Englishman's home being, in theory at least, his castle—anyone can sue a trespasser for damages. And the Court may award him an injunction—that is, an Order, forbidding any repetition of the wrongful behaviour. So you and your colleagues may have to consider taking that sort of action against the people who attempt to break up your meeting.

But there is one much more important, practical, immediate and valuable remedy given by the law to those who trespass against you. You may eject the unwanted guest. If necessary, you may employ 'reasonable force' to do so.

How much force is 'reasonable'? That depends on all the circumstances. You should employ no force at all until you have asked the trespasser to leave and he has refused. Then a polite frog-march will normally suffice. Anything more desperate (which goes beyond that which is reasonably necessary to get rid of the individual) would be frowned upon. A refusal to leave is not a licence to inflict actual or grievous bodily harm on the offender.

In the unlikely event of your being threatened with some weapon, you are entitled to defend yourself. The man who offers force whilst engaged in trespassing is likely to have little luck if he complains that too much force was used against him. But generally speaking, your stewards—or some of the younger and more powerful members of your audience—should have no difficulty in hustling the intruder out of the room or hall. Actions in

law taken by ousted trespassers, alleging that unreasonable force
was used against them, are almost unknown.

The chairman, then, should not descend into the arena of
physical force. He should direct that the stewards or others do
the ejecting. But he should not hesitate. He must be firm—make
his decision and stick to it.

Of course, the decision may be wrong. It may prove to be a
tactical error. But dither and all is lost. You are far more likely
to make the wrong decision effective if you move with determination and due speed than to achieve the correct results by acting
with perfect moderation, when your indecision becomes apparent
to the meeting. Act—and act swiftly.

Suppose, though, that in fact the alleged trespasser had every
right to be present and that you, as chairman, make a mistake
in having him ejected. Suppose, for instance, that you take
umbrage at something said by a member of staff at an employees'
meeting and you require him to leave the premises. You may
have been quite wrong. He may have been wrongfully dismissed
and entitled to claim damages against the company. But that still
gave him no right whatsoever to remain, contrary to your wishes.
You were entitled to eject him. His remedy lay elsewhere.

In a small meeting, there should be no difficulty in getting
trespassers to leave. Indicate the nearest convenient route and
they act unlawfully if they do not make use of it. If the meeting
is a larger one, then stewards should have been appointed beforehand. They are under the authority of the chairman. He may
require them to take any necessary measures to deal with disorder. They act on his instructions. If he tells them to eject a
trespasser, they may do so.

Incidentally, even the stewards have no right to require trespassers to identify themselves. By all means let names and
addresses be asked for. But if they are refused, no offence is
committed. The chairman appoints the stewards and they have
considerable powers. But they are not the police.

The police should be called in as the ultimate resort. If the
police have reasonable grounds for believing that there is likely
to be a breach of the peace or that such a breach is 'imminent',

they may enter the meeting even without your consent. If you genuinely believe that a breach of the peace may result, you may call them in and they are bound to come to your assistance. And it is statute—as well as 'common law' rules, built up through centuries of usage—which lends weight to the arm of the law, where there is likely to be disorder at a public meeting.

79 *Public order*

'Any person who in any public place or in any public meeting uses threatening, abusive or insulting words or behaviour with intent to provoke a breach of the peace or whereby a breach of the peace is likely to be occasioned, shall be guilty of an offence.' (Section 5 of *The Public Order Act, 1936*). Penalty? Up to three months' imprisonment or a £50 fine or both. And 'a constable may without warrant arrest any person reasonably suspected by him to be committing an offence under Section . . . 5 of this Act.'

*   *   *

So if you are chairing a public meeting, the police have a good deal more power than yourself. Those who break up your proceedings are not only offending against good taste, and good manners and destroying your goodwill, but they may well be committing a criminal offence which is regarded more seriously by the law than many people realize.

Note in particular:

'Threatening, abusive or insulting words or behaviour' is a

very broad phrase. But it does not cover the case of the firm, straightforward, and outspoken dissenter, who causes chaos by using words which stir up trouble but which are not 'threatening, abusive or insulting' in the ordinary meaning of those words;

The trouble-maker may be guilty of the offence either where he intends to create or provoke a breach of the peace or where such is the likely result of his words or behaviour—either will do;

'Public meeting' is defined as including 'any meeting in a public place and any meeting which the public or any section thereof are permitted to attend, whether on payment or otherwise';

'Public place' is defined as meaning 'any highway, public park or garden, any sea beach, and any public bridge, road, footway, lane, court, square, passage or alley, whether a thoroughfare or not; and includes any open space to which, for the time being, the public have or are permitted to have access, whether on payment or otherwise';

It follows that these rules are most likely to apply to you in respect of a meeting in a private place to which the public or any section of it are invited or permitted to attend. Your shareholders are a section of the public.

For amusement, note that it has been held that these rules are 'not designed to create a new offence as between neighbours engaged in abusing each other'. They are, however, directed at those who abuse (amongst others) the chairman.

*   *   *

Any person who in a public place or at any public meeting uses threatening, abusive or insulting words or behaviour or distributes or displays any writing, sign or visible representation which is threatening, insulting or abusive, with intent to provoke a breach of the peace or whereby a breach of the peace is likely to be occasioned, is guilty of an offence. (Section 5 of *The Public Order Act, 1936*—as amended by *The Public Order Act, 1963*, and *The Race Relations Act, 1965*).

Any person who at a lawful public meeting acts in a disorderly manner for the purpose of preventing the transaction of the business for which the meeting was called together shall be guilty of an offence. And so is any person who incites another to commit the offence (*The Public Meeting Act, 1908*).

If any constable reasonably suspects any person of attempting to break up a public meeting, he may—at the request of the chairman of that meeting—require the interrupter immediately to give his name and address. If he refuses or fails to do so or gives a false name and address, then he commits an offence. If the constable reasonably suspects him of giving false particulars —or if he refuses to give any particulars at all—he may be arrested without a warrant. (Section 6 of *The Public Order Act, 1936*).

*   *   *

Finally, remember a few more rules on police powers:

They are not entitled to enter private premises without either the invitation of the occupiers or a warrant.

They are not bound to eject trespassers from private premises (but see Chapter 78). However, if there is an actual breach of the peace, they are bound to take action.

When the police have reasonable grounds for believing that a breach of the peace is likely to be committed, they may enter a meeting held on private premises, even without a warrant. But in practice, the odds against this happening are considerable.

When you need the help of the police, ask for it—and do not wait until things get desperate. As we have seen, they have enough power, if they need it. But the mere knowledge of their presence usually obviates the need.

80 Introducing the guest

However well you know the person you are about to introduce, have his name written down in front of you. The chances of your mind going blank are remote. But it happens. The most famous occasion? During the 1966 Election when a local Conservative party chairman was introducing Mr Edward Heath. 'In the short time since our guest of honour has become leader of the party,' he thundered, 'his name has become a household word. I am proud, honoured and delighted to introduce to you our future Prime Minister, Mr ... er ... er ... er ...' Calamity.

Or: 'The name of our guest is a household word in the trade. Ladies and gentlemen, Mr ... er ... er ... er ...'

'Our guest needs no introduction ... without further ado, I am pleased to introduce to you Sir Robert ... er ... er ... er ...'

This sort of gaffe can never be undone. And it is possible even when you have done your homework. But it is far more likely without preparation. This business of 'the speaker needs no introduction' generally implies that the chairman has not bothered to find out anything about the speaker. Let your secretary dip into *Who's Who ... The Wine Producers' Year Book ... The International Dictionary of Great Millionaires ...* or whatever the appropriate reference work happens to be. Alternatively, get someone to phone up the man's assistant or secretary or manager and get some details of his doings. Even better, hunt around for a personal and friendly anecdote. The less it appears that you had to do research, the better—but the more research you do, the more effective your introduction is likely to be.

If the speaker arrives and you have no information about him, do not despair. Speakers appreciate being asked. Take the man on one side and say to him quietly, with your pencil in one hand: 'I am to have the pleasure of introducing you to our audience. Which of your many offices would you like me to mention? How would you like to be introduced?'

Every speaker has his foibles. He may not want you to say that he is an ex-president of the Undertakers' Society—he may have been defeated in a recent and bitter election contest. He may prefer to forget that he was the author of a book which resulted in a libel action. On the other hand, he may especially want you to remind his audience that he is an ex-president of the Oxford Union . . . formerly secretary to Sir James Director . . . a champion golfer, as well as a prominent industrialist or trade union leader.

Or suppose that you are introducing a man who has really fought his way up the ladder. Maybe he would like you to refer to his humble origins. Or perhaps he would prefer to forget them. Unless someone has given you the tip off, you cannot know. The number of potential bricks to be dropped is immense.

At a recent dinner, a famous, generous and charitable business-man was introduced to his audience as the man who 'not only conceived the idea of the . . . Girls Boarding School but had personally raised the very large sum needed to establish it.' Unfortunately, the chairman had omitted to check on how the school was going. Had he done so, he would have discovered that there were only eight applicants for the 120 places and that the entire venture was a flop which the guest of honour was not anxious to recall. The mixture of embarrassed silence and delighted laughter which greeted this *faux pas* reflected in no way upon the affection which the audience had for the gentleman concerned, whom everyone knew to be a first-class man. But it made the audience feel sorry for him—and for the chairman. The fact that the chairman was another voluntary worker in good causes and a popular man of business in no way excused an error which could so easily have been avoided.

If you are too busy to prepare your introduction, then get someone else to do it (either the preparation or, if necessary, the introduction itself) for you. There is no law to prevent a chairman from saying: 'I shall now ask his ex-mentor/disciple/managing director (or as the case may be) to introduce our guest to you.' It does not happen very often—which makes it all the more delightful when it does.

So speak of your guest's known achievements. By all means couple this with friendly or flattering references to his firm or his forebears. But the following are to be avoided:

'We are very pleased to have Mr Jackson with us tonight. His father is a very famous figure in the industry and we know that, in listening to his son, we shall have a treat awaiting us . . .'

Little better is: 'Mr Bloggs is the distinguished son of famous parents . . .'

Much worse (but often happening in practice): 'Lord Bloggs is unfortunately unable to be with us tonight. But we are pleased that Lady Bloggs has consented to speak to us. Without further ado, I introduce Lady Bloggs.'

This is not to say that a word could not have been introduced to compliment Lord and Lady Bloggs on their splendid and happy partnership. But the disappointment at the absence of the original guest must not be made apparent. Anyway, has Lady Bloggs herself nothing to commend her other than her good taste in husbands? The Honourable James Bloggs inherited his courtesy title. But surely he has done something with his life which the chairman ought to explain? The guests will be curious to hear something of the background of their speaker. Heredity is not all.

Try this: 'This is an industry which is proud of its family connections. Many of us are old colleagues and friends of William Harness. We have been delighted to see the active part taken by his son, Roger, in our great charity. Naturally, we honour him because he is the son of our old and distinguished friend. But it is in his own right that he is invited to speak to us tonight. His achievements are many. He is . . . he was . . . and we are confident that he will be a leader in our industry for many years to come. Ladies and gentlemen, Mr Roger Harness . . .'

Or: 'Tonight, we are honoured by Lady Bloggs. It is true that her husband was to have addressed us. I will not repeat the gaffe of the chairman who once introduced the wife in circumstances such as these by saying: "Sir William's misfortune in being ill is our good luck. We are indeed happy to welcome his wife in his place." We are delighted that the reason for Lord Bloggs' absence is that he is busy selling his goods overseas and hence keeping up his company's magnificent record in the field. We are fortunate that he has been good enough to leave his wife behind, in England—and to trust her in our company this evening. He is ...'

If (as so often happens) the speaker is a last-minute substitute, do not apologize for the fact. 'We were to have had Mr Hodge to speak to us, but he has let us down at the last minute. We are grateful to Mr Black, his assistant, for stepping into the breach. Ladies and gentlemen, Mr Black.' That just will not do. There are two decent alternatives. Either ignore altogether the fact that Mr Hodge has let you down. Everyone will know it. The word will have gone around. And it may be much less embarrassing if nothing is said. Alternatively, make a virtue out of necessity. Thus:

'Ladies and gentlemen. I know that you will all have been very sorry to have heard that our proposed guest, Mr Arthur Hodge, has been struck down by the 'flu. But equally, you will be pleased to learn that he is making a good recovery. He sends his greetings to us all—I have a telegram from him here.' (That was intelligent of Mr Hodge, incidentally.) 'It wishes us every good fortune. And I know that you will want me to reply, on behalf of us all, wishing him the most speedy recovery.

'I cannot tell Mr Black how grateful we are to him for having agreed to come to us at such very short notice. His readiness to step into the breach is just one indication of his loyalty to our organization ... of one reason at least why he has earned the affection of all of his colleagues ... He is ... he was ... he will be ...'

Or: 'Our good friend and proposed guest, Mr Arthur Hodge has, alas, been called abroad on urgent business. We know that he would never have let us down had there been any possible alternative. We wish him success in his venture—may he bring home the bacon—or, to be more precise, may he have every success in exporting the prize pigs. And we are very much obliged to him for having on our behalf asked Mr Robert Rook to address us in his place.

'Mr Rook is already well known to us. He is . . . he was . . he will be . . . We know the pressure of work upon Mr Rook and we are extremely grateful to him for honouring us by joining us this evening. Ladies and gentlemen, Mr Rook . . .'

There are, of course, occasions when the speaker should not be introduced. For instance: 'I shall ask our chairman, Edward Smith, to propose the loyal toast.' Or: 'Thank you, Mr Hodge. I am pleased to ask our treasurer, Richard Bright, to propose the vote of thanks.'

The chairman, then, sets the tone and calls the tune. He has many important duties, one of the most vital of which is the introduction of the speakers. He should treat his job seriously. He should apply the same rules to the brief speeches of introduction as he would to longer efforts. Introduction needs a beginning, a body, an end. The opening and closing sentences matter. Careful preparation (which, as usual, must be as unobtrusive as possible when the speech is in fact made) is important. A bad introduction can ruin a good speech—and a potentially fine meeting.

81 *Handling the speaker*

No area of a chairman's duties is so potentially hazardous as handling the guest speaker. Here are a few hints:

As we saw in the last chapter, the importance of remembering his name can scarcely be exaggerated. And if you are not quite sure how to pronounce it, ask him. If his name is to be put in a programme, toast list, brochure or other document, check that the spelling is correct. People are very touchy about their names.

Ascertain in advance as much as you can about the speaker. Several members of the Royal Family are renowned for their splendid memories. They come into a room and promptly recognize people and even remember where they last met. This is partly because they have good memories, but mainly because they do their homework. The best way to flatter your speaker is to remember all about him. The surest way to antagonize him is to be indifferent to him and to his past achievements.

If he has incurred expenses, remember to invite him to let you know. (See Chapter 40).

Remember to say thank you—and to write and repeat your thanks afterwards. You can never express gratitude too often.

Whilst trying to ensure that the speaker gets a fair hearing, be careful not to interrupt him too often. Competent speakers can handle their own audiences and prefer, where possible, to do so. The chairman should exercise his authority with moderation.

Prime the speaker in advance as to the length of time you want him to speak, and ask him whether he would like to be reminded when he is a few minutes away from the appointed end. Most speakers will gladly agree, and will not then resent a reminder. If necessary, push a note in front of the speaker, with: 'FIVE MINUTES TO GO' in large letters. But to do this without pré-arrangement can upset the speaker and your friendship with him.

*   *   *

Much of the chairman's job is done before the meeting actually begins. If he reads this book beforehand, he should do better at the time. Otherwise, he can bring it with him . . . in a plain, white cover if he prefers. . . .

So all that remains is to wish you—in the role speaker or the chairman—the very best of luck. However experienced and able you may be . . . however carefully you follow the rules we have given . . . whatever the occasion . . . there is no substitute for good fortune. Whether you are on your feet or in the chair, may you be blessed with success.

And I mean this sincerely..
However, let me say this....
Possibly you may feel - as I do..
Furthermore, I would add - as a postscript
FINALLY - let me
In conclusion
ZZZZZZZ
ZZZZ

Appendices

Extracts from Table A of The Companies Act, 1948

Table A contains a model set of regulations for the management of a company limited by shares. All or part of Table A is, more often than not, incorporated into the Articles of a company. Individual Articles may be (and often are) excluded or modified. But most are not. Here are those Articles of Table A which apply to meetings.

* * *

PART I

REGULATIONS FOR THE MANAGEMENT OF A COMPANY LIMITED BY SHARES, NOT BEING A PRIVATE COMPANY

Share Capital and Variation of Rights

2. Without prejudice to any special rights previously conferred on the holders of any existing shares or class of shares, any share in the company may be issued with such preferred, deferred or other special rights or such restrictions, whether in regard to dividend, voting, return of capital or otherwise as the company may from time to time by ordinary resolution determine.

3. Subject to the provisions of section 58 of the Act, any preference shares may, with the sanction of an ordinary resolution, be issued on the terms that they are, or at the option of the company are liable, to be redeemed on such terms and in such manner as the company before the issue of the shares may by special resolution determine.

4. If at any time the share capital is divided into different classes of shares, the rights attached to any class (unless otherwise provided by the terms of issue of the shares of that class) may, whether or not the company is being

wound up, be varied with the consent in writing of the holders of three-fourths of the issued shares of that class, or with the sanction of an extraordinary resolution passed at a separate general meeting of the holders of the shares of the class. To every such separate general meeting the provisions of these regulations relating to general meetings shall apply, but so that the necessary quorum shall be two persons at least holding or representing by proxy one-third of the issued shares of the class and that any holder of shares of the class present in person or by proxy may demand a poll.

Conversion of Shares into Stock

40. The company may by ordinary resolution convert any paid-up shares into stock and reconvert any stock into paid-up shares of any denomination.

Alteration of Capital

44. The company may from time to time by ordinary resolution increase the share capital by such sum, to be divided into shares of such amount, as the resolution shall prescribe.

45. The company may by ordinary resolution—
    (a) consolidate and divide all or any of its share capital into shares of larger amount than its existing shares;
    (b) sub-divide its existing shares, or any of them, into shares of smaller amount than is fixed by the memorandum of association subject, nevertheless, to the provisions of section 61 (1) (d) of the Act;
    (c) cancel any shares which, at the date of the passing of the resolution, have not been taken or agreed to be taken by any person.

46. The company may by special resolution reduce its share capital, any capital redemption reserve fund or any share premium account in any manner and with, and subject to, any incident authorized, and consent required, by law.

General Meetings

47. The company shall in each year hold a general meeting as its annual general meeting in addition to any other meetings in that year, and shall specify the meeting as such in the notices calling it; and not more than

fifteen months shall elapse between the date of one annual general meeting
of the company and that of the next. Provided that so long as the company
holds its first annual general meeting within eighteen months of its
incorporation, it need not hold it in the year of its incorporation or in the
following year. The annual general meeting shall be held at such time
and place as the directors shall appoint.

48. All general meetings other than annual general meetings shall be
called extraordinary general meetings.

49. The directors may, whenever they think fit, convene an extraordinary
general meeting, and extraordinary general meetings shall also be convened on such requisition, or, in default, may be convened by such
requisitions, as provided by section 132 of the Act. If at any time there
are not within the United Kingdom sufficient directors capable of acting
to form a quorum, any director or any two members of the company
may convene an extraordinary general meeting in the same manner as
nearly as possible as that in which meetings may be convened by the
directors.

Notice of General Meetings

50. An annual general meeting and a meeting called for the passing of
a special resolution shall be called by twenty-one days' notice in writing at
the least, and a meeting of the company other than an annual general
meeting or a meeting for the passing of a special resolution shall be
called by fourteen days' notice in writing at the least. The notice shall be
exclusive of the day on which it is served or deemed to be served and of the
day for which it is given, and shall specify the place, the day and the
hour of meeting and, in case of special business, the general nature of that
business, and shall be given, in manner hereinafter mentioned or in
such other manner, if any, as may be prescribed by the company in general
meeting, to such persons as are, under the regulations of the company,
entitled to receive such notices from the company :
  Provided that a meeting of the company shall, notwithstanding that it
is called by shorter notice than that specified in this regulation, be deemed
to have been duly called if it is so agreed—
  (a) in the case of a meeting called as the annual general meeting, by
      all the members entitled to attend and vote thereat; and
  (b) in the case of any other meeting, by a majority in number of
      the members having a right to attend and vote at the meeting,
      being a majority together holding not less than 95 per cent. in
      nominal value of the shares giving that right.

51. The accidental omission to give notice of a meeting to, or the non-receipt of notice of a meeting by, any person entitled to receive notice shall not invalidate the proceedings at that meeting.

Proceedings at General Meetings

52. All business shall be deemed special that is transacted at an extraordinary general meeting, and also that is transacted at an annual general meeting, with the exception of declaring a dividend, the consideration of the accounts, balance sheets, and the reports of the directors and auditors, the election of directors in the place of those retiring and the appointment of, and the fixing of the remuneration of, the auditors.

53. No business shall be transacted at any general meeting unless a quorum of members is present at the time when the meeting proceeds to business; save as herein otherwise provided, three members present in person shall be a quorum.

54. If within half an hour from the time appointed for the meeting a quorum is not present, the meeting, if convened upon the requisition of members, shall be dissolved; in any other case it shall stand adjourned to the same day in the next week, at the same time and place or to such other day and at such other time and place as the directors may determine, and if at the adjourned meeting a quorum is not present within half an hour from the time appointed for the meeting, the members present shall be a quorum.

55. The chairman, if any, of the board of directors shall preside as chairman at every general meeting of the company, or if there is no such chairman, or if he shall not be present within fifteen minutes after the time appointed for the holding of the meeting or is unwilling to act the directors present shall elect one of their number to be chairman of the meeting.

56. If at any meeting no director is willing to act as chairman or if no director is present within fifteen minutes after the time appointed for holding the meeting, the members present shall choose one of their number to be chairman of the meeting.

57. The chairman may, with the consent of any meeting at which a quorum is present (and shall if so directed by the meeting), adjourn the meeting from time to time and from place to place, but no business shall be transacted at any adjourned meeting other than the business left

unfinished at the meeting from which the adjournment took place. When a meeting is adjourned for thirty days or more, notice of the adjourned meeting shall be given as in the case of an original meeting. Save as aforesaid it shall not be necessary to give any notice of an adjournment or of the business to be transacted at an adjourned meeting.

58. At any general meeting a resolution put to the vote of the meeting shall be decided on a show of hands unless a poll is (before or on the declaration of the result of the show of hands) demanded—

    (*a*) by the chairman; or

    (*b*) by at least three members present in person or by proxy; or

    (*c*) by any member or members present in person or by proxy and representing not less than one-tenth of the total voting rights of all the members having the right to vote at the meeting; or

    (*d*) by a member or members holding shares in the company conferring a right to vote at the meeting being shares on which an aggregate sum has been paid up equal to not less than one-tenth of the total sum paid up on all the shares conferring that right.

Unless a poll be so demanded a declaration by the chairman that a resolution has on a show of hands been carried or carried unanimously or by a particular majority, or lost and an entry to that effect in the book containing the minutes of the proceedings of the company shall be conclusive evidence of the fact without proof of the number or proportion of the votes recorded in favour of or against such resolution.

The demand for a poll may be withdrawn.

59. Except as provided in regulation 61, if a poll is duly demanded it shall be taken in such manner as the chairman directs, and the result of the poll shall be deemed to be the resolution of the meeting at which the poll was demanded.

60. In the case of an equality of votes, whether on a show of hands or on a poll, the chairman of the meeting at which the show of hands takes place or at which the poll is demanded, shall be entitled to a second or casting vote.

61. A poll demanded on the election of a chairman or on a question of adjournment shall be taken forthwith. A poll demanded on any other question shall be taken at such time as the chairman of the meeting directs, and any business other than that upon which a poll has been demanded may be proceeded with pending the taking of the poll.

Votes of Members

62. Subject to any rights or restrictions for the time being attached to any class or classes of shares, on a show of hands every member present in person shall have one vote, and on a poll every member shall have one vote for each share of which he is the holder.

63. In the case of joint holders the vote of the senior who tenders a vote, whether in person or by proxy, shall be accepted to the exclusion of the votes of the other joint holders; and for this purpose seniority shall be determined by the order in which the names stand in the register of members.

64. A member of unsound mind, or in respect of whom an order has been made by any court having jurisdiction in lunacy, may vote, whether on a show of hands or on a poll, by his committee, receiver, curator bonis, or other person in the nature of a committee, receiver or curator bonis appointed by that court, and any such committee, receiver, curator bonis or other person may, on a poll, vote by proxy.

65. No member shall be entitled to vote at any general meeting unless all calls or other sums presently payable by him in respect of shares in the company have been paid.

66. No objection shall be raised to the qualification of any voter except at the meeting or adjourned meeting at which the vote objected to is given or tendered, and every vote not disallowed at such meeting shall be valid for all purposes. Any such objection made in due time shall be referred to the chairman of the meeting, whose decision shall be final and conclusive.

67. On a poll votes may be given either personally or by proxy.

68. The instrument appointing a proxy shall be in writing under the hand of the appointer or of his attorney duly authorized in writing, or, if the appointer is a corporation, either under seal, or under the hand of an officer or attorney duly authorized. A proxy need not be a member of the company.

69. The instrument appointing a proxy and the power of attorney or other authority, if any, under which it is signed or a notarially certified copy of that power or authority shall be deposited at the registered office of the company or at such other place within the United Kingdom as is

specified for that purpose in the notice convening the meeting, not less than 48 hours before the time for holding the meeting or adjourned meeting, at which the person named in the instrument proposes to vote, or, in the case of a poll, not less than 24 hours before the time appointed for the taking of the poll, and in default the instrument of proxy shall not be treated as valid.

70. An instrument appointing a proxy shall be in the following form or a form as near thereto as circumstances admit—

Limited

I/We,   , of   , in the county of   , being a member/members of the above-named company, hereby appoint
of   , or failing him,
of   , as my/our proxy to vote for me/us on my/our behalf at the [annual or extraordinary, as the case may be] general meeting of the company to be held on the   day of   19
and at any adjournment thereof.
     Signed this   day of   19   .'

71. Where it is desired to afford members an opportunity of voting for or against a resolution the instrument appointing a proxy shall be in the following form or a form as near thereto as circumstances admit—

'I/We,   , of
in the county of   , being a member/members of the above-named company, here appoint
of   , or failing him
of   , as my/our proxy to vote for me/us on my/our behalf at the [annual or extraordinary, as the case may be] general meeting of the company, to be held on the   day of   19   ,
and at any adjournment thereof
     Signed this   day of   19

This form is to be used *in favour of / against the resolution. Unless otherwise instructed, the proxy will vote as he thinks fit.
     *Strike out whichever is not desired.'

72. The instrument appointing a proxy shall be deemed to confer authority to demand or join in demanding a poll.

73. A vote given in accordance with the terms of an instrument of proxy shall be valid notwithstanding the previous death or insanity of the principal or revocation of the proxy or of the authority under which the proxy was executed, or the transfer of the share in respect of which the proxy is given, provided that no intimation in writing of such death,

insanity, revocation or transfer as aforesaid shall have been received by the company at the office before the commencement of the meeting or adjourned meeting at which the proxy is used.

Directors

75. The number of the directors and the names of the first directors shall be determined in writing by the subscribers of the memorandum of association or a majority of them.

76. The remuneration of the directors shall from time to time be determined by the company in general meeting. Such remuneration shall be deemed to accrue from day to day. The directors may also be paid all travelling, hotel and other expenses properly incurred by them in attending and returning from meetings of the directors or any committee of the directors or general meetings of the company or in connection with the business of the company.

77. The shareholding qualification for directors may be fixed by the company in general meeting, and unless and until so fixed no qualification shall be required.

78. A director of the company may be or become a director or other officer of, or otherwise interested in, any company promoted by the company or in which the company may be interested as shareholder or otherwise, and no such director shall be accountable to the company for any remuneration or other benefits received by him as a director or officer of, or from his interest in, such other company unless the company otherwise direct.

Powers and Duties of Directors

80. The business of the company shall be managed by the directors, who may pay all expenses incurred in promoting and registering the company, and may exercise all such powers of the company as are not, by the Act or by these regulations, required to be exercised by the company in general meeting, subject, nevertheless, to any of these regulations, to the provisions of the Act and to such regulations, being not inconsistent with the aforesaid regulations or provisions, as may be prescribed by the company in general meeting; but no regulation made by the company in general meeting shall invalidate any prior act of the directors which would have been valid if that regulation had not been made.

84.—(1) A director who is in any way, whether directly or indirectly, interested in a contract or proposed contract with the company shall declare the nature of his interest at a meeting of the directors in accordance with section 199 of the Act.

(2) A director shall not vote in respect of any contract or arrangement in which he is interested, and if he shall do so his vote shall not be counted, nor shall he be counted in the quorum present at the meeting, but neither of these prohibitions shall apply to—

(a) any arrangement for giving any director any security or indemnity in respect of money lent by him to or obligations undertaken by him for the benefit of the company; or

(b) to any arrangement for the giving by the company of any security to a third party in respect of a debt or obligation of the company for which the director himself has assumed responsibility in whole or in part under a guarantee or indemnity or by the deposit of a security; or

(c) any contract by a director to subscribe for or underwrite shares or debentures of the company; or

(d) any contract or arrangement with any other company in which he is interested only as an officer of the company or as holder of shares or other securities;

and these prohibitions may at any time be suspended or relaxed to any extent, and either generally or in respect of any particular contract, arrangement or transaction, by the company in general meeting.

(3) A director may hold any other office or place of profit under the company (other than the office of auditor) in conjunction with his office of director for such period and on such terms (as to remuneration and otherwise) as the directors may determine and no director or intending director shall be disqualified by his office from contracting with the company either with regard to his tenure of any such other office or place of profit or as vendor, purchaser or otherwise, nor shall any such contract, or any contract or arrangement entered into by or on behalf of the company in which any director is in any way interested, be liable to be avoided, nor shall any director so contracting or being so interested be liable to account to the company for any profit realized by any such contract or arrangement by reason of such director holding that office or of the fiduciary relation thereby established.

(4) A director, notwithstanding his interest, may be counted in the quorum present at any meeting whereat he or any other director is appointed to hold any such office or place of profit under the company or whereat the terms of any such appointment are arranged, and he may vote on any such appointment or arrangement other than his own appointment or the arrangement of the terms thereof.

(5) Any director may act by himself or his firm in a professional

capacity for the company, and he or his firm shall be entitled to remuneration for professional services as if he were not a director; provided that nothing herein contained shall authorize a director or his firm to act as auditor to the company.

86. The directors shall cause minutes to be made in books provided for the purpose—
- (*a*) of all appointments of officers made by the directors;
- (*b*) of the names of the directors present at each meeting of the directors and of any committee of the directors;
- (*c*) of all resolutions and proceedings at all meetings of the company, and of the directors, and of committees of directors;

and every director present at any meeting of directors or committee of directors shall sign his name in a book to be kept for that purpose.

87. The directors on behalf of the company may pay a gratuity or pension or allowance on retirement to any director who has held any other salaried office or place of profit with the company or to his widow or dependants and may make contributions to any fund and pay premiums for the purchase or provision of any such gratuity, pension or allowance.

Disqualification of Directors

88. The office of director shall be vacated if the director—
- (*a*) ceases to be a director by virtue of section 182 or 185 of the Act; or
- (*b*) becomes bankrupt or makes any arrangement or composition with his creditors generally; or
- (*c*) becomes prohibited from being a director by reason of any order made under section 188 of the Act; or
- (*d*) becomes of unsound mind; or
- (*e*) resigns his office by notice in writing to the company; or
- (*f*) shall for more than six months have been absent without permission of the directors from meetings of the directors held during that period.

Rotation of Directors

89. At the first annual general meeting of the company all the directors shall retire from office, and at the annual general meeting in every subsequent year one-third of the directors for the time being, or, if their number is not three or a multiple of three, then the number nearest one-third, shall retire from office.

90. The directors to retire in every year shall be those who have been longest in office since their last election, but as between persons who became directors on the same day those to retire shall (unless they otherwise agree among themselves) be determined by lot.

91. A retiring director shall be eligible for re-election.

92. The company at the meeting at which a director retires in manner aforesaid may fill the vacated office by electing a person thereto, and in default the retiring director shall if offering himself for re-election be deemed to have been re-elected, unless at such meeting it is expressly resolved not to fill such vacated office or unless a resolution for the re-election of such director shall have been put to the meeting and lost.

93. No person other than a director retiring at the meeting shall unless recommended by the directors be eligible for election to the office of director at any general meeting unless not less than three nor more than twenty-one days before the date appointed for the meeting there shall have been left at the registered office of the company notice in writing, signed by a member duly qualified to attend and vote at the meeting for which such notice is given, of his intention to propose such person for election, and also notice in writing signed by that person of his willingness to be elected.

94. The company may from time to time by ordinary resolution increase or reduce the number of directors, and may also determine in what rotation the increased or reduced number is to go out of office.

95. The directors shall have power at any time, and from time to time, to appoint any person to be a director, either to fill a casual vacancy or as an addition to the existing directors, but so that the total number of directors shall not at any time exceed the number fixed in accordance with these regulations. Any director so appointed shall hold office only until the next following annual general meeting, and shall then be eligible for re-election but shall not be taken into account in determining the directors who are to retire by rotation at such meeting.

96. The company may by ordinary resolution, of which special notice has been given in accordance with section 142 of the Act, remove any director before the expiration of his period of office notwithstanding anything in these regulations or in any agreement between the company and such director. Such removal shall be without prejudice to any claim such director may have for damages for breach of any contract of service between him and the company.

97. The company may by ordinary resolution appoint another person in place of a director removed from office under the immediately preceding regulation, and without prejudice to the powers of the directors under regulation 95 the company in general meeting may appoint any person to be a director either to fill a casual vacancy or as an additional director. A person appointed in place of a director so removed or to fill such a vacancy shall be subject to retirement at the same time as if he had become a director on the day on which the director in whose place he is appointed was last elected a director.

Proceedings of Directors

98. The directors may meet together for the despatch of business, adjourn, and otherwise regulate their meetings, as they think fit. Questions arising at any meeting shall be decided by a majority of votes. In case of an equality of votes, the chairman shall have a second or casting vote. A director may, and the secretary on the requisition of a director shall, at any time summon a meeting of the directors. It shall not be necessary to give notice of a meeting of directors to any director for the time being absent from the United Kingdom.

99. The quorum necessary for the transaction of the business of the directors may be fixed by the directors, and unless so fixed shall be two.

100. The continuing directors may act notwithstanding any vacancy in their body, but, if and so long as their number is reduced below the number fixed by or pursuant to the regulations of the company as the necessary quorum of directors, the continuing directors or director may act for the purpose of increasing the number of directors to that number, or of summoning a general meeting of the company, but for no other purpose.

101. The directors may elect a chairman of their meetings and determine the period for which he is to hold office; but if no such chairman is elected, or if at any meeting the chairman is not present within five minutes after the time appointed for holding the same, the directors present may choose one of their number to be chairman of the meeting.

102. The directors may delegate any of their powers to committees consisting of such member or members of their body as they think fit; any committee so formed shall in the exercise of the powers so delegated conform to any regulations that may be imposed on it by the directors.

103. A committee may elect a chairman of its meetings; if no such chairman is elected, or if at any meeting the chairman is not present within five minutes after the time appointed for holding the same, the members present may choose one of their number to be chairman of the meeting.

104. A committee may meet and adjourn as it thinks proper. Questions arising at any meeting shall be determined by a majority of votes of the members present, and in the case of an equality of votes the chairman shall have a second or casting vote.

105. All acts done by any meeting of the directors or of a committee of directors or by any person acting as a director shall, notwithstanding that it be afterwards discovered that there was some defect in the appointment of any such director or person acting as aforesaid, or that they or any of them were disqualified, be as valid as if every such person had been duly appointed and was qualified to be a director.

106. A resolution in writing, signed by all the directors for the time being entitled to receive notice of a meeting of the directors, shall be as valid and effectual as if it had been passed at a meeting of the directors duly convened and held.

Managing Director

107. The directors may from time to time appoint one or more of their body to the office of managing director for such period and on such terms as they think fit, and, subject to the terms of any agreement entered into in any particular case, may revoke such appointment. A director so appointed shall not, whilst holding that office, be subject to retirement by rotation or be taken into account in determining the rotation of retirement of directors, but his appointment shall be automatically determined if he cease from any cause to be a director.

108. A managing director shall receive such remuneration (whether by way of salary, commission or participation in profits, or partly in one way and partly in another) as the directors may determine.

109. The directors may entrust to and confer upon a managing director any of the powers exercisable by them upon such terms and conditions and with such restrictions as they may think fit, and either collaterally with or to the exclusion of their own powers and may from time to time revoke, withdraw, alter or vary all or any of such powers.

Secretary

110. The secretary shall be appointed by the directors for such term, at such remuneration and upon such conditions as they may think fit; and any secretary so appointed may be removed by them.

111. No person shall be appointed or hold office as secretary who is—
  (*a*) the sole director of the company; or
  (*b*) a corporation the sole director of which is the sole director of the company; or
  (*c*) the sole director of a corporation which is the sole director of the company.

112. A provision of the Act or these regulations requiring or authorizing a thing to be done by or to a director and the secretary shall not be satisfied by its being done by or to the same person acting both as director and as, or in place of, the secretary.

Dividends and Reserve

114. The company in general meeting may declare dividends, but no dividend shall exceed the amount recommended by the directors.

Notices

131. A notice may be given by the company to any member either personally or by sending it by post to him or to his registered address, or (if he has no registered address within the United Kingdom) to the address, if any, within the United Kingdom supplied by him to the company for the giving of notice to him. Where a notice is sent by post, service of the notice shall be deemed to be effected by properly addressing, pre-paying, and posting a letter containing the notice, and to have been effected in the case of a notice of a meeting at the expiration of 24 hours after the letter containing the same is posted, and in any other case at the time at which the letter would be delivered in the ordinary course of post.

132. A notice may be given by the company to the joint holders of a share by giving the notice to the joint holder first named in the register of members in respect of the share.

133. A notice may be given by the company to the persons entitled to a share in consequence of the death or bankruptcy of a member by sending

it through the post in a prepaid letter addressed to them by name, or by the title of representatives of the deceased, or trustee of the bankrupt, or by any like description, at the address, if any, within the United Kingdom supplied for the purpose by the persons claiming to be so entitled, or (until such an address has been so supplied) by giving the notice in any manner in which the same might have been given if the death or bankruptcy had not occurred.

134. Notice of every general meeting shall be given in any manner hereinbefore authorized to—

> (*a*) every member except those members who (having no registered address within the United Kingdom) have not supplied to the company an address within the United Kingdom for the giving of notices to them;
>
> (*b*) every person upon whom the ownership of a share devolves by reason of his being a legal personal representative or a trustee in bankruptcy of a member where the member but for his death or bankruptcy would be entitled to receive notice of the meeting; and
>
> (*c*) the auditor for the time being of the company.

No other person shall be entitled to receive notices of general meetings.

Winding up

135. If the company shall be wound up the liquidator may, with the sanction of an extraordinary resolution of the company and any other sanction required by the Act, divide amongst the members in specie or kind the whole or any part of the assets of the company (whether they shall consist of property of the same kind or not) and may, for such purposes set such value as he deems fair upon any property to be divided as aforesaid and may determine how such division shall be carried out as between the members or different classes of members. The liquidator may, with the like sanction, vest the whole or any part of such assets in trustees upon such trusts for the benefit of the contributories as the liquidator, with the like sanction, shall think fit, but so that no member shall be compelled to accept any shares or other securities whereon there is any liability.

PART II

REGULATIONS FOR THE MANAGEMENT OF
A PRIVATE COMPANY LIMITED BY SHARES

1. The regulations contained in Part I of Table A (with the exception of regulations 24 and 53) shall apply.

4. No business shall be transacted at any general meeting unless a quorum of members is present at the time when the meeting proceeds to business; save as herein otherwise provided two members present in person or by proxy shall be a quorum.

5. Subject to the provisions of the Act, a resolution in writing signed by all the members for the time being entitled to receive notice of and to attend and vote at general meetings (or being corporations by their duly authorized representatives) shall be as valid and effective as if the same had been passed at a general meeting of the company duly convened and held.

Note: Regulations 3 and 4 of this Part are alternative to regulations 24 and 53 respectively of Part I.

Table C

ARTICLES OF ASSOCIATION OF A COMPANY
LIMITED BY GUARANTEE AND NOT HAVING
A SHARE CAPITAL

Members

2. The number of members with which the company proposes to be registered is 500 but the directors may from time to time register an increase of members.

3. The subscribers to the memorandum of association and such other persons as the directors shall admit to membership shall be members of the company.

General Meetings

4. The company shall in each year hold a general meeting as its annual general meeting in addition to any other meetings in that year, and shall specify the meeting as such in the notices calling it; and not more than fifteen months shall elapse between the date of one annual general meeting of the company and that of the next. Provided that so long as the company holds its first annual general meeting within eighteen months of its incorporation, it need not hold it in the year of its incorporation or in the following year. The annual general meeting shall be held at such time and place as the directors shall appoint.

5. All general meetings other than annual general meetings shall be called extraordinary general meetings.

6. The directors may, whenever they think fit, convene an extraordinary general meeting, and extraordinary general meetings shall also be convened on such requisition, or, in default, may be convened by such requisitionists, as provided by section 132 of the Act. If at any time there are not within the United Kingdom sufficient directors capable of acting to form a quorum, any director or any two members of the company may convene an extraordinary general meeting in the same manner as nearly as possible as that in which meetings may be convened by the directors.

Notice of General Meetings

7. An annual general meeting and a meeting called for the passing of a special resolution shall be called by twenty-one days' notice in writing at the least, and a meeting of the company other than an annual general meeting or a meeting for the passing of a special resolution shall be called by fourteen days' notice in writing at the least. The notice shall be exclusive of the day on which it is served or deemed to be served and of the day for which it is given, and shall specify the place, the day and the hour of meeting and, in case of special business, the general nature of that business and shall be given, in manner hereinafter mentioned or in such other manner, if any, as may be prescribed by the company in general meeting, to such persons as are, under the articles of the company, entitled to receive such notices from the company:
　Provided that a meeting of the company shall, notwithstanding that it is called by shorter notice than that specified in this article be deemed to have been duly called if it is so agreed—
  (a) in the case of a meeting called as the annual general meeting, by all the members entitled to attend and vote thereat; and
  (b) in the case of any other meeting, by a majority in number of the members having a right to attend and vote at the meeting, being a majority together representing not less than ninety-five per cent. of the total voting rights at that meeting of all the members.

8. The accidental omission to give notice of a meeting to, or the non-receipt of notice of a meeting by, any person entitled to receive notice shall not invalidate the proceedings at that meeting.

Proceedings at General Meetings

9. All business shall be deemed special that is transacted at an extra-

ordinary general meeting, and also all that is transacted at an annual general meeting, with the exception of declaring a dividend, the consideration of the accounts, balance sheets, and the reports of the directors and auditors, the election of directors in the place of those retiring and the appointment of, and the fixing of the remuneration, of the auditors.

10. No business shall be transacted at any general meeting unless a quorum of members is present at the time when the meeting proceeds to business; save as herein otherwise provided, three members present in person shall be a quorum.

11. If within half an hour from the time appointed for the meeting a quorum is not present, the meeting, if convened upon the requisition of members, shall be dissolved; in any other case it shall stand adjourned to the same day in the next week, at the same time and place, or to such other day and at such other time and place as the directors may determine, and if at the adjourned meeting a quorum is not present within half an hour from the time appointed for the meeting the members present shall be a quorum.

12. The chairman, if any, of the board of directors shall preside as chairman at every general meeting of the company, or if there is no such chairman, or if he shall not be present within fifteen minutes after the time appointed for the holding of the meeting or is unwilling to act the directors present shall elect one of their number to be chairman of the meeting.

13. If at any meeting no director is willing to act as chairman or if no director is present within fifteen minutes after the time appointed for holding the meeting, the members present shall choose one of their number to be chairman of the meeting.

14. The chairman may, with the consent of any meeting at which a quorum is present (and shall if so directed by the meeting), adjourn the meeting from time to time and from place to place, but no business shall be transacted at any adjourned meeting other than the business left unfinished at the meeting from which the adjournment took place. When a meeting is adjourned for thirty days or more, notice of the adjourned meeting shall be given as in the case of an original meeting. Save as aforesaid it shall not be necessary to give any notice of an adjournment or of the business to be transacted at an adjourned meeting.

15. At any general meeting a resolution put to the vote of the meeting

shall be decided on a show of hands unless a poll is (before or on the declaration of the result of the show of hands) demanded—

(a) by the chairman; or

(b) by at least three members present in person or by proxy; or

(c) by any member or members present in person or by proxy and representing not less than one-tenth of the total voting rights of all the members having the right to vote at the meeting.

Unless a poll be so demanded a declaration by the chairman that a resolution has on a show of hands been carried or carried unanimously, or by a particular majority, or lost and an entry to that effect in the book containing the minutes of proceedings of the company shall be conclusive evidence of the fact without proof of the number or proportion of the votes recorded in favour of or against such resolution.

The demand for a poll may be withdrawn.

16. Except as provided in article 18, if a poll is duly demanded it shall be taken in such manner as the chairman directs, and the result of the poll shall be deemed to be the resolution of the meeting at which the poll was demanded.

17. In the case of an equality of votes, whether on a show of hands or on a poll, the chairman of the meeting at which the show of hands takes place or at which the poll is demanded, shall be entitled to a second or casting vote.

18. A poll demanded on the election of a chairman, or on a question of adjournment, shall be taken forthwith. A poll demanded on any other question shall be taken at such time as the chairman of the meeting directs, and any business other than that upon which a poll had been demanded may be proceeded with pending the taking of the poll.

19. Subject to the provisions of the Act a resolution in writing signed by all the members for the time being entitled to receive notice of and to attend and vote at general meetings (or being corporations by their duly authorized representatives) shall be as valid and effective as if the same had been passed at a general meeting of the company duly convened and held.

Votes of Members

20. Every member shall have one vote.

21. A member of unsound mind, or in respect of whom an order has been

made by any court having jurisdiction in lunacy, may vote, whether on a show of hands or on a poll, by his committee, receiver, curator bonis or other person in the nature of a committee, receiver or curator bonis appointed by that court, and any such committee, receiver, curator bonis or other person may, on a poll, vote by proxy.

22. No member shall be entitled to vote at any general meeting unless all moneys presently payable by him to the company have been paid.

23. On a poll votes may be given either personally or by proxy.

24. The instrument appointing a proxy shall be in writing under the hand of the appointer or of his attorney duly authorized in writing, or, if the appointer is a corporation, either under seal or under the hand of an officer or attorney duly authorized. A proxy need not be a member of the company.

25. The instrument appointing a proxy and the power of attorney or other authority, if any, under which it is signed or a notarially certified copy of that power or authority shall be deposited at the registered office of the company or at such other place within the United Kingdom as is specified for that purpose in the notice convening the meeting, not less than 48 hours before the time for holding the meeting or adjourned meeting at which the person named in the instrument proposes to vote, or, in the case of a poll, not less than 24 hours before the time appointed for the taking of the poll, and in default the instrument of proxy shall not be treated as valid.

26. An instrument appointing a proxy shall be in the following form or a form as near thereto as circumstances admit—

Limited.

I/We   of   in the county of
                                           , being a member/members
of the above named company, hereby appoint
of   or failing him
                              of
as my/our proxy to vote for me/us on my/our behalf at the [annual or extraordinary, as the case may be] general meeting of the company to be held on the   day of
                    19   , and at any adjournment thereof.
        Signed this   day of   19   .

27. Where it is desired to afford members an opportunity of voting for

or against a resolution the instrument appointing a proxy shall be in the
following form or a form as near thereto as circumstances admit—

                                                                   Limited.

    I/We   , of
in the county of   , being a
member/members of the above named company, hereby appoint
                                              of
or failing him   of   '
                , as my/our proxy to vote for me/us
on my/our behalf at the [annual or extraordinary, as the case
may be] general meeting of the company to be held on the
              day of   19 , and at
any adjournment thereof.

        Signed this   day of   19 .
                       *in favour of
This form is to be used ————————— the resolution. Unless
                       against
otherwise instructed, the proxy will vote as he thinks fit.
        * Strike out whichever is not desired.'

28. The instrument appointing a proxy shall be deemed to confer
authority to demand or join in demanding a poll.

29. A vote given in accordance with the terms of an instrument of proxy
shall be valid notwithstanding the previous death or insanity of the
principal or revocation of the proxy or of the authority under which the
proxy was executed, provided that no intimation in writing of such death,
insanity or revocation as aforesaid shall have been received by the company at the office before the commencement of the meeting or adjourned
meeting at which the proxy is used.

Corporations acting by Representatives at Meetings

30. Any corporation which is a member of the company may by resolution
of its directors or other governing body authorize such person as it thinks
fit to act as its representative at any meeting of the company, and the
person so authorized shall be entitled to exercise the same powers on
behalf of the corporation which he represents as that corporation could
exercise if it were an individual member of the company.

Directors

31. The number of the directors and the names of the first directors shall

be determined in writing by the subscribers of the memorandum of association or a majority of them.

32. The remuneration of the directors shall from time to time be determined by the company in general meeting. Such remuneration shall be deemed to accrue from day to day. The directors shall also be paid all travelling, hotel and other expenses properly incurred by them in attending and returning from meetings of the directors of any committee of the directors or general meetings of the company or in connection with the business of the company.

Borrowing Powers

33. The directors may exercise all the powers of the company to borrow money, and to mortgage or charge its undertaking and property, or any part thereof, and to issue debentures, debenture stock and other securities, whether outright or as security for any debt, liability or obligation of the company or of any third party.

Powers and Duties of Directors

34. The business of the company shall be managed by the directors, who may pay all expenses incurred in promoting and registering the company, and may exercise all such powers of the company as are not, by the Act or by these articles, required to be exercised by the company in general meeting, subject nevertheless to the provisions of the Act or the articles and to such regulations, being not inconsistent with the aforesaid provisions, as may be prescribed by the company in general meeting; but no regulation made by the company in general meeting shall invalidate any prior act of the directors which would have been valid if that regulation had not been made.

35. The directors may from time to time and at any time by power of attorney appoint any company, firm or person or body of persons, whether nominated directly or indirectly by the directors, to be the attorney or attorneys of the company for such purposes and with such powers, authorities and discretions (not exceeding those vested in or exercisable by the directors under these articles) and for such period and subject to such conditions as they may think fit, and any such powers of attorney may contain such provisions for the protection and convenience of persons dealing with any such attorney as the directors may think fit and may also authorize any such attorney to delegate all or any of the powers, authorities and discretions vested in him.

36. All cheques, promissory notes, drafts, bills of exchange and other negotiable instruments, and all receipts for moneys paid to the company, shall be signed, drawn, accepted, endorsed, or otherwise executed, as the case may be, in such manner as the directors shall from time to time by resolution determine.

37. The directors shall cause minutes to be made in books provided for the purpose—
   (a) of all appointments of officers made by the directors;
   (b) of the names of the directors present at each meeting of the directors and of any committee of the directors;
   (c) of all resolutions and proceedings at all meetings of the company, and of the directors, and of committees of directors;

and every director present at any meeting of directors or committee of directors shall sign his name in a book to be kept for that purpose.

Disqualification of Directors

38. The office of director shall be vacated if the director—
   (a) without the consent of the company in general meeting holds any other office of profit under the company; or
   (b) becomes bankrupt or makes any arrangement or composition with his creditors generally; or
   (c) becomes prohibited from being a director by reason of any order made under section 188 of the Act; or
   (d) becomes of unsound mind; or
   (e) resigns his office by notice in writing to the company; or
   (f) ceases to be a director by virtue of section 185 of the Act;
   (g) is directly or indirectly interested in any contract with the company and fails to declare the nature of his interest in manner required by section 199 of the Act.

   A director shall not vote in respect of any contract in which he is interested or any matter arising thereout, and if he does so vote his vote shall not be counted.

Rotation of Directors

39. At the first annual general meeting of the company all the directors shall retire from office, and at the annual general meeting in every subsequent year one-third of the directors for the time being, or, if their number is not three or a multiple of three, then the number nearest one-third, shall retire from office.

40. The directors to retire in every year shall be those who have been longest in office since their last election, but as between persons who became directors on the same day those to retire shall (unless they otherwise agree among themselves) be determined by lot.

41. A retiring director shall be eligible for re-election.

42. The company at the meeting at which a director retires in manner aforesaid may fill the vacated office by electing a person thereto, and in default the retiring director shall, if offering himself for re-election, be deemed to have been re-elected, unless at such meeting it is expressly resolved not to fill such vacated office or unless a resolution for the re-election of such director shall have been put to the meeting and lost.

43. No person other than a director retiring at the meeting shall unless recommended by the directors be eligible for election to the office of director at any general meeting unless, not less than three nor more than twenty-one days before the date appointed for the meeting, there shall have been left at the registered office of the company notice in writing, signed by a member duly qualified to attend and vote at the meeting for which such notice is given, of his intention to propose such person for election, and also notice in writing signed by that person of his willingness to be elected.

44. The company may from time to time by ordinary resolution increase or reduce the number of directors, and may also determine in what rotation the increased or reduced number is to go out of office.

45. The directors shall have power at any time, and from time to time, to appoint any person to be a director, either to fill a casual vacancy or as an addition to the existing directors, but so that the total number of directors shall not at any time exceed the number fixed in accordance with these articles. Any director so appointed shall hold office only until the next following annual general meeting, and shall then be eligible for re-election, but shall not be taken into account in determining the directors who are to retire by rotation at such meeting.

46. The company may by ordinary resolution, of which special notice has been given in accordance with section 142 of the Act, remove any director before the expiration of his period of office notwithstanding anything in these articles or in any agreement between the company and such director. Such removal shall be without prejudice to any claim such director may have for damages for breach of any contract of service between him and the company.

47. The company may by ordinary resolution appoint another person in place of a director removed from office under the immediately preceding article. Without prejudice to the powers of the directors under article 45 the company in general meeting may appoint any person to be a director either to fill a casual vacancy or as an additional director. The person appointed to fill such a vacancy shall be subject to retirement at the same time as if he had become a director on the day on which the director in whose place he is appointed was last elected a director.

Proceedings of Directors

48. The directors may meet together for the despatch of business, adjourn, and otherwise regulate their meetings, as they think fit. Questions arising at any meeting shall be decided by a majority of votes. In the case of an equality of votes the chairman shall have a second or casting vote. A director may, and the secretary on the requisition of a director shall, at any time summon a meeting of the directors. It shall not be necessary to give notice of a meeting of directors to any director for the time being absent from the United Kingdom.

49. The quorum necessary for the transaction of the business of the directors may be fixed by the directors, and unless so fixed shall be two.

50. The continuing directors may act notwithstanding any vacancy in their body, but, if and so long as their number is reduced below the number fixed by or pursuant to the articles of the company as the necessary quorum of directors, the continuing directors or director may act for the purpose of increasing the number of directors to that number, or of summoning a general meeting of the company, but for no other purpose.

51. The directors may elect a chairman of their meetings and determine the period for which he is to hold office; but, if no such chairman is elected, or if at any meeting the chairman is not present within five minutes after the time appointed for holding the same, the directors present may choose one of their number to be chairman of the meeting.

52. The directors may delegate any of their powers to committees consisting of such member or members of their body as they think fit: any committee so formed shall in the exercise of the powers so delegated conform to any regulations that may be imposed on it by the directors.

53. A committee may elect a chairman of its meetings; if no such chairman is elected, or if at any meeting the chairman is not present within five minutes after the time appointed for holding the same, the members

present may choose one of their number to be chairman of the meeting.

54. A committee may meet and adjourn as it thinks proper. Questions arising at any meeting shall be determined by a majority of votes of the members present, and in the case of an equality of votes the chairman shall have a second or casting vote.

55. All acts done by any meeting of the directors or of a committee of directors, or by any person acting as a director, shall notwithstanding that it be afterwards discovered that there was some defect in the appointment of any such director or person acting as aforesaid, or that they or any of them were disqualified, be as valid as if every such person had been duly appointed and was qualified to be a director.

56. A resolution in writing, signed by all the directors for the time being entitled to receive notice of a meeting of the directors, shall be as valid and effectual as if it had been passed at a meeting of the directors duly convened and held.

Secretary

57. The secretary shall be appointed by the directors for such term, at such remuneration and upon such conditions as they may think fit; and any secretary so appointed may be removed by them.

58. A provision of the Act or these articles requiring or authorizing a thing to be done by or to a director and the secretary shall not be satisfied by its being done by or to the same person acting both as director and as, or in place of, the secretary.

Extracts from The Companies Act, 1948

The bulk of the consolidated code of statute law concerning companies is contained in the Companies Act, 1948. The following are the Sections of greatest importance to those concerned with company meetings.

Meetings and Proceedings

130.—(1) Every company limited by shares and every company limited by guarantee and having a share capital shall, within a period of not less than one month nor more than three months from the date at which the company is entitled to commence business, hold a general meeting of the members of the company, which shall be called 'the statutory meeting'.

(2) The directors shall, at least fourteen days before the day on which the meeting is held, forward a report (in this Act referred to as 'the statutory report') to every member of the company.

Provided that if the statutory report is forwarded later than is required by this subsection, it shall, notwithstanding that fact, be deemed to have been duly forwarded if it is so agreed by all the members entitled to attend and vote at the meeting.

(3) The statutory report shall be certified by not less than two directors of the company and shall state—

    (a) the total number of shares allotted, distinguishing shares allotted as fully or partly paid up otherwise than in cash, and stating in the case of shares partly paid up the extent to which they are so paid up, and in either case the consideration for which they have been allotted;

    (b) the total amount of cash received by the company in respect of all the shares allotted, distinguished as aforesaid;

    (c) an abstract of the receipts of the company and of the payments made thereout, up to a date within seven days of the date of the report, exhibiting under distinctive headings the receipts of the company from shares and debentures and other sources, the payments made thereout, and particulars concerning the balance remaining in hand, and an account or estimate of the preliminary expenses of the company;

(*d*) the names, addresses and descriptions of the directors, auditors, if any, managers, if any, and secretary of the company; and

(*e*) the particulars of any contract the modification of which is to be submitted to the meeting for its approval, together with the particulars of the modification or proposed modification.

(4) The statutory report shall, so far as it relates to the shares allotted by the company, and to the cash received in respect of such shares, and to the receipts and payments of the company on capital account, be certified as correct by the auditors, if any, of the company.

(5) The directors shall cause a copy of the statutory report, certified as required by this section, to be delivered to the registrar of companies for registration forthwith after the sending thereof to the members of the company.

(6) The directors shall cause a list showing the names, descriptions and addresses of the members of the company, and the number of shares held by them respectively, to be produced at the commencement of the meeting and to remain open and accessible to any member of the company during the continuance of the meeting.

(7) The members of the company present at the meeting shall be at liberty to discuss any matter relating to the formation of the company, or arising out of the statutory report, whether previous notice has been given or not, but no resolution of which notice has not been given in accordance with the articles may be passed.

(8) The meeting may adjourn from time to time, and at any adjourned meeting any resolution of which notice has been given in accordance with the articles, either before or subsequently to the former meeting, may be passed, and the adjourned meeting shall have the same powers as an original meeting.

(9) In the event of any default in complying with the provisions of this section, every director of the company who is knowingly and wilfully guilty of the default or, in the case of default by the company, every officer of the company who is in default shall be liable to a fine not exceeding fifty pounds.

(10) This section shall not apply to a private company.

131.—(1) Every company shall in each year hold a general meeting as its annual general meeting in addition to any other meetings in that year, and shall specify the meeting as such in the notices calling it; and not more than fifteen months shall elapse between the date of one annual general meeting of a company and that of the next:

Provided that, so long as a company holds its first annual general meeting within eighteen months of its incorporation, it need not hold it in the year of its incorporation or in the following year.

(2) If default is made in holding a meeting of the company in accordance with the foregoing subsection, the Board of Trade may, on the application of any member of the company, call, or direct the calling of, a general meeting of the company and give such ancillary or consequential directions as the Board think expedient, including directions modifying or supplementing, in relation to the calling, holding and conducting of the meeting, the operation of the company's articles; and it is hereby declared that the directions that may be given under this subsection include a direction that one member of the company present in person or by proxy shall be deemed to constitute a meeting.

(3) A general meeting held in pursuance of the last foregoing subsection shall, subject to any directions of the Board of Trade, be deemed to be an annual general meeting of the company; but, where a meeting so held is not held in the year in which the default in holding the company's annual general meeting occurred, the meeting so held shall not be treated as the annual general meeting for the year in which it is held unless at that meeting the company resolves that it shall be so treated.

(4) Where a company resolves that a meeting shall be so treated, a copy of the resolution shall, within fifteen days after the passing thereof, be forwarded to the registrar of companies and recorded by him.

(5) If default is made in holding a meeting of the company in accordance with subsection (1) of this section, or in complying with any directions of the Board of Trade under subsection (2) thereof, the company and every officer of the company who is in default shall be liable to a fine not exceeding fifty pounds, and if default is made in complying with subsection (4) of this section, the company and every officer of the company who is in default shall be liable to a default fine of two pounds.

132.—(1) The directors of a company, notwithstanding anything in its articles, shall, on the requisition of members of the company holding at the date of the deposit of the requisition not less than one-tenth of such of the paid-up capital of the company as at the date of the deposit carries the right of voting at general meetings of the company, or, in the case of a company not having a share capital, members of the company representing not less than one-tenth of the total voting rights of all the members having at the said date a right to vote at general meetings of the company, forthwith proceed duly to convene an extraordinary general meeting of the company.

(2) The requisition must state the objects of the meeting, and must be signed by the requisitionists and deposited at the registered office of the

company, and may consist of several documents in like form each signed by one or more requisitionists.

(3) If the directors do not within twenty-one days from the date of the deposit of the requisition proceed duly to convene a meeting, the requisitionists, or any of them representing more than one half of the total voting rights of all of them, may themselves convene a meeting, but any meeting so convened shall not be held after the expiration of three months from the said date.

(4) A meeting convened under this section by the requisitionists shall be convened in the same manner, as nearly as possible, as that in which meetings are to be convened by directors.

(5) Any reasonable expenses incurred by the requisitionists by reason of the failure of the directors duly to convene a meeting shall be repaid to the requisitionists by the company, and any sum so repaid shall be retained by the company out of any sums due or to become due from the company by way of fees or other remuneration in respect of their services to such of the directors as were in default.

(6) For the purposes of this section the directors shall, in the case of a meeting at which a resolution is to be proposed as a special resolution, be deemed not to have duly convened the meeting if they do not give such notice thereof as is required by section 141 of this Act.

133.—(1) Any provision of a company's articles shall be void in so far as it provides for the calling of a meeting of the company (other than an adjourned meeting) by a shorter notice than—

    (a) in the case of the annual general meeting, twenty-one days' notice in writing; and

    (b) in the case of a meeting other than an annual general meeting or a meeting for the passing of a special resolution, fourteen days' notice in writing in the case of a company other than an unlimited company and seven days' notice in writing in the case of an unlimited company.

(2) Save in so far as the articles of a company make other provision in that behalf (not being a provision avoided by the foregoing subsection) a meeting of the company (other than an adjourned meeting) may be called—

    (a) in the case of the annual general meeting, by twenty-one days' notice in writing; and

    (b) in the case of a meeting other than an annual general meeting or a meeting for the passing of a special resolution, by fourteen days' notice in writing in the case of a company other than an unlimited company and by seven days' notice in writing in the case of an unlimited company.

(3) A meeting of a company shall, notwithstanding that it is called by shorter notice than that specified in the last foregoing subsection or in the company's articles, as the case may be, be deemed to have been duly called if it is so agreed—

    (*a*) in the case of a meeting called as the annual general meeting, by all the members entitled to attend and vote thereat; and

    (*b*) in the case of any other meeting, by a majority in number of the members having a right to attend and vote at the meeting, being a majority together holding not less than ninety-five per cent. in nominal value of the shares giving a right to attend and vote at the meeting, or, in the case of a company not having a share capital, together representing not less than ninety-five per cent. of the total voting rights at that meeting of all the members.

134. The following provisions shall have effect in so far as the articles of the company do not make other provision in that behalf:—

    (*a*) notice of the meeting of a company shall be served on every member of the company in the manner in which notices are required to be served by Table A, and for the purpose of this paragraph the expression 'Table A' means that Table as for the time being in force;

    (*b*) two or more members holding not less than one-tenth of the issued share capital or, if the company has not a share capital, not less than five per cent. in number of the members of the company may call a meeting;

    (*c*) in the case of a private company two members, and in the case of any other company three members, personally present shall be a quorum;

    (*d*) any member elected by the members present at a meeting may be chairman thereof;

    (*e*) in the case of a company originally having a share capital, every member shall have one vote in respect of each share or each ten pounds of stock held by him, and in any other case every member shall have one vote.

135.—(1) If for any reason it is impracticable to call a meeting of a company in any manner in which meetings of that company may be called, or to conduct the meeting of the company in manner prescribed by the articles or this Act, the court may, either of its own motion or on the application of any director of the company or of any member of the company who would be entitled to vote at the meeting, order a meeting of the company to be called, held and conducted in such manner as the court thinks fit, and where any such order is made may give such ancillary or consequential directions as it thinks expedient; and it is hereby declared that the directions that may be given under this subsection include a direction that one member of the company present in person or by proxy shall be deemed to constitute a meeting.

(2) Any meeting called, held and conducted in accordance with an order under the foregoing subsection shall for all purposes be deemed to be a meeting of the company duly called, held and conducted.

136.—(1) Any member of a company entitled to attend and vote at a meeting of the company shall be entitled to appoint another person (whether a member or not) as his proxy to attend and vote instead of him, and a proxy appointed to attend and vote instead of a member of a private company shall also have the same right as the member to speak at the meeting:

Provided that, unless the articles otherwise provide,—

    (*a*) this subsection shall not apply in the case of a company not having a share capital; and

    (*b*) a member of a private company shall not be entitled to appoint more than one proxy to attend on the same occasion; and

    (*c*) a proxy shall not be entitled to vote except on a poll.

(2) In every notice calling a meeting of a company having a share capital there shall appear with reasonable prominence a statement that a member entitled to attend and vote is entitled to appoint a proxy or, where that is allowed, one or more proxies to attend and vote instead of him, and that a proxy need not also be a member; and if default is made in complying with this subsection as respects any meeting, every officer of the company who is in default shall be liable to a fine not exceeding fifty pounds.

(3) Any provision contained in a company's articles shall be void in so far as it would have the effect of requiring the instrument appointing a proxy, or any other document necessary to show the validity of or otherwise relating to the appointment of a proxy, to be received by the company or any other person more than forty-eight hours before a meeting or adjourned meeting in order that the appointment may be effective thereat.

(4) If for the purpose of any meeting of a company invitations to appoint as proxy a person or one of a number of persons specified in the invitations are issued at the company's expense to some only of the members entitled to be sent a notice of the meeting and to vote thereat by proxy, every officer of the company who knowingly and wilfully authorizes or permits their issue as aforesaid shall be liable to a fine not exceeding one hundred pounds:

Provided that an officer shall not be liable under this subsection by reason only of the issue to a member at his request in writing of a form of appointment naming the proxy or of a list of persons willing to act as proxy if the form or list is available on request in writing to every member entitled to vote at the meeting by proxy.

(5) This section shall apply to meetings of any class of members of a company as it applies to general meetings of the company.

137.—(1) Any provision contained in a company's articles shall be void in so far as it would have the effect either—

> (a) of excluding the right to demand a poll at a general meeting on any question other than the election of the chairman of the meeting or the adjournment of the meeting; or
>
> (b) of making ineffective a demand for a poll on any such question which is made either—
>
>> (i) by not less than five members having the right to vote at the meeting; or
>>
>> (ii) by a member or members representing not less than one tenth of the total voting rights of all the members having the right to vote at the meeting; or
>>
>> (iii) by a member or members holding shares in the company conferring a right to vote at the meeting, being shares on which an aggregate sum has been paid up equal to not less than one tenth of the total sum paid up on all the shares conferring that right.

(2) The instrument appointing a proxy to vote at a meeting of a company shall be deemed also to confer authority to demand or join in demanding a poll, and for the purposes of the foregoing subsection a demand by a person as proxy for a member shall be the same as a demand by the member.

138. On a poll taken at a meeting of a company or a meeting of any class of members of a company, a member entitled to more than one vote need not, if he votes, use all his votes or cast all the votes he uses in the same way.

139.—(1) A corporation, whether a company within the meaning of this Act or not, may—

> (a) if it is a member of another corporation, being a company within the meaning of this Act, by resolution of its directors or other governing body authorize such person as it thinks fit to act as its representative at any meeting of the company or at any meeting of any class of members of the company.
>
> (b) if it is a creditor (including a holder of debentures) of another corporation, being a company within the meaning of this Act, by resolution of its directors or other governing body authorize such person as it thinks fit to act as its representative at any meeting of any creditors of the company held in pursuance of this Act or of

any rules made thereunder, or in pursuance of the provisions contained in any debenture or trust deed, as the case may be.

(2) A person authorized as aforesaid shall be entitled to exercise the same powers on behalf of the corporation which he represents as that corporation could exercise if it were an individual shareholder, creditor or holder of debentures of that other company.

140.—(1) Subject to the following provisions of this section it shall be the duty of a company, on the requisition in writing of such number of members as is hereinafter specified and (unless the company otherwise resolves) at the expense of the requisitionists,—

    (a) to give to members of the company entitled to receive notice of the next annual general meeting notice of any resolution which may properly be moved and is intended to be moved at that meeting;

    (b) to circulate to members entitled to have notice of any general meeting sent to them any statement of not more than one thousand words with respect to the matter referred to in any proposed resolution or the business to be dealt with at that meeting.

(2) The number of members necessary for a requisition under the foregoing subsection shall be—

    (a) any number of members representing not less than one twentieth of the total voting rights of all the members having at the date of the requisition a right to vote at the meeting to which the requisition relates; or

    (b) not less than one hundred members holding shares in the company on which there has been paid up an average sum, per member, of not less than one hundred pounds.

(3) Notice of any such resolution shall be given, and any such statement shall be circulated, to members of the company entitled to have notice of the meeting sent to them by serving a copy of the resolution or statement on each such member in any manner permitted for service of notice of the meeting, and notice of any such resolution shall be given to any other member of the company by giving notice of the general effect of the resolution in any manner permitted for giving him notice of meetings of the company:

Provided that the copy shall be served, or notice of the effect of the resolution shall be given, as the case may be, in the same manner and, so far as practicable, at the same time as notice of the meeting and, where it is not practicable for it to be served or given at that time, it shall be served or given as soon as practicable thereafter.

(4) A company shall not be bound under this section to give notice of any resolution or to circulate any statement unless—

(*a*) a copy of the requisition signed by the requisitionists (or two or more copies which between them contain the signatures of all the requisitionists) is deposited at the registered office of the company—

    (i) in the case of a requisition requiring notice of a resolution, not less than six weeks before the meeting; and

    (ii) in the case of any other requisition, not less than one week before the meeting; and

(*b*) there is deposited or tendered with the requisition a sum reasonably sufficient to meet the company's expenses in giving effect thereto:

Provided that if, after a copy of a requisition requiring notice of a resolution has been deposited at the registered office of the company, an annual general meeting is called for a date six weeks or less after the copy has been deposited, the copy though not deposited within the time required by this subsection shall be deemed to have been properly deposited for the purposes thereof.

(5) The company shall also not be bound under this section to circulate any statement if, on the application either of the company or of any other person who claims to be aggrieved, the court is satisfied that the rights conferred by this section are being abused to secure needless publicity for defamatory matter; and the court may order the company's costs on an application under this section to be paid in whole or in part by the requisitionists, notwithstanding that they are not parties to the application.

(6) Notwithstanding anything in the company's articles, the business which may be dealt with at an annual general meeting shall include any resolution of which notice is given in accordance with this section, and for the purposes of this subsection notice shall be deemed to have been given notwithstanding the accidental omission, in giving it, of one or more members.

(7) In the event of any default in complying with the provisions of this section, every officer of the company who is in default shall be liable to a fine not exceeding five hundred pounds.

141.—(1) A resolution shall be an extraordinary resolution when it has been passed by a majority of not less than three fourths of such members as, being entitled so to do, vote in person or, where proxies are allowed, by proxy, at a general meeting of which notice specifying the intention to propose the resolution as an extraordinary resolution has been duly given.

(2) A resolution shall be a special resolution when it has been passed by such a majority as is required for the passing of an extraordinary resolution and at a general meeting of which not less than twenty-one

days' notice, specifying the intention to propose the resolution as a special resolution, has been duly given:

Provided that, if it is so agreed by a majority in number of the members having the right to attend and vote at any such meeting, being a majority together holding not less than ninety-five per cent. in nominal value of the shares giving that right, or, in the case of a company not having a share capital, together representing not less than ninety-five per cent. of the total voting rights at that meeting of all the members, a resolution may be proposed and passed as a special resolution at a meeting of which less than twenty-one days' notice has been given.

(3) At any meeting at which an extraordinary resolution or a special resolution is submitted to be passed, a declaration of the chairman that the resolution is carried shall, unless a poll is demanded, be conclusive evidence of the fact without proof of the number or proportion of the votes recorded in favour of or against the resolution.

(4) In computing the majority on a poll demanded on the question that an extraordinary resolution or a special resolution be passed, reference shall be had to the number of votes cast for and against the resolution.

(5) For the purposes of this section, notice of a meeting shall be deemed to be duly given and the meeting to be duly held when the notice is given and the meeting held in manner provided by this Act or the articles.

142. Where by any provision hereafter contained in this Act special notice is required of a resolution, the resolution shall not be effective unless notice of the intention to move it has been given to the company not less than twenty-eight days before the meeting at which it is moved, and the company shall give its members notice of any such resolution at the same time and in the same manner as it gives notice of the meeting or, if that is not practicable, shall give them notice thereof, either by advertisement in a newspaper having an appropriate circulation or in any other mode allowed by the articles, not less than twenty-one days before the meeting:

Provided that if, after notice of the intention to move such a resolution has been given to the company, a meeting is called for a date twenty-eight days or less after the notice has been given, the notice though not given within the time required by this subsection shall be deemed to have been properly given for the purposes thereof.

143.—(1) A printed copy of every resolution or agreement to which this section applies shall, within fifteen days after the passing or making thereof, be forwarded to the registrar of companies and recorded by him:

(2) Where articles have been registered, a copy of every such resolution or agreement for the time being in force shall be embodied in or annexed

to every copy of the articles issued after the passing of the resolution or the making of the agreement.

(3) Where articles have not been registered, a printed copy of every such resolution or agreement shall be forwarded to any member at his request on payment of one shilling or such less sum as the company may direct.

(4) This section shall apply to—

(a) special resolutions;

(b) extraordinary resolutions;

(c) resolutions which have been agreed to by all the members of a company, but which, if not so agreed to, would not have been effective for their purpose unless, as the case may be, they had been passed as special resolutions or as extraordinary resolutions;

(d) resolutions or agreements which have been agreed to by all the members of some class of shareholders but which, if not so agreed to, would not have been effective for their purpose unless they had been passed by some particular majority or otherwise in some particular manner, and all resolutions or agreements which effectively bind all the members of any class of shareholders though not agreed to by all those members;

(e) resolutions requiring a company to be wound up voluntarily, passed under paragraph (a) of subsection (1) of section 278 of this Act.

(5) If a company fails to comply with subsection (1) of this section, the company and every officer of the company who is in default shall be liable to a default fine of two pounds.

(6) If a company fails to comply with subsection (2) or subsection (3) of this section, the company and every officer of the company who is in default shall be liable to a fine not exceeding one pound for each copy in respect of which default is made.

(7) For the purposes of the two last foregoing subsections, a liquidator of the company shall be deemed to be an officer of the company.

144. Where a resolution is passed at an adjourned meeting of—

(a) a company;

(b) the holders of any class of shares in a company;

(c) the directors of a company;

the resolution shall for all purposes be treated as having been passed on the date on which it was in fact passed, and shall not be deemed to have been passed on any earlier date.

145.—(1) Every company shall cause minutes of all proceedings of general meetings, all proceedings at meetings of its directors and, where there are managers, all proceedings at meetings of its managers to be entered in books kept for that purpose.

(2) Any such minute if purporting to be signed by the chairman of the meeting at which the proceedings were had, or by the chairman of the next succeeding meeting, shall be evidence of the proceedings.

(3) Where minutes have been made in accordance with the provisions of this section of the proceedings at any general meeting of the company or meeting of directors or managers, then, until the contrary is proved, the meeting shall be deemed to have been duly held and convened, and all proceedings had thereat to have been duly had, and all appointments of directors, managers or liquidators shall be deemed to be valid.

(4) If a company fails to comply with subsection (1) of this section, the company and every officer of the company who is in default shall be liable to a default fine.

146.—(1) The books containing the minutes of proceedings of any general meeting of a company held on or after the first day of November, nineteen hundred and twenty-nine, shall be kept at the registered office of the company, and shall during business hours (subject to such reasonable restrictions as the company may by its articles or in general meeting impose, so that not less than two hours in each day be allowed for inspection) be open to the inspection of any member without charge.

(2) Any member shall be entitled to be furnished within seven days after he has made a request in that behalf to the company with a copy of any such minutes as aforesaid at a charge not exceeding sixpence for every hundred words.

(3) If any inspection required under this section is refused or if any copy required under this section is not sent within the proper time, the company and every officer of the company who is in default shall be liable in respect of each offence to a fine not exceeding two pounds and further to a default fine of two pounds.

(4) In the case of any such refusal or default, the court may by order compel an immediate inspection of the books in respect of all proceedings of general meetings or direct that the copies required shall be sent to the persons requiring them.

Committees of Inspection

252.—(1) When a winding-up order has been made by the court in England, it shall be the business of the separate meetings of creditors and contributories summoned for the purpose of determining whether or not an application should be made to the court for appointing a liquidator in place of the official receiver, to determine further whether or not an application is to be made to the court for the appointment of a committee of inspection to act with the liquidator and who are to be members of the committee if appointed.

(2) When a winding-up order has been made by the court in Scotland, the liquidator shall summon separate meetings of the creditors and contributories of the company for the purpose of determining whether or not an application is to be made to the court for the appointment of a committee of inspection to act with the liquidator and who are to be the members of the committee if appointed:

Provided that, where the winding-up order has been made on the ground that the company is unable to pay its debts, it shall not be necessary for the liquidator to summon a meeting of the contributories.

(3) The court may make any appointment and order required to give effect to any such determination, and if there is a difference between the determinations of the meetings of the creditors and contributories in respect of the matters aforesaid the court shall decide the difference and make such order thereon as the court may think fit.

253.—(1) A committee of inspection appointed in pursuance of this Act shall consist of creditors and contributories of the company or persons holding general powers of attorney from creditors or contributories in such proportions as may be agreed on by the meetings of creditors and contributories or as, in case of difference, may be determined by the court:

Provided that, where in Scotland a winding-up order has been made on the ground that a company is unable to pay its debts, the committee shall consist of creditors or persons holding general powers of attorney from creditors.

(2) The committee shall meet at such times as they from time to time appoint, and, failing such appointment, at least once a month, and the liquidator or any member of the committee may also call a meeting of the committee as and when he thinks necessary.

(3) The committee may act by a majority of their members present at a meeting but shall not act unless a majority of the committee are present.

(4) A member of the committee may resign by notice in writing signed by him and delivered to the liquidator.

(5) If a member of the committee becomes bankrupt or compounds or arranges with his creditors or is absent from five consecutive meetings of the committee without the leave of those members who together with himself represent the creditors or contributories, as the case may be, his office shall thereupon become vacant.

(6) A member of the committee may be removed by an ordinary resolution at a meeting of creditors, if he represents creditors, or of contributories, if he represents contributories, of which seven days' notice has been given, stating the object of the meeting.

(7) On a vacancy occurring in the committee the liquidator shall forth-with summon a meeting of creditors or of contributories, as the case may require, to fill the vacancy, and the meeting may, by resolution, reappoint the same or appoint another creditor or contributory to fill the vacancy:

Provided that if the liquidator, having regard to the position in the winding up, is of the opinion that it is unnecessary for the vacancy to be filled he may apply to the court and the court may make an order that the vacancy shall not be filled, or shall not be filled except in such circumstances as may be specified in the order.

(8) The continuing members of the committee, if not less than two, may act notwithstanding any vacancy in the committee.

254. Where in the case of a winding up in England there is no committee of inspection, the Board of Trade may, on the application of the liquidator, do any act or thing or give any direction or permission which is by this Act authorized or required to be done or given by the committee.

Extracts from
The Companies Act, 1967

The 1967 Companies Act considerably increased the information which must be laid before a company in general meeting. It did so primarily by abolishing the status of an 'exempt private company'—that is, a private company exempt from providing similar information to that required of a public company. But the main provisions as to what must be laid before a company meeting are contained in the following Sections.

Accounts

3.—(1) Subject to the provisions of this section, where, at the end of its financial year, a company has subsidiaries, there shall, in the case of each subsidiary, be stated in, or in a note on, or statement annexed to, the company's accounts laid before it in general meeting—

(a) the subsidiary's name;

(b) if it be incorporated in Great Britain and if it be registered in England and the company be registered in Scotland (or vice versa), the country in which it is registered, and if it be incorporated outside Great Britain, the country in which it is incorporated; and

(c) in relation to shares of each class of the subsidiary held by the company, the identity of the class and the proportion of the nominal value of the issued shares of that class represented by the shares held.

(2) For the purposes of the foregoing subsection, shares of a body corporate shall be treated as being held, or as not being held, by another such body if they would, be virtue of section 154(3) of the principal Act, be treated as being held or, as the case may be, as not being held by that other body for the purpose of determining whether the first-mentioned body is its subsidiary; and the particulars required by the foregoing

subsection shall include with reference to the proportion of the nominal value of the issued shares of a class represented by shares held by a company, a statement of the extent (if any) to which it consists in shares held by, or by a nominee for, a subsidiary of the company and the extent (if any) to which it consists in shares held by, or by a nominee for, the company itself.

(3) Subsection (1) of this section shall not require the disclosure of information with respect to a body corporate which is the subsidiary of another and is incorporated outside the United Kingdom or, being incorporated in the United Kingdom, carries on business outside the United Kingdom if the disclosure would, in the opinion of the directors of that other, be harmful to the business of that other or of any of its subsidiaries and the Board of Trade agree that the information need not be disclosed.

(4) If, in the opinion of the directors of a company having, at the end of its financial year, subsidiaries, the number of them is such that compliance with subsection (1) of this section would result in particulars of excessive length being given, compliance with that subsection shall not be requisite except in the case of the subsidiaries carrying on the businesses the results of the carrying on of which, in the opinion of the directors, principally affected the amount of the profit or loss of the company and its subsidiaries or the amount of the assets of the company and its subsidiaries.

(5) Where, in the case of a company, advantage is taken of the last foregoing subsection,—

(a) there must be included in the statement required by this section the information that it deals only with the subsidiaries carrying on such businesses as are referred to in that subsection; and

(b) the particulars given in compliance with subsection (1) of this section, together with those which, but for the fact that advantage is so taken, would have to be given, shall be annexed to the annual return first made by the company after its accounts have been laid before it in general meeting.

(6) If a company fails to satisfy an obligation imposed on it by the last foregoing subsection to annex particulars to a return, the company and every officer who is in default shall be liable to a default fine.

4.—(1) Subject to the provisions of this section, if, at the end of its financial year, a company holds shares of any class comprised in the equity share capital of another body corporate (not being its subsidiary) exceeding in nominal value one tenth of the nominal value of the issued shares of that class, there shall be stated in, or in a note on, or statement annexed to, the accounts of the company laid before it in general meeting—

(*a*) the name of that other body corporate and—

    (i) if it be incorporated in Great Britain and if it be registered in England and the company be registered in Scotland (or vice-versa), the country in which it is registered; and

    (ii) if it be incorporated outside Great Britain, the country in which it is incorporated;

(*b*) the identity of the class and the proportion of the nominal value of the issued shares of that class represented by the shares held; and

(*c*) if the company also holds shares in that other body corporate of another class (whether or not comprised in its equity share capital), or of other classes (whether or not so comprised), the like particulars as respects that other class or, as the case may be, each of those other classes.

(2) If, at the end of its financial year, a company holds shares in another body corporate (not being its subsidiary) and the amount of all the shares therein which it holds (as stated or included in its accounts laid before it in general meeting) exceeds one tenth of the amount of its assets (as so stated), there shall be stated in, or in a note on, or statement annexed to, those accounts—

(*a*) the name of that other body corporate and—

    (i) if it be incorporated in Great Britain and if it be registered in England and the company be registered in Scotland (or vice versa), the country in which it is registered; and

    (ii) if it be incorporated outside Great Britain, the country in which it is incorporated; and

(*b*) in relation to shares in that other body corporate of each class held, the identity of the class and the proportion of the nominal value of the issued shares of that class represented by the shares held.

(3) Neither of the foregoing subsections shall require the disclosure by a company of information with respect to another body corporate if that other body is incorporated outside the United Kingdom or, being incorporated in the United Kingdom, carries on business outside the United Kingdom if the disclosure would, in the opinion of the directors of the company, be harmful to the business of the company or of that other body and the Board of Trade agree that the information need not be disclosed.

(4) If, at the end of its financial year a company falls within subsection (1) of this section in relation to more bodies corporate than one, and the number of them is such that, in the opinion of the directors, compliance with that subsection would result in particulars of excessive length being given, compliance with that subsection shall not be requisite except in the case of the bodies carrying on the businesses the results of the carrying on of which, in the opinion of the directors, principally affected

the amount of the profit or loss of the company or the amount of its assets.

(5) Where, in the case of a company, advantage is taken of the last foregoing subsection,—

> (a) there must be included in the statement dealing with the bodies last mentioned in that subsection the information that it deals only with them; and
>
> (b) the particulars given in compliance with subsection (1) of this section, together with those which, but for the fact that advantage is so taken, would have to be so given, shall be annexed to the annual return first made by the company after its accounts have been laid before it in general meeting.

(6) If a company fails to satisfy an obligation imposed on it by the last foregoing subsection to annex particulars to a return, the company and every officer of the company who is in default shall be liable to a default fine.

(7) For the purposes of this section, shares of a body corporate shall be treated as being held, or as not being held, by another such body if they would, by virtue of section 154(3) of the principal Act (but on the assumption that paragraph (b)(ii) had been omitted therefrom), be treated as being held or, as the case may be, as not being held by that other body for the purpose of determining whether the first-mentioned body is its subsidiary.

(8) In this section 'equity capital' has the meaning assigned to it by section 154(5) of the principal Act.

5.—(1) Subject to the following subsection, where, at the end of its financial year, a company is the subsidiary of another body corporate, there shall be stated in, or in a note on, or statement annexed to, the company's accounts laid before it in general meeting the name of the body corporate regarded by the directors as being the company's ultimate holding company and, if known to them, the country in which it is incorporated.

(2) The foregoing subsection shall not require the disclosure by a company which carries on business outside the United Kingdom of information with respect to the body corporate regarded by the directors as being its ultimate holding company if the disclosure would, in their opinion, be harmful to the business of that holding company or of the first-mentioned company or any other of that holding company's subsidiaries and the Board of Trade agree that the information need not be disclosed.

6.—(1) In any accounts of a company laid before it in general meeting, or in a statement annexed thereto, there shall, so far as the information is contained in the company's books and papers or the company has the right to obtain it from the persons concerned,—

(*a*) if one person has been chairman throughout the financial year, be shown his emoluments (unless his duties as chairman were wholly or mainly discharged outside the United Kingdom), and if not, be shown with respect to each person who has been chairman during the year, his emoluments so far as attributable to the period during which he was chairman (unless his duties as chairman were wholly or mainly so discharged);

(*b*) with respect to all the directors (other than any who discharged their duties as such wholly or mainly outside the United Kingdom), be shown the number (if any) who had no emoluments or whose several emoluments amounted to not more than £2,500 and, by reference to each pair of adjacent points on a scale whereon the lowest point is £2,500 and the succeeding ones are successive integral multiples of £2,500, the number (if any) whose several emoluments exceed the lower point but did not exceed the higher.

(2) If, of the directors of a company (other than any who discharged their duties as such wholly or mainly outside the United Kingdom), the emoluments of one only (so far as ascertainable from information contained in the company's books and papers or obtainable by right by the company from him) exceed the relevant amount, his emoluments (so far as so ascertainable) shall also be shown in the said accounts or in a statement annexed thereto; and if, of the directors of a company (other than any who discharged their duties as such wholly or mainly outside the United Kingdom), the emoluments (so far as so ascertainable) of each of two or more exceed the relevant amount, the emoluments (so far as so ascertainable) of him (or them, in the case of equality) who had the greater or, as the case may be, the greatest shall also be shown in the said accounts or in a statement annexed thereto.

(3) For the purposes of this section there shall be brought into account as emoluments of any person all such amounts (other than contributions paid in respect of him under any pension scheme) as in his case are, by virtue of section 196 of the principal Act (disclosure of aggregates of directors' salaries, pensions, &c.), required to be included in the amount shown under subsection (1)(*a*) of that section.

(4) If, in the case of any accounts, the requirements of this section are not complied with, it shall be the duty of the auditors of the company by whom the accounts are examined to include in their report thereon, so far as they are reasonably able to do so, a statement giving the required particulars.

(5) In section 198 of the principal Act (general duty to make disclosure for the purposes of section 195 to 197). the reference in subsection (1) to sections 195 and 196 of that Act and the reference in subsection (3) to the said section 196 shall each be construed as including a reference to this section.

(6) A company which is neither a holding company nor a subsidiary of another body corporate shall not be subject to the requirements of this section as respects a financial year in the case of which the amount shown in its accounts under section 196(1)(a) of the principal Act does not exceed £7,500.

(7) In this section—

    (a) 'chairman', in relation to a company, means the person elected by the directors of the company to be chairman of their meetings and includes a person who, though not so elected, holds any office (however designated) which, in accordance with the constitution of the company, carries with it functions substantially similar to those discharged by a person so elected; and

    (b) 'the relevant amount'—

        (i) if one person has been chairman throughout the year, means the amount of his emoluments;

        (ii) if not, means an amount equal to the aggregate of the emoluments, so far as attributable to the period during which he was chairman, of each person who has been chairman during the year.

7.—(1) In any accounts of a company laid before it in general meeting, or in a statement annexed thereto, there shall be shown, so far as the information is contained in the company's books and papers or the company has the right to obtain it from the persons concerned,—

    (a) the number of directors who have waived rights to receive emoluments which, but for the waiver, would have fallen to be included in the amount shown in those accounts under section 196(1)(a) of the principal Act;

    (b) the aggregate amount of the said emoluments.

(2) For the purposes of this section—

    (a) it shall be assumed that a sum not receivable in respect of a period would have been paid at the time at which it was due to be paid;

    (b) a sum not so receivable that was payable only on demand, being a sum the right to receive which has been waived, shall be deemed to have been due for payment at the time of the waiver.

(3) Subsections (4), (5) and (6) of the last foregoing section shall, with the substitution, for references to that section, of references to this section, apply for the purposes of this section as they apply for the purposes of that section.

8.—(1) In any accounts of a company laid before it in general meeting, or in a statement annexed thereto, there shall be shown by reference to each pair of adjacent points on a scale whereon the lowest point is £10,000 and the succeeding ones are successive integral multiples of £2,500 beginning with that in the case of which the multiplier is five, the number (if any) of persons in the company's employment whose several emoluments exceeded the lower point but did not exceed the higher, other than,—

(a) directors of the company; and

(b) persons, other than directors of the company, being persons who,—

(i) if employed by the company throughout the financial year to which the accounts relate, worked wholly or mainly during that year outside the United Kingdom; or

(ii) if employed by the company for part only of that year, worked wholly or mainly during that part outside the United Kingdom.

(2) For the purposes of this section, a person's emoluments shall include any paid to or receivable by him from the company, the company's subsidiaries and any other person in respect of his services as a person in the employment of the company or a subsidiary thereof or as a director of a subsidiary thereof (except sums to be accounted for to the company or any of its subsidiaries) and 'emoluments', in relation to a person, includes fees and percentages, any sums paid by way of expenses allowance in so far as those sums are charged to United Kingdom income tax, and the estimated money value of any other benefits received by him otherwise than in cash.

(3) The amounts to be brought into account for the purpose of complying with subsection (1) above as respects a financial year shall be the sums receivable in respect of that year, whenever paid, or, in the case of sums not receivable in respect of a period, the sums paid during that year, so, however, that where—

(a) any sums are not brought into account for the relevant financial year on the ground that the person receiving them is liable to account therefor as mentioned in the last foregoing subsection, but the liability is wholly or partly released or is not enforced within a period of two years; or

(b) any sums paid to a person by way of expenses allowance are charged to United Kingdom income tax after the end of the relevant financial year;

those sums shall, to the extent to which the liability is released or not enforced or they are charged as aforesaid, as the case may be, be brought into account for the purpose of complying with subsection (1) above on the first occasion in which it is practicable to do so.

(4) If, in the case of any accounts, the requirements of this section are not complied with, it shall be the duty of the auditors of the company by whom the accounts are examined to include in their report thereon, so far

as they are reasonably able to do so, a statement giving the required particulars.

(5) References in subsection (2) above to a company's subsidiary—

(*a*) in relation to a person who is or was, while employed by the company a director, by virtue of the company's nomination, direct or indirect, of any other body corporate, shall, subject to the following paragraph, include that body corporate, whether or not it is or was in fact the company's subsidiary; and

(*b*) shall be taken as referring to a subsidiary at the time the services were rendered.

9. Schedule 8 to the principal Act shall be amended in accordance with the provisions of Schedule 1 to this Act and shall, accordingly, have effect as set out in Schedule 2 to this Act.

Audit

14.—(1) The auditors of a company shall make a report to the members on the accounts examined by them, and on every balance sheet, every profit and loss account and all group accounts laid before the company in general meeting during their tenure of office.

(2) The auditors' report shall be read before the company in general meeting and shall be open to inspection by any member.

(3) The report shall—

(*a*) except in the case of a company that is entitled to avail itself, and has availed itself, of the benefit of any of the provisions of Part III of Schedule 8 to the principal Act, state whether in the auditors' opinion the company's balance sheet and profit and loss account and (if it is a holding company submitting group accounts) the group accounts have been properly prepared in accordance with the provisions of the principal Act and this Act and whether in their opinion a true and fair view is given—

(i) in the case of the balance sheet, of the state of the company's affairs as at the end of its financial year;

(ii) in the case of the profit and loss account (if it be not framed as a consolidated profit and loss account), of the company's profit or loss for its financial year;

(iii) in the case of group accounts submitted by a holding company, of the state of affairs and profit or loss of the company and its subsidiaries dealt with thereby, so far as concerns members of the company;

(*b*) in the said excepted case, state whether in the auditors' opinion the company's balance sheet and profit and loss account and (if it

is a holding company submitting group accounts) the group
accounts have been properly prepared in accordance with the
provisions of the principal Act and this Act.

(4) It shall be the duty of the auditors of a company, in preparing their
report under this section, to carry out such investigations as will enable
them to form an opinion as to the following matters, that is to say,—

    (*a*) whether proper books of account have been kept by the company
       and proper returns adequate for their audit have been received
       from branches not visited by them; and

    (*b*) whether the company's balance sheet and (unless it is framed as a
       consolidated profit and loss account) profit and loss account are
       in agreement with the books of account and returns;

and if the auditors are of opinion that proper books of account have not
been kept by the company or that proper returns adequate for their audit
have not been received from branches not visited by them, or if the
balance sheet and (unless it is framed as a consolidated profit and loss
account) profit and loss account are not in agreement with the books of
account and return, the auditors shall state that fact in their report.

(5) Every auditor of a company shall have a right of access at all times
to the books and accounts and vouchers of the company, and shall be
entitled to require from the officers of the company such information and
explanation as he thinks necessary for the performance of the duties of the
auditors.

(6) If the auditors fail to obtain all the information and explanations
which, to the best of their knowledge and belief, are necessary for the
purposes of their audit, they shall state that fact in their report.

(7) The auditors of a company shall be entitled to attend any general
meeting of the company and to receive all notices of, and other com-
munications relating to, any general meeting which any member of the
company is entitled to receive, and to be heard at any general meeting
which they attend on any part of the business of the meeting which
concerns them as auditors.

(8) The foregoing provisions of this section shall have effect in place of
section 162 of, and Schedule 9 to, the principal Act, and, accordingly,—

    (*a*) that section and that Schedule shall cease to have effect;

    (*b*) section 438 of the principal Act shall have effect as if the pro-
       visions of subsections (1) and (5) of this section were provisions
       of that Act specified in Schedule 15 thereto;

    (*c*) in regulation 130 of Table A and article 65 of Table C in Schedule
       to the principal Act, for references to sections 159 to 162 of that
       Act there shall be substituted references to sections 159 to 161 of
       that Act and this section; and

    (*d*) n paragraph 24(2) of Schedule 2 to the Betting, Gaming and
       Lotteries Act, 1963 (which applies the said Schedule 9 to auditors'

reports on accounts of certain pool promoters), for the reference
to the said Schedule 9 there shall be substituted a reference to
subsections (3), (4) and (6) of this section.

Directors' Report

15. In the nine next following sections, 'the directors' report' means the
report by the directors of a company which, by section 157(1) of the
principal Act, is required to be attached to every balance sheet of the
company laid before it in general meeting.

16.—(1) The directors' report shall state the names of the persons who, at
any time during the financial year, were directors of the company and the
principal activities of the company and of its subsidiaries in the course of
that year and any significant change in those activities in that year, and
shall also—

(a) if significant changes in the fixed assets of the company or of any
of its subsidiaries have occurred in that year, contain particulars
of the changes, and, if, in the case of such of those assets as
consist in interests in land, the market value thereof (as at the end
of that year) differs substantially from the amount at which they
are included in the balance sheet and the difference is, in the
opinion of the directors, of such significance as to require that the
attention of members of the company or of holders of debentures
thereof should be drawn thereto, indicate the difference with
such degree of precision as is practicable;

(b) if, in that year, the company has issued any shares, state the
reason for making the issue, the classes of shares issued and, as
respects each class of shares, the number issued and the consideration received by the company for the issue, and if, in that year, it
has issued any debentures, state the reason for making the issue,
the classes of debentures issued and, as respects each class of
debentures, the amounts issued and the consideration received
by the company for the issue;

(c) if, at the end of that year, there subsists a contract with the
company in which a director of the company has, or at any time
in that year had, in any way, whether directly or indirectly, an
interest, or there has, at any time in that year, subsisted a contract
with the company in which a director of the company had, at any
time in that year, in any way, whether directly or indirectly, an
interest (being, in either case, in the opinion of the directors, a
contract of significance in relation to the company's business and
in which the director's interest is or was material), contain—

(i) a statement of the fact of the contractor's subsisting or, as the case may be, having subsisted;

(ii) the names of the parties to the contract (other than the company);

(iii) the name of the director (if not a party to the contract);

(iv) an indication of the nature of the contract; and

(v) an indication of the nature of the director's interest in the contract;

(*d*) if, at the end of that year, there subsist arrangements to which the company is a party, being arrangements whose objects are, or one of whose objects is, to enable directors of the company to acquire benefits by means of the acquisition of shares in, or debentures of, the company or any other body corporate, or there have, at any time in that year, subsisted such arrangements as aforesaid to which the company was a party, contain a statement explaining the effect of the arrangements and giving the names of the persons who at any time in that year were directors of the company and held, or whose nominees held, shares or debentures acquired in pursuance of the arrangements;

(*e*) as respects each person who, at the end of that year, was a director of the company, state whether or not, according to the register kept by the company for the purposes of the following provisions of this Part of this Act relating to the obligation of a director of a company to notify it of interests of his in shares in, or debentures of, the company and of every other body corporate, being the company's subsidiary or holding company or a subsidiary of the company's holding company, he was, at the end of that year, interested in shares in, or debentures of, the company or any other such body corporate and, if he was, the number and amount of shares in, and debentures of, each body (specifying it) in which, according to that register, he was, at the beginning of that year (or, if he was not then a director, when he became a director), interested in shares in, or debentures of, the company or any other such body corporate and, if he was, the number and amount of shares in, and debentures of, each body (specifying it) in which, acording to that register, he was interested at the beginning of that year or, as the case may be, when he became a director;

(*f*) contain particulars of any matters (other than those required to be dealt with by the following provisions of this Part of this Act) so far as they are material for the appreciation of the state of the company's affairs by its members, being matters the disclosure of which will not, in the opinion of the directors, be harmful to the business of the company or of any of its subsidiaries.

(2) As respects a company entitled to the benefit of any provision con-

tained in Part III (exceptions for special classes of company) of Schedule 8 to the principal Act, the foregoing subsection shall have effect as if paragraph (*a*) were omitted.

(3) The references, in paragraph (*c*) of subsection (1) above, to a contract do not include references to a director's contract of service or to a contract between the company and another body corporate, being a contract in which a director of the company has or had an interest by virtue only of his being a director of that other body.

(4) An interest in shares or debentures which, under the provisions of this Part of this Act referred to in paragraph (*e*) of subsection (1) above, falls to be treated as being the interest of a director shall be so treated for the purposes of that paragraph, and the references in that paragraph to the time when a person became a director shall, in the case of a person who became a director on more than one occasion, be construed as referring to the time when he first became a director.

17.—(1) If, in the course of a financial year, a company (being one subject to the requirements of paragraph 13A of Schedule 8 to the principal Act but not being one that has subsidiaries at the end of that year and submits in respect of that year group accounts prepared as consolidated accounts) has carried on business of two or more classes (other than banking or discounting or a class prescribed for the purposes of sub-paragraph (2) of that paragraph) that, in the opinion of the directors, differ substantially from each other, there shall be contained in the director's report relating to that year a statement of—

(*a*) the proportions in which the turnover for that year (so far as stated in the accounts in respect of that year in pursuance of that Schedule) is divided amongst those classes (describing them); and

(*b*) as regards business of each class, the extent or approximate extent (expressed, in either case, in monetary terms) to which, in the opinion of the directors, the carrying on of business of that class contributed to, or restricted, the profit or loss of the company for that year before taxation.

(2) If—

(*a*) a company has subsidiaries at the end of its financial year and submits in respect of that year group accounts prepared as consolidated accounts; and

(*b*) the company and the subsidiaries dealt with by the accounts carried on between them in the course of the year business of two or more classes (other than banking or discounting or a class prescribed for the purposes of paragraph 13A(2) of Schedule 8 to the principal Act) that, in the opinion of the directors, differ substantially from each other;

there shall be contained in the directors' report relating to that year a statement of—

    (i) the proportions in which the turnover for that year (so far as stated in the accounts in respect of that year in pursuance of that Schedule) is divided amongst those classes (describing them); and

    (ii) as regards business of each class, the extent or approximate extent (expressed, in either case, in monetary terms) to which, in the opinion of the directors of the company, the carrying on of business of that class contributed to, or restricted, the profit or loss for that year (before taxation) of the company and the subsidiaries dealt with by the accounts.

(3) For the purposes of this section, classes of business which, in the opinion of the directors, do not differ substantially from each other shall be treated as one class.

18.—(1) If, at the end of a financial year, a company does not have subsidiaries, there shall be contained in the directors' report relating to that year a statement of—

    (a) the average number of persons employed by it in each week in that year; and

    (b) the aggregate remuneration paid or payable in respect of that year to the persons by reference to whom the number stated under the foregoing paragraph is ascertained.

(2) If, at the end of a financial year, a company has subsidiaries, there shall be contained in the directors' report relating to that year a statement of—

    (a) the average number of persons employed between them in each week in that year by the company and the subsidiaries; and

    (b) the aggregate remuneration paid or payable in respect of that year to the persons by reference to whom the number stated under the foregoing paragraph is ascertained.

(3) The number to be stated under subsection (1)(a) above shall be the quotient derived by dividing, by the number of weeks in the financial year, the number derived by ascertaining, in relation to each of those weeks, the number of persons who, under contracts of service, were employed in the week (whether throughout it or not) by the company and adding up the numbers ascertained, and the number to be stated under subsection (2)(a) above shall be the quotient derived by dividing, by the number of weeks in the financial year, the number derived by ascertaining, in relation to each of those weeks, the number of persons who, under contracts of service, were employed between them in the week (whether throughout it or not) by the company and its subsidiaries and adding up the numbers ascertained.

(4) The remuneration to be taken into account for the purposes of sub-sections (1)(*b*) and (2)(*b*) above is the gross remuneration paid or payable in respect of the financial year; and for this purpose 'remuneration' shall include bonuses (whether payable under contract or not).

(5) This section shall not apply to a company if the number that, but for this subsection, would fall to be stated under subsection (1)(*a*) or (2)(*a*) above is less than 100, nor shall it apply to a company that is a wholly owned subsidiary of a company incorporated in Great Britain.

(6) For the purposes of this section, no regard shall be had to a person who worked wholly or mainly outside the United Kingdom.

(7) In this section, 'wholly owned subsidiary' shall be construed in accordance with section 150(4) of the principal Act.

19.—(1) If a company (not being the wholly owned subsidiary of a company incorporated in Great Britain) has, in a financial year, given money for political purposes or charitable purposes or both, there shall (if it exceeded £50 in amount) be contained in the directors' report relating to that year, in the case of each of the purposes for which money has been given, a statement of the amount of money given therefor and, in the case of political purposes for which money has been given, the following particulars, so far as applicable, namely—

(*a*) the name of each person to whom money has been given for those purposes exceeding £50 in amount and the amount of money given;

(*b*) if money exceeding £50 in amount has been given by way of donation or subscription to a political party, the identity of the party and the amount of money given.

(2) The foregoing subsection shall not have effect in the case of a company which, at the end of a financial year, has subsidiaries which have, in that year, given money as mentioned in the foregoing subsection, but is not itself the wholly owned subsidiary of a company incorporated in Great Britain; but in such a case there shall (if the amount of money so given in that year by the company and the subsidiaries between them exceeds £50) be contained in the directors' report relating to that year, in the case of each of the purposes for which money has been given by the company and the subsidiaries between them, a statement of the amount of money given therefor and, in the case of political purposes for which money has been given, the like particulars, so far as applicable, as are required by the foregoing subsection.

(3) For the purposes of this section a company shall be treated as giving money for political purposes if, directly or indirectly,—

(*a*) it gives a donation or subscription to a political party of the United Kingdom or of any part thereof; or (*b*) it gives a donation or subscription to a person who, to its knowledge, is carrying on, or proposing to carry on, any activities which can, at the time at which the donation or subscription was given, reasonably be regarded as likely to affect public support for such a political party as aforesaid.

(4) For the purposes of this section, money given for charitable purposes to a person who, when it was given, was ordinarily resident outside the United Kingdom shall be left out of account.

(5) In this section, 'charitable purposes' means purposes which are exclusively charitable and 'wholly owned subsidiary' shall be construed in accordance with section 150(4) of the principal Act; and, as respects Scotland, 'charitable' shall be construed in the same way as if it were contained in the Income Tax Acts.

20.—(1) If, at the end of a financial year, a company subject to the requirements of paragraph 13A of Schedule 8 to the principal Act whose business consists in, or includes, the supplying of goods does not have subsidiaries, then, unless the turnover for that year (so far as stated in the accounts in respect of that year in pursuance of that paragraph) does not exceed £50,000, there shall be contained in the directors' report relating to that year—

(*a*) if, in that year, goods have been exported by the company from the United Kingdom, a statement of the value of the goods that have been so exported from the United Kingdom during that year;

(*b*) if, in that year, no goods have been so exported from the United Kingdom, a statement of that fact.

(2) If, at the end of a financial year, a company has subsidiaries, then, except in a case in which neither the business of the company nor that of any of the subsidiaries consists in, or includes, the supplying of goods, or a case in which the company submits in respect of that year group accounts prepared as consolidated accounts in respect of itself and all its subsidiaries and the turnover (so far as stated therein in pursuance of the said paragraph 13A) does not exceed £50,000, there shall be included in the directors' report relating to that year—

(*a*) unless, in the case of the company and of each of its subsidiaries, no goods have been exported by it in that year from the United Kingdom, a statement of the aggregate of the values of the goods which, in the case of the company and of each of the subsidiaries, have been exported by it in that year from the United Kingdom;

(*b*) if, in the case of the company and of each of its subsidiaries, no goods have been exported by it in that year from the United Kingdom, a statement of that fact.

(3) For the purposes of this section, goods exported by a company as the agent of another person shall be disregarded.

(4) The foregoing provisions of this section shall not require the disclosure of information in the directors' report of a company if the directors thereof satisfy the Board of Trade that it is in the national interest that the information should not be disclosed.

21. None of sections 16 to 20 (both inclusive) of this Act shall apply to a report attached to a balance sheet of a company laid before it in general meeting in respect of a financial year ending before that section comes into operation.

22. Where advantage is taken of the proviso to section 163 of the principal Act to show an item in the directors' report instead of in the accounts, the report shall also show the corresponding amount for (or, as the case may require, as at the end of) the immediately preceding financial year of that item, except where that amount would not have had to be shown had the item been shown in the accounts.

23. If any person being a director of a company fails to take all reasonable steps to secure compliance with section 157(1) of the principal Act and with the requirements of the foregoing provisions of this Part of this Act with respect to the directors' report, he shall, in respect of each offence, be liable on summary conviction to imprisonment for a term not exceeding six months or to a fine not exceeding £200:
Provided that—
   (a) in any proceedings against a person in respect of an offence under this section, it shall be a defence to prove that he had reasonable ground to believe, and did believe, that a competent and reliable person was charged with the duty of seeing that the said section 157(1) was, or the said requirements were, as the case may be, complied with and was in a position to discharge that duty; and
   (b) a person shall not be sentenced to imprisonment for any such offence unless, in the opinion of the court dealing with the case, the offence was committed wilfully.

24. Section 158 of the principal Act (which confers upon members of a company, holders of debentures of a company and persons who, though not members or holders of debentures of a company, are entitled to receive notices of general meetings of a company, rights to receive copies of every balance sheet, together with copies of the auditors' report) shall have effect as if references to the auditors' report included references to the directors' report.

Re-registration of Companies

43.—(1) A company which, at the coming into operation of this section, is registered as limited or thereafter is so registered (otherwise than in pursuance of the next following section) may be re-registered under the principal Act as unlimited in pursuance of an application in that behalf complying with the requirement of the next following subsection, framed in the prescribed form and signed by a director or by the secretary of the company and lodged with the registrar of companies in England or Scotland (according as the registered office is situate in England or Scotland) together with the documents mentioned in subsection (3) of this section.

(2) The said requirement is that the application must—

(*a*) set out such alterations in the company's memorandum as, —

(i) if it is to have a share capital, are requisite to bring it, both in substance and in form, into conformity with the requirements imposed by the principal Act with respect to the substance and form of the memorandum of a company to be formed under that Act as an unlimited company having a share capital; or

(ii) if it is not to have a share capital, are requisite in the circumstances; and

(*b*) if articles have been registered, set out such alterations therein and additions thereto as,—

(i) if it is to have a share capital, are requisite to bring them, both in substance and in form, into conformity with the requirements imposed by the principal Act with respect to the substance and form of the articles of a company to be formed thereunder as an unlimited company having a share capital; or

(ii) if it is not to have a share capital, are requisite in the circumstances; and

if articles have not been registered, have annexed thereto, and request the registration of, printed articles, bearing the same stamp as if they contained in a deed, being, if the company is to have a share capital, articles complying with the said requirements and, if not, articles appropriate to the circumstances.

(3) The documents referred to in subsection (1) above are—

(*a*) the prescribed form of assent to the company's being registered as unlimited subscribed by or on behalf of all the members of the company;

(*b*) a statutory declaration made by the directors of the company that the persons by whom or on whose behalf the form of assent is subscribed constitute the whole membership of the company and, if any of the members have not subscribed that form themselves, that the directors have taken all reasonable steps to satisfy themselves that each person who subscribed it on behalf of a member was lawfully empowered so to do;

(c) a printed copy of the memorandum incorporating the alterations therein set out in the application; and

(d) if articles have been registered, a printed copy thereof incorporating the alterations therein and additions thereto set out in the application.

(4) The registrar shall retain the application and other documents lodged with him under subsection (1) of this section, shall, if articles are annexed to the application, register them and shall issue to the company a certificate of incorporation appropriate to the status to be assumed by the company by virtue of this section; and upon the issue of the certificate—

(a) the status of the company shall, by virtue of the issue, be changed from limited to unlimited; and

(b) the alterations in the memorandum set out in the application and (if articles have been previously registered) any alterations and additions to the articles so set out shall, notwithstanding anything in the principal Act, take effect as if duly made by resolution of the company and the provisions of the principal Act shall apply to the memorandum and articles as altered or added to by virtue of this section accordingly.

(5) A certificate of incorporation issued by virtue of this section shall be conclusive evidence that the requirements of this section with respect to re-registration and of matters precedent and incidental thereto have been complied with, and that the company was authorized to be re-registered under the principal Act in pursuance of this section and was duly so re-registered.

(6) Where a company is re-registered in pursuance of this section, a person who, at the time when the application for it to be re-registered was lodged, was a past member of the company and did not thereafter again become a member thereof shall not, in the event of the company's being wound up, be liable to contribute to the assets of the company more than he would have been liable to contribute thereto had it not been so re-registered.

(7) For the purposes of this section—

(a) subscription to a form of assent by the legal personal representative of a deceased member of a company shall be deemed to be subscription by him;

(b) a trustee in bankruptcy of a person who is a member of a company shall, to the exclusion of that person, be deemed to be a member of the company.

(8) In this section, 'prescribed' means prescribed by regulations made by the Board of Trade by statutory instrument.

44.—(1) A company which, at the coming into operation of this section, is registered as unlimited or thereafter is so registered (otherwise than by virtue of the last foregoing section) may be re-registered under the principal Act as limited if a special resolution that it should be so re-registered (complying with the requirement of the next following subsection) is passed and an application in that behalf, framed in the prescribed form and signed by a director or by the secretary of the company, is lodged with the registrar of companies in England or Scotland (according as the registered office of the company is situate in England or Scotland) together with the documents mentioned in subsection (3) of this section not earlier than the day on which the copy of the resolution forwarded to him in pursuance of section 143 of the principal Act is received by him.

(2) The said requirement is that the resolution—

(*a*) must state the manner in which the liability of the members of the company is to be limited and, if the company is to have a share capital, what that capital is to be; and

(*b*) must—

(i) if the company is to be limited by guarantee, provide for the making of such alterations in its memorandum and such alterations in and additions to its articles as are requisite to bring the memorandum and articles, both in substance and in form, into conformity with the requirements of the principal Act with respect to the substance and form of the memorandum and articles of a company to be formed thereunder whose condition as to mode of limitation of liability and possession of a share capital (or want of it) will be similar to the condition of the company as to those matters which will obtain upon its re-registration;

(ii) if the company is to be limited by shares, provide for the making of such alterations in its memorandum as are requisite to bring it, both in substance and in form, into conformity with the requirements of the principal Act with respect to the substance and form of the memorandum of a company to be formed thereunder as a company so limited, and such alterations in and additions to its articles as are requisite in the circumstances.

(3) The documents referred to in subsection (1) above are a printed copy of the memorandum as altered in pursuance of the resolution and a printed copy of the articles as so altered.

(4) The registrar shall retain the application and other documents

lodged with him under subsection (1) above and shall issue to the company a certificate of incorporation appropriate to the status to be assumed by the company by virtue of this section; and upon the issue of the certificate—

    (*a*) the status of the company shall, by virtue of the issue, be changed from unlimited to limited; and

    (*b*) the alterations in the memorandum specified in the resolution and the alterations in, and additions to, the articles so specified shall, notwithstanding anything in the principal Act, take effect.

(5) A certificate of incorporation issued by virtue of this section shall be conclusive evidence that the requirements of this section with respect to re-registration and of matters precedent and incidental thereto have been complied with, and that the company was authorized to be re-registered under the principal Act in pursuance of this section and was duly so re-registered.

(6) Section 64 of the principal Act (power of unlimited company by resolution for registration as a limited company to provide for reserve share capital) shall have effect as if, for the reference to its resolution for registration as a limited company in pursuance of that Act, there were substituted a reference to its resolution for registration as a limited company in pursuance of that Act or re-registration as a limited company in pursuance of this section.

(7) In the event of the winding up of a company re-registered in pursuance of this section, the following provisions shall have effect: —

    (*a*) not withstanding paragraph (*a*) of subsection (1) of section 212 of the principal Act (which section relates to the liability as contributories of past and present members), a past member of the company who was a member thereof at the time of re-registration shall, if the winding up commences within the period of three years beginning with the day on which the company is re-registered, be liable to contribute to the assets of the company in respect of debts and liabilities of its contracted before that time;

    (*b*) where no persons who were members of the company at that time are existing members of the company, a person who, at that time, was a present or past member thereof shall, subject to the said paragraph (*a*) and to the foregoing paragraph, but notwithstanding paragraph (*c*) of the said subsection (1), be liable to contribute as aforesaid notwithstanding that the existing members have satisfied the contributions required to be made by them in pursuance of the principal Act;

    (*c*) notwithstanding paragraphs (*d*) and (*e*) of the said subsection (1), there shall be no limit on the amount which a person who, at that time, was a past or present member of the company is liable to contribute as aforesaid.

(8) In section 112 of the Stamp Act 1891 (which charges a duty on the capital of limited liability companies), the first reference to a company to be registered with limited liability shall be construed as including a reference to a company to be re-registered in pursuance of this section with such liability.

(9) In this section 'prescribed' means prescribed by regulations made by the Board of Trade by statutory instrument.

APPENDIX 4

Extracts from The Employment Protection Act, 1975

Insolvency

Priority of
certain debts.
on insolvency
1914 c. 59.

1913 c. 20.
1948 c. 38.

63.—(1) An amount to which this section applies shall be treated for the purposes of—

    (*a*) section 33 of the Bankruptcy Act 1914 ;

    (*b*) section 118 of the Bankruptcy (Scotland) Act 1913 ; and

    (*c*) section 319 of the Companies Act 1948 ;

as if it were wages payable by the employer to the employee in respect of the period for which it is payable.

(2) This section applies to any amount owed by an employer to an employee in respect of—

    (*a*) a guarantee payment ;

    (*b*) remuneration on suspension on medical grounds under section 29 above ;

    (*c*) any payment for time off under section 57(4) or 61(3) above ;

    (*d*) remuneration under a protective award made under section 101 below.

Employee's
rights on
insolvency of
employer.

64.—(1) If on an application made to him in writing by an employee the Secretary of State is satisfied—

    (*a*) that the employer of that employee has become insolvent ; and

    (*b*) that on the relevant date the employee was entitled to be paid the whole or part of any debt to which this section applies,

the Secretary of State shall, subject to the provisions of this section, pay the employee out of the Redundancy Fund the amount to which in the opinion of the Secretary of State the employee is entitled in respect of that debt.

(2) In this section the " relevant date " in relation to a debt means the date on which the employer became insolvent or the

date of the termination of the employee's employment, whichever is the later.

(3) This section applies to the following debts: —

(a) any arrears of pay in respect of a period or periods not exceeding in the aggregate eight weeks ;

(b) any amount which the employer is liable to pay the employee for the period of notice required by section 1(1) or (2) of the Contracts of Employment Act 1972 1972 c. 53. (minimum period of notice) or for any failure of the employer to give the period of notice required by section 1(1) of that Act ;

(c) any holiday pay in respect of a period or periods of holiday, not exceeding six weeks in all, to which the employee became entitled during the 12 months immediately preceding the relevant date ;

(d) any basic award of compensation for unfair dismissal ;

(e) any reasonable sum by way of reimbursement of the whole or part of any fee or premium paid by an apprentice or articled clerk.

(4) For the purposes of subsection (3)(a) above any such amount as is referred to in section 63(2) above shall be treated as if it were arrears of pay.

(5) The total amount payable to an employee in respect of any debt mentioned in subsection (3) above, where the amount of that debt is referable to a period of time, shall not exceed £80 in respect of any one week or, in respect of a shorter period, an amount bearing the same proportion to £80 as that shorter period bears to a week.

(6) The Secretary of State may vary the limit referred to in subsection (5) above after a review under section 86 below, by order made in accordance with that section.

(7) A sum shall be taken to be reasonable for the purposes of subsection (3)(e) above in a case where a trustee in bankruptcy or liquidator has been or is required to be appointed if it is admitted to be reasonable by the trustee in bankruptcy or liquidator under section 34 of the Bankruptcy Act 1914 (preferential 1914 c. 59. claims of apprentices and articled clerks), whether as originally enacted or as applied to the winding up of a company by section 317 of the Companies Act 1948.   1948 c. 38.

(8) Subsection (7) above shall not apply to Scotland, but in Scotland a sum shall be taken to be reasonable for the purposes of subsection (3)(e) above in a case where a trustee in bankruptcy or liquidator has been or is required to be appointed if it is admitted by the trustee in bankruptcy or the liquidator for the purposes of the bankruptcy or winding up.

(9) The provisions of subsections (10) and (11) below shall apply in a case where one of the following officers (hereafter in this section referred to as the " relevant officer ") has been or is required to be appointed in connection with the employer's insolvency, that is to say, a trustee in bankruptcy, a liquidator, a receiver or manager, or a trustee under a composition or arrangement between the employer and his creditors or under a trust deed for his creditors executed by the employer ; and in this subsection " liquidator " and " receiver " include the Official Receiver in his capacity as a provisional liquidator or interim receiver.

(10) Subject to subsection (11) below, the Secretary of State shall not in such a case make any payment under this section in respect of any debt until he has received a statement from the relevant officer of the amount of that debt which appears to have been owed to the employee on the relevant date and to remain unpaid ; and the relevant officer shall, on request by the Secretary of State, provide him, as soon as reasonably practicable, with such a statement.

(11) Where—

(a) a period of six months has elapsed since the application for a payment under this section was received by the Secretary of State, but no such payment has been made ;

(b) the Secretary of State is satisfied that a payment under this section should be made ; and

(c) it appears to the Secretary of State that there is likely to be further delay before he receives a statement about the debt in question,

then, the Secretary of State may, if the applicant so requests or, if the Secretary of State thinks fit, without such a request, make a payment under this section, notwithstanding that no such statement has been received.

Payment
of unpaid
contributions
to occupational
pension
scheme.

65.—(1) If, on an application made to him in writing by the persons competent to act in respect of an occupational pension scheme, the Secretary of State is satisfied that an employer has become insolvent and that at the time that he did so there remained unpaid relevant contributions falling to be paid by him to the scheme, the Secretary of State shall, subject to the provisions of this section, pay into the resources of the scheme out of the Redundancy Fund the sum which in his opinion is payable in respect of the unpaid relevant contributions.

(2) In this section " relevant contributions " means contributions falling to be paid by an employer in accordance with an occupational pension scheme, either on his own account or on behalf of an employee ; and for the purposes of this section a contribution of any amount shall not be treated as falling

to be paid on behalf of an employee unless a sum equal to that amount has been deducted from the pay of the employee by way of a contribution from him.

(3) The sum payable under this section in respect of unpaid contributions of an employer on his own account to an occupational pension scheme shall be the least of the following amounts—

(a) the balance of relevant contributions remaining unpaid on the date when he became insolvent and payable by the employer on his own account to the scheme in respect of the 12 months immediately preceding that date;

(b) the amount certified by an actuary to be necessary for the purpose of meeting the liability of the scheme on dissolution to pay the benefits provided by the scheme to or in respect of the employees of the employer;

(c) an amount equal to 10 per cent. of the total amount of remuneration paid or payable to those employees in respect of the 12 months immediately preceding the date on which the employer became insolvent.

(4) For the purposes of subsection (3)(c) above, "remuneration" includes holiday pay, maternity pay and any such payment as is referred to in section 63(2) above.

(5) Any sum payable under this section in respect of unpaid contributions on behalf of an employee shall not exceed the amount deducted from the pay of the employee in respect of the employee's contributions to the occupational pension scheme during the 12 months immediately preceding the date on which the employer became insolvent.

(6) The provisions of subsections (7) to (9) below shall apply in a case where one of the following officers (hereafter in this section referred to as the "relevant officer") has been or is required to be appointed in connection with the employers' insolvency, that is to say, a trustee in bankruptcy, a liquidator, a receiver or manager, or a trustee under a composition or arrangement between the employer and his creditors or under a trust deed for his creditors executed by the employer; and in this subsection "liquidator" and "receiver" include the Official Receiver in his capacity as a provisional liquidator or interim receiver.

(7) Subject to subsection (9) below, the Secretary of State shall not in such a case make any payment under this section in respect of unpaid relevant contributions until he has received a statement from the relevant officer of the amount of relevant contributions which appear to have been unpaid on the date on which the employer became insolvent and to remain unpaid; and the relevant officer shall, on request by the Secretary of State

provide him, as soon as reasonably practicable, with such a statement.

(8) Subject to subsection (9) below, an amount shall be taken to be payable, paid or deducted as mentioned in subsection (3)(a) or (c) or subsection (5) above, only if it is so certified by the relevant officer.

(9) Where—

> (a) a period of six months has elapsed since the application for a payment under this section was received by the Secretary of State, but no such payment has been made ;

> (b) the Secretary of State is satisfied that a payment under this section should be made ; and

> (c) it appears to the Secretary of State that there is likely to be further delay before he receives a statement or certificate about the contributions in question,

then, the Secretary of State may, if the applicants so request or, if the Secretary of State thinks fit, without such a request, make a payment under this section, notwithstanding that no such statement or certificate has been received.

Complaint to industrial tribunal.

66.—(1) A person who has applied for a payment under section 64 above may, within the period of three months beginning with the date on which the decision of the Secretary of State on that application was communicated to him or, if that is not reasonably practicable, within such further period as is reasonable, present a complaint to an industrial tribunal that—

> (a) the Secretary of State has failed to make any such payment ; or

> (b) any such payment made by the Secretary of State is less than the amount which should have been paid.

(2) Any persons who are competent to act in respect of an occupational pension scheme and who have applied for a payment to be made under section 65 above into the resources of the scheme may, within the period of three months beginning with the date on which the decision of the Secretary of State on that application was communicated to them, or, if that is not reasonably practicable, within such further period as is reasonable, present a complaint to an industrial tribunal that—

> (a) the Secretary of State has failed to make any such payment ; or

> (b) any such payment made by him is less than the amount which should have been paid.

(3) Where an industrial tribunal finds that the Secretary of State ought to make a payment under section 64 or 65 above, it shall make a declaration to that effect and shall also declare the amount of any such payment which it finds the Secretary of State ought to make.

67.—(1) Where in pursuance of section 64 above the Secretary of State makes any payment to an employee in respect of any debt to which that section applies—

   (*a*) any rights and remedies of the employee in respect of that debt (or, if the Secretary of State has paid only part of it, in respect of that part) shall, on the making of the payment, become rights and remedies of the Secretary of State ; and

   (*b*) any decision of an industrial tribunal requiring an employer to pay that debt to the employee shall have the effect that the debt or, as the case may be, that part of it which the Secretary of State has paid, is to be paid to the Secretary of State.

(2) There shall be included among the rights and remedies which become rights and remedies of the Secretary of State in accordance with subsection (1)(*a*) above any right to be paid in priority to other creditors of the employer in accordance with—

   (*a*) section 33 of the Bankruptcy Act 1914 ;   1914 c. 59.

   (*b*) section 118 of the Bankruptcy (Scotland) Act 1913 ; 1913 c. 20. and

   (*c*) section 319 of the Companies Act 1948,   1948 c. 38.

and the Secretary of State shall be entitled to be so paid in priority to any other unsatisfied claim of the employee ; and in computing for the purposes of any of those provisions any limit on the amount of sums to be so paid any sums paid to the Secretary of State shall be treated as if they had been paid to the employee.

(3) Where in pursuance of section 65 above the Secretary of State makes any payment into the resources of an occupational pension scheme in respect of any contributions to the scheme, any rights and remedies in respect of those contributions belonging to the persons competent to act in respect of the scheme shall, on the making of the payment, become rights and remedies of the Secretary of State.

(4) Any sum recovered by the Secretary of State in exercising any right or pursuing any remedy which is his by virtue of this section shall be paid into the Redundancy Fund.

68.—(1) Where an application is made to the Secretary of State under section 64 or 65 above in respect of a debt owed, or contributions to an occupational pension scheme falling to be made, by an employer, the Secretary of State may require—

   (*a*) the employer to provide him with such information as the Secretary of State may reasonably require for the purpose of determining whether the application is well-founded ; and

(b) any person having the custody or control of any relevant records or other documents to produce for examination on behalf of the Secretary of State any such document in that person's custody or under his control which is of such a description as the Secretary of State may require.

(2) Any such requirement shall be made by notice in writing given to the person on whom the requirement is imposed and may be varied or revoked by a subsequent notice so given.

(3) If a person refuses or wilfully neglects to furnish any information or produce any document which he has been required to furnish or produce by a notice under this section he shall be liable on summary conviction to a fine not exceeding £100.

(4) If a person, in purporting to comply with a requirement of a notice under this section, knowingly or recklessly makes any false statement he shall be liable on summary conviction to a fine not exceeding £400.

Interpretation of ss. 64 to 68.

69.—(1) For the purposes of sections 64 to 68 above an employer shall be taken to be insolvent if, but only if, in England and Wales,—

(a) he becomes bankrupt or makes a composition or arrangement with his creditors or a receiving order is made against him ;

1914 c. 59.

(b) he has died and an order is made under section 130 of the Bankruptcy Act 1914 for the administration of his estate according to the law of bankruptcy, or by virtue of an order of the court his estate is being administered in accordance with rules set out in Part I of Schedule 1 to the Administration of Estates Act 1925 ; or

1925 c. 23.

(c) where the employer is a company, a winding up order is made or a resolution for voluntary winding up is passed with respect to it, or a receiver or manager of its undertaking is duly appointed, or possession is taken, by or on behalf of the holders of any debentures secured by a floating charge, of any property of the company comprised in or subject to the charge.

(2) For the purposes of sections 64 to 68 above an employer shall be taken to be insolvent if, but only if, in Scotland,—

(a) an award of sequestration is made on his estate or he executes a trust deed for his creditors or enters into a composition contract ;

1913 c. 20.

(b) he has died and a judicial factor appointed under section 163 of the Bankruptcy (Scotland) Act 1913 is required by that section to divide his insolvent estate among his creditors ; or (*c*) where the employer is a company, a winding up order is made or a resolution for voluntary winding up is passed with respect to it or a receiver of its undertaking is duly appointed.

(3) In sections 64 to 68 above—

" holiday pay " means—

(*a*) pay in respect of a holiday actually taken ; or

(*b*) any accrued holiday pay which under the employee's contract of employment would in the ordinary course have become payable to him in respect of the period of a holiday if his employment with the employer had continued until he became entitled to a holiday ;

" occupational pension scheme " means any scheme or arrangement which provides or is capable of providing, in relation to employees in any description of employment, benefits (in the form of pensions or otherwise) payable to or in respect of any such employees on the termination of their employment or on their death or retirement ;

and any reference in those sections to the resources of such a scheme is a reference to the funds out of which the benefits provided by the scheme are from time to time payable.

Extracts from The Companies (Winding-up) Rules, 1949

General Meetings of Creditors and Contributories
in relation to a Winding-up by the Court

121. Unless the Court otherwise directs, the meetings of creditors and contributories under section 239 of the Act (hereinafter referred to as the first meetings of creditors and contributories) shall be held within one month or if a Special Manager has been appointed then within six weeks after the date of the winding-up order. The dates of such meetings shall be fixed and they shall be summoned by the Official Receiver.

122. The Official Receiver shall forthwith give notice of the dates fixed by him for the first meetings of creditors and contributories to the Board of Trade, who shall gazette the same.

123. The first meetings of creditors and contributories shall be summoned as hereinafter provided.

124. The notices of first meetings of creditors and contributories may be in Forms 71 and 72 in the Appendix, and the notices to creditors shall state a time within which the creditors must lodge their proofs in order to entitle them to vote at the first meeting.

125. The Official Receiver shall also give to each of the Officers of the Company, who in his opinion ought to attend the first meetings of creditors and contributories, seven days' notice of the time and place appointed for each meeting. The notice may either be delivered personally or sent by prepaid post letter, as may be convenient. It shall be the duty of every Officer who receives notice of such meeting to attend if so required by the Official Receiver, and if any such Officer fails to attend the Official Receiver shall report such failure to the Court.

126.—(1) The Official Receiver shall also, as soon as practicable, send to each creditor mentioned in the Company's Statement of Affairs, and to each person appearing from the Company's books or otherwise to be a contributory of the Company a summary of the Company's Statement of Affairs, including the causes of its failure, and any observations thereon which the Official Receiver may think fit to make. The proceedings at a meeting shall not be invalidated by reason of any summary or notice required by these Rules not having been sent or received before the meeting.

(2) Where prior to the winding-up order the company has commenced to be wound up voluntarily the Official Receiver may, if in his absolute discretion he sees fit so to do, send to the persons aforesaid or any of them an account of such voluntary winding-up showing how such winding-up has been conducted and how the property of the Company has been disposed of and any observations which the Official Receiver may think fit to make on such account or on the voluntary winding-up.

General Meetings of Creditors and Contributories in relation to Winding-up by the Court and of Creditors in relation to a Creditors' Voluntary Winding-up

127.—(1) In addition to the first meetings of creditors and contributories and in addition also to meetings of creditors and contributories directed to be held by the Court under section 346 of the Act (hereinafter referred to as Court meetings of creditors and contributories), the Liquidator in any winding-up by the Court may himself from time to time subject to the provisions of the Act and the control of the Court summon, hold and conduct meetings of the creditors or contributories (hereinafter referred to as Liquidator's meetings of creditors and contributories) for the purpose of ascertaining their wishes in all matters relating to the winding-up.

(2) In any creditors' voluntary winding-up the Liquidator may himself from time to time summon, hold and conduct meetings of creditors for the purpose of ascertaining their wishes in all matters relating to the winding-up (such meetings and all meetings of creditors which a Liquidator or a Company is by the Act required to convene in or immediately before such a voluntary winding-up and all meetings convened by a creditor in a voluntary winding-up under these Rules are hereinafter called voluntary liquidation meetings).

128. Except where and so far as the nature of the subject-matter or the context may otherwise require the Rules as to meetings hereinafter set out shall apply to first meetings, Court meetings, Liquidator's meetings of creditors and contributories, and voluntary liquidation meetings, but so nevertheless that the said Rules shall take effect as to first meetings subject and without prejudice to any express provisions of the Act and

as to Court meetings subject and without prejudice to any express directions of the Court.

129.—(1) The Official Receiver or Liquidator shall summon all meetings
of creditors and contributories by giving not less than seven days' notice
of the time and place thereof in the London Gazette and in a local
paper; and shall not less than seven days before the day appointed for
the meeting send by post to every person appearing by the Company's
books to be a creditor of the Company notice of the meeting of creditors,
and to every person appearing by the Company's books or otherwise to be
a contributory of the Company notice of the meetings of contributories.

(2) The notice to each creditor shall be sent to the address given in
his proof, or if he has not proved to the address given in the Statement
of Affairs of the Company, if any, or to such other address as may be
known to the person summoning the meeting. The notice to each contributory shall be sent to the address mentioned in the Company's
books as the address of such contributory, or to such other address as may
be known to the person summoning the meeting.

(3) In the case of meetings under section 297 of the Act the continuing Liquidator or if there is no continuing Liquidator any creditor
may summon the meeting.

(4) This Rule shall not apply to meetings under section 293 or section
300 of the Act.

130. A certificate by the Official Receiver or other officer of the Court, or
by the clerk of any such person, or an affidavit by the Liquidator, or
creditor, or his solicitor, or the clerk of either of such persons, or as the
case may be by some officer of the Company or its solicitor or the clerk of
such Company or solicitor, that the notice of any meeting has been duly
posted, shall be sufficient evidence of such notice having been duly sent to
the person to whom the same was addressed.

131. Every meeting shall be held at such place as is in the opinion of the
person convening the same most convenient for the majority of the
creditors or contributories or both. Different times or places or both may
if thought expedient be named for the meetings of creditors and for the
meetings of contributories.

132. The costs of summoning a meeting of creditors or contributories at
the instance of any person other than the Official Receiver or Liquidator
shall be paid by the person at whose instance it is summoned who shall
before the meeting is summoned deposit with the Official Receiver or
Liquidator (as the case may be) such sum as may be required by the

Official Receiver or Liquidator as security for the payment of such costs. The costs of summoning such meeting of creditors or contributories, including all disbursements for printing, stationery, postage and the hire of room, shall be calculated at the following rate for each creditor or contributory to whom notice is required to be sent, namely, two shillings per creditor or contributory for the first 20 creditors or contributories, one shilling per creditor or contributory for the next 30 creditors or contributories, sixpence per creditor or contributory for any number of creditors or contributories after the first 50. The said costs shall be repaid out of the assets of the Company if the Court shall by order or if the creditors or contributories (as the case may be) shall by resolution so direct. This Rule shall not apply to meetings under sections 293 or 297 of the Act.

133. Where a meeting is summoned by the Official Receiver or the Liquidator, he or someone nominated by him shall be Chairman of the meeting. At every other meeting of creditors or contributories the Chairman shall be such person as the meeting by resolution shall appoint. This Rule shall not apply to meetings under section 293 of the Act.

134. At a meeting of creditors a resolution shall be deemed to be passed when a majority in number and value of the creditors present personally or by proxy and voting on the resolution have voted in favour of the resolution, and at a meeting of the contributories a resolution shall be deemed to be passed when a majority in number and value of the contributories present personally or by proxy, and voting on the resolution, have voted in favour of the resolution, the value of the contributories being determined according to the number of votes conferred on each contributory by the regulations of the Company.

135. The Official Receiver or as the case may be the Liquidator shall file with the Registrar a copy certified by him of every resolution of a meeting of creditors or contributories in a winding-up by the Court.

136. Where a meeting of creditors or contributories is summoned by notice the proceedings and resolutions at the meeting shall unless the Court otherwise orders be valid notwithstanding that some creditors or contributories may not have received the notice sent to them.

137. The Chairman may with the consent of the meeting adjourn it from time to time and from place to place, but the adjourned meeting shall be held at the same place as the original meeting unless in the resolution for adjournment another place is specified or unless the Court otherwise orders.

138—(1) A meeting may not act for any purpose except the election of a chairman, the proving of debts and the adjournment of the meeting unless there are present or represented thereat in the case of a creditors' meeting at least three creditors entitled to vote or in the case of a meeting of contributories at least three contributories or all the creditors entitled to vote or all the contributories if the number of creditors entitled to vote or the number of contributories as the case may be shall not exceed three.

(2) If within half an hour from the time appointed for the meeting a quorum of creditors or contributories, as the case may be, is not present or represented, the meeting shall be adjourned to the same day in the following week at the same time and place or to such other day or time or place as the chairman may appoint, but so that the day appointed shall be not less than seven nor more than twenty-one days from the day from which the meeting was adjourned.

139. In the case of a first meeting of creditors or of an adjournment thereof a person shall not be entitled to vote as a creditor unless he has duly lodged with the Official Receiver, not later than the time mentioned for that purpose in the notice convening the meeting or adjourned meeting, a proof of the debt which he claims to be due to him from the Company. In the case of a Court meeting or Liquidator's meeting of creditors a person shall not be entitled to vote as a creditor unless he has lodged with the Official Receiver or Liquidator a proof of the debt which he claims to be due to him from the Company and such proof has been admitted wholly or in part before the date on which the meeting is held: Provided that this and the next four following Rules shall not apply to a Court meeting of creditors held prior to the first meeting of creditors.

This Rule shall not apply to any creditors or class of creditors who by virtue of the Rules or any directions given thereunder are not required to prove their debts or to any voluntary liquidation meeting.

140. A creditor shall not vote in respect of any unliquidated or contingent debt or any debt the value of which is not ascertained, nor shall a creditor vote in respect of any debt on or secured by a current bill of exchange or promissory note held by him unless he is willing to treat the liability to him thereon of every person who is liable thereon antecedently to the Company, and against whom a Receiving Order in Bankruptcy has not been made, as a security in his hands, and to estimate the value thereof, and for the purposes of voting, but not for the purposes of dividend, to deduct it from his proof.

141. For the purpose of voting, a secured creditor shall, unless he surrenders his security, state in his proof or in a voluntary liquidation in such a statement as is hereinafter mentioned the particulars of his security, the date when it was given, and the value at which he assesses it, and

shall be entitled to vote only in respect of the balance (if any) due to him after deducting the value of his security. If he votes in respect of his whole debt he shall be deemed to have surrendered his security, unless the Court on application is satisfied that the omission to value the security has arisen from inadvertence.

142. The Official Receiver or Liquidator may, within twenty-eight days after a proof or in a voluntary liquidation a statement estimating the value of a security as aforesaid has been used in voting at a meeting, require the creditor to give up the security for the benefit of the creditors generally on payment of the value so estimated with an addition thereto of twenty per cent: Provided that where a creditor has valued his security he may at any time before being required to give it up correct the valuation by a new proof and deduct the new value from his debt, but in that case the said addition of twenty per cent. shall not be made if the security is required to be given up.

143. The Chairman shall have power to admit or reject a proof for the purpose of voting, but his decision shall be subject to appeal to the Court. If he is in doubt whether a proof shall be admitted or rejected he shall mark it as objected to and allow the creditor to vote subject to the vote being declared invalid in the event of the objection being sustained.

144. For the purpose of voting at any voluntary liquidation meetings, a secured creditor shall, unless he surrender his security, lodge with the Liquidator or, where there is no Liquidator, at the Registered Office of the Company, before the meeting a statement giving the particulars of his security, the date when it was given and the value at which he assesses it.

145.—(1) The Chairman shall cause minutes of the proceedings at the meeting to be drawn up and fairly entered in a book kept for that purpose and the minutes shall be signed by him or by the Chairman of the next ensuing meeting.

(2) A list of creditors and contributories present at every meeting shall be made and kept as in Form 74 in the Appendix.

Proxies in relation to a Winding-up by the Court and to Meetings of Creditors in a Creditors' Voluntary Winding-up

146. A creditor or a contributory may vote either in person or by proxy. Where a person is authorized in manner provided by section 139 of the Act to represent a corporation at any meeting of creditors or contributories such person shall produce to the Official Receiver or Liquidator or other the Chairman of the meeting a copy of the resolution so authorizing

him. Such copy must either be under the seal of the corporation or must be certified to be a true copy by the secretary or a director of the corporation. The succeeding Rules as to proxies shall not (unless otherwise directed by the Court) apply to a Court meeting of creditors or contributories prior to the first meeting.

147. Every instrument of proxy shall be in accordance with the appropriate form in the Appendix.

148. General and special forms of proxy shall be sent to the creditors and contributories with the notice summoning the meeting, and neither the name nor description of the Official Receiver or Liquidator or any other person shall be printed or inserted in the body of any instrument of proxy before it is so sent.

149. A creditor or a contributory may give a general proxy to any person.

150. A creditor or a contributory may give a special proxy to any person to vote at any specified meeting or adjournment thereof:
   (*a*) for or against the appointment or continuance in office of any specified person as Liquidator or Member of the Committee of Inspection, and;
   (*b*) on all questions relating to any matter other than those above referred to and arising at the meeting or an adjournment thereof.

151. Where it appears to the satisfaction of the Court that any solicitation has been used by or on behalf of a Liquidator in obtaining proxies or in procuring his appointment as Liquidator except by the direction of a meeting of creditors or contributories, the Court if it thinks fit may order that no remuneration be allowed to the person by whom or on whose behalf the solicitation was exercised notwithstanding any resolution of the Committee of Inspection or of the creditors or contributories to the contrary.

152. A creditor or a contributory in a winding-up by the Court may appoint the Official Receiver or Liquidator and in a voluntary winding-up the Liquidator or if there is no Liquidator the Chairman of a meeting to act as his general or special proxy.

153. No person acting either under a general or a special proxy shall vote in favour of any resolution which would directly or indirectly place himself, his partner or employer in a position to receive any remuneration out of the estate of the Company otherwise than as a creditor rate-

ably with the other creditors of the Company: Provided that where any person holds special proxies to vote for an application to the Court in favour of the appointment of himself as Liquidator he may use the said proxies and vote accordingly.

154.—(1) A proxy intended to be used at the first meeting of creditors or contributories, or an adjournment thereof, shall be lodged with the Official Receiver not later than the time mentioned for that purpose in the notice convening the meeting or the adjourned meeting, which time shall be not earlier than twelve o'clock at noon of the day but one before, nor later than twelve o'clock at noon of the day before the day appointed for such meeting, unless the Court otherwise directs.

(2) In every other case a proxy shall be lodged with the Official Receiver or Liquidator in a winding-up by the Court, with the Company at its Registered Office for a meeting under section 293 of the Act, and with the Liquidator or if there is no Liquidator with the person named in the notice convening the meeting to receive the same in a voluntary winding-up not later than four o'clock in the afternoon of the day before the meeting or adjourned meeting at which it is to be used.

(3) No person shall be appointed a general or special proxy who is a minor.

155. Where an Official Receiver who holds any proxies cannot attend the meeting for which they are given, he may, in writing, depute some person under his official control to use the proxies on his behalf and in such manner as he may direct.

156. The proxy of a creditor blind or incapable of writing may be accepted if such creditor has attached his signature or mark thereon in the presence of a witness, who shall add to his signature his description and residence: Provided that such witness shall have certified at the foot of the proxy that all such insertions have been made at the request and in the presence of the creditor before he attached his signature or mark.

Form No. 80. (Rule 147.)
GENERAL PROXY
(*Title.*)

I/We,   of   , a creditor [*or* contributory],
hereby appoint (1)   to be my/our general proxy to vote
at the Meeting of Creditors [*or* Contributories] to be held in the above
matter on the   day of   19   , or at any
adjournment thereof.

Dated this   day of   19
                         [Signed] (2)

NOTES

(1.) The person appointed general proxy may in a winding-up by the
Court be the Official Receiver, the Liquidator, or such other person as the
creditor [or contributory] may approve, and in a voluntary winding up
the Liquidator or if there is no Liquidator the chairman of a meeting but
not the Official Receiver. The proxy form should be altered accordingly.

(2.) If a firm, sign the firm's trading title, and add 'by *A.B.*, a partner
in the said firm.' If the appointor is a corporation, then the Form of
Proxy must be under its Common Seal or under the hand of some officer
duly authorized in that behalf, and the fact that the officer is so
authorized must be so stated.

(3.) The proxy form when signed must be lodged by the time and at
the address named for that purpose in the notice convening the meeting
at which it is to be used.

Form No. 81. (Rule 147.)
SPECIAL PROXY
(*Title.*)

I/We,   of   , a creditor [*or* contributory], hereby
appoint(1)   as my/our proxy at the meeting of creditors
[*or* contributories] to be held on the   day of   19   ,
or at any adjournment thereof, to vote (*a*)   the resolution Nod.
                    in the notice convening.

Dated this   day of   19
                         [Signed] (2)

(*a*) Here insert the word 'for' or the word 'against' as the case may
require, and specify the particular resolution.

NOTES

(1.) The person appointed proxy may in a winding up by the Court be the Official Receiver, the Liquidator, or such other person as the creditor [or contributory] may approve, and in a voluntary winding up the Liquidator or if there is no Liquidator the chairman of a meeting but not the Official Receiver. The proxy form should be altered accordingly. A creditor [or contributory] may give a special proxy to any person to vote at any specified meeting or adjournment thereof on all or any of the following matters: —

(*a*) For or against the appointment or continuance in office of any specified person as liquidator or as member of the committee of inspection;

(*b*) On all questions relating to any matter, other than those above referred to, arising at a specified meeting or adjournment thereof.

(2.) If a firm, sign the firm's trading title, and add 'by *A.B.*, partner in the said firm.' If the appointor is a corporation, then the form must be under its common seal or under the hand of some officer duly authorized in that behalf, and the fact that he is so authorized must be so stated.

(3.) The proxy form when signed must be lodged by the time and at the address named for that purpose in the notice convening the meeting at which it is to be used.

APPENDIX 6

The Bankruptcy Act, 1914 — The First Schedule – Meeting of Creditors

1. The first meeting of creditors shall be summoned for a day not later than fourteen days after the date of the receiving order, unless the court for any special reason deems it expedient that the meeting be summoned for a later day.

2. The Official Receiver shall summon the meeting by giving not less than six clear days' notice of the time and place thereof in the *London Gazette* and in a local paper.

3. The Official Receiver shall also, as soon as practicable, send to each creditor mentioned in the debtor's statement of affairs, a notice of the time and place of the first meeting of creditors, accompanied by a summary of the debtors' statement of affairs, including the cause of his failure, and any observations thereon which the Official Receiver may think fit to make; but the proceedings at the first meeting shall not be invalidated by reason of any such notice or summary not having been sent or received before the meeting.

4. The meeting shall be held at such place as in the opinion of the Official Receiver is most convenient for the majority of the creditors.

5. The Official Receiver or the trustee may at any time summon a meeting of creditors, and shall do so whenever so directed by the Court, or so requested by a creditor in accordance with the provisions of this Act.

6. Meetings subsequent to the first meeting shall be summoned by sending notice of the time and place thereof to each creditor at the address given in the debtor's statement of affairs, or at such other address as may be known to the person summoning the meeting.

7. The Official Receiver, or some person nominated by him shall be the chairman at the first meeting. The chairman at subsequent meetings shall be such person as the meeting by resolution appoint.

8. A person shall not be entitled to vote as a creditor at the first or any other meeting of creditors unless he has duly proved a debt provable

in bankruptcy to be due to him from the debtor, and the proof has been duly lodged before the time appointed for the meeting.

9. A creditor shall not vote at any such meeting in respect of any un-liquidated or contingent debt, or any debt the value of which is not ascertained.

10. For the purpose of voting, a secured creditor shall, unless he sur-renders his security, state in his proof the particulars of his security, the date when it was given, and the value at which he assesses it, and shall be entitled to vote only in respect of the balance (if any) due to him, after deducting the value of his security. If he votes in respect of his whole debt he shall be deemed to have surrendered his security unless the Court on application is satisfied that the omission to value the security has arisen from inadvertence.

11. A creditor shall not vote in respect of any debt on or secured by a current bill of exchange or promissory note held by him, unless he is will-ing to treat the liability to him thereon of every person who is liable thereon antecendently to the debtor, and against whom a receiving order has not been made, as a security in his hands, and to estimate the value thereof, and for the purposes of voting, but not for the purposes of divi-dend, to deduct it from his proof.

12. It shall be competent to the trustee or to the Official Receiver, within twenty-eight days after a proof estimating the value of a security as afore-said has been made use of in voting at any meeting, to require the creditor to give up the security for the benefit of the creditors generally on payment of the value so estimated, with an addition thereto of twenty per centum: provided that where a creditor has put a value on such security, he may, at any time before he has been required to give up such security as aforesaid, correct such valuation by a new proof, and deduct such new value from his debt, but in that case such addition to twenty per centum shall not be made if the trustee requires the security to be given up.

13. If a receiving order is made against one partner of a firm, any creditor to whom that partner is indebted jointly with the other partners of the firm, or any of them, may prove his debt for the purpose of voting at any meeting of creditors, and shall be entitled to vote thereat.

14. The chairman of a meeting shall have power to admit or reject a proof for the purpose of voting, but his decision shall be subject to appeal to the Court. If he is in doubt whether the proof of a creditor should be admitted or rejected he shall mark the proof as objected to and shall allow the creditor to vote, subject to the vote being declared invalid in the event of the objection being sustained.

15. A creditor may vote either in person or by proxy.

16. Every instrument of proxy shall be in the prescribed form, and shall be issued by the Official Receiver of the debtor's estate, or by some other

Official Receiver, or, after the appointment of a trustee, by the trustee, and every insertion therein shall be in the handwriting of the person giving the proxy or of any manager or clerk, or other person in his regular employment, or of any commissioner to administer oaths in the Supreme Court.

17. General and special forms of proxy shall be sent to the creditors, together with a notice summoning a meeting of creditors, and neither the name nor the description of the Official Receiver, or of any other person, shall be printed or inserted in the body of any instrument or proxy before it is so sent.

18. A creditor may give a general proxy to his manager or clerk, or any other person in his regular employment. In such case the instrument of proxy shall state the relation in which the person to act thereunder stands to the creditor.

19. A creditor may give a special proxy to any person to vote at any specified meeting or adjournment thereof on all or any of the following matters:

    (*a*) For or against any specific proposal for a composition or scheme of arrangement;

    (*b*) For or against the appointment of any specified person as trustee at a specified rate of remuneration, or as member of the committee of inspection, or for or against the continuance in office of any specified person as trustee or member of a committee of inspection;

    (*c*) On all questions relating to any matter other than those above referred to, arising at any specified meeting or adjournment thereof.

20. A proxy shall not be used unless it is deposited with the Official Receiver or trustee before the meeting at which it is to be used.

21. Where it appears to the satisfaction of the Court that any solicitation has been used by or on behalf of a trustee or receiver in obtaining proxies, or in procuring the trusteeship or receivership, except by the direction of a meeting of creditors, the Court shall have power, if it thinks fit, to order that no remuneration shall be allowed to the person by whom or on whose behalf such solicitation may have been exercised, notwithstanding any resolution of the committee of inspection or of the creditors to the contrary.

22. A creditor may appoint the Official Receiver of the debtor's estate to act in manner prescribed as his general or special proxy.

23. The chairman of a meeting may, with the consent of the meeting, adjourn the meeting from time to time and from place to place.

24. A meeting shall not be competent to act for any purpose, except the election of a chairman, the proving of debts, and the adjournment of

the meeting unless there are present, or represented thereat, at least three creditors, or all the creditors if their number does not exceed three.

25. If within half an hour from the time appointed for the meeting a quorum of creditors is not present or represented, the meeting shall be adjourned to the same day in the following week at the same time and place, or to such other day as the chairman may appoint, not being less than seven nor more than twenty-one days.

26. The chairman of every meeting shall cause minutes of the proceedings at the meeting to be drawn up and fairly entered in a book kept for that purpose, and the minutes shall be signed by him or by the chairman of the next ensuing meeting.

27. No person acting either under a general or special proxy shall vote in favour of any resolution which would directly or indirectly place himself, his partner or employer, in a position to receive any remuneration out of the estate of the debtor otherwise than as a creditor rateably with the other creditors of the debtor: provided that where any person holds special proxies to vote for the appointment of himself as trustee he may use the said proxies and vote accordingly.

28. The vote of the trustee, or of his partner, clerk, solicitor, or solicitor's clerk, either as creditor or as proxy for a creditor, shall not be reckoned in the majority required for passing any resolution affecting the remuneration or conduct of the trustee.

Index